Marketing Research That Won't Break the Bank

Marketing Research That Won't Break the Bank

A Practical Guide to Getting the Information You Need

Alan R. Andreasen

Foreword by William A. Smith

The Second Edition of *Cheap But Good Marketing Research*
Prepared with the assistance of the
Academy for Educational Development

JOSSEY-BASS
A Wiley Imprint
www.josseybass.com

Published by Jossey-Bass
A Wiley Imprint
989 Market Street, San Francisco, CA 94103-1741   www.josseybass.com

Jossey-Bass books and products are available through most bookstores. To contact Jossey-Bass
directly call our Customer Care Department within the U.S. at 800-956-7739, outside the U.S.
at (317) 572-3986 or fax (317) 572-4002.

Jossey-Bass also publishes its books in a variety of electronic formats. Some content that appears in
print may not be available in electronic books.

Library of Congress Cataloging-in-Publication Data:
Andreasen, Alan R., date.
    Marketing research that won't break the bank: a practical guide to getting the information
you need/Alan R. Andreasen; foreword by William A. Smith.—1st ed.
        p. cm.—(The Jossey-Bass nonprofit and public management series)
    Includes bibliographical references and index.
    ISBN 0-7879-6419-0 (alk. paper)
    1. Marketing research. I. Title. II. Series.
    HF5415.2 .A486 2002
    658.8'3—dc21

                                                                    2002010335

Printed in the United States of America
FIRST EDITION
HB Printing   10 9 8 7 6 5 4 3 2 1

The Jossey-Bass
Nonprofit and Public Management Series

Contents

Part One: Planning a Low-Cost Research Program

For Seymour Sudman (in memoriam) and Jean Manning

Foreword

Managers in a wide range of organizations with limited budgets face daunting challenges in competitive marketplaces. Their training and experience make it clear to them that to be successful, their strategies and tactics must emerge from a clear, in-depth understanding of their target markets, their competitors, and the environment in which they all operate. Yet these managers lack the resources to routinely hire the best researchers, contract for the latest databases and information services, or staff a large research department.

This is true of thousands of managers in the private sector—the start-up innovator, the niche marketer, the neighborhood entrepreneur. It is even truer in the nonprofit world, where budgets for almost everyone are very limited but where managers have immense challenges set for them or that they set for themselves.

This book is designed to help such managers increase their effectiveness through the creative and judicious use of low-cost sources of information. It provides insight on how to use the Web, do low-cost surveys and focus groups, be clever at observing customers and competitors, use simple experiments to test tactics and strategies, and create internal records that yield maximum creative insight.

This book is valuable also for the frameworks it offers to help managers with limited budgets in two other ways. First, it helps those who may be reluctant to entertain the idea of conducting a significant amount of research by addressing head-on the myths that may be unnecessarily holding them back. It confronts such misconceptions as "research is only for big decisions" or "most research is a waste" or, the most important myth, "market research is too expensive." The simple truths that put the lie to these myths go a long way toward helping the reluctant investigator move out of the marketplace fog to crisp, clear insights into what is transpiring with key target groups, major competitors, regulators, and others whose perceptions, attitudes, actions, and future plans will have major impact on the marketer's success.

The second source of help is what the author calls backward marketing research. This simple concept has been proved to reduce the waste and increase the impact of research significantly in a wide range of organizations, including some very large ones, such as the DDB Needham advertising agency. It starts with a simple premise: if research does not help managers make decisions, it is not useful and a waste of resources (including the manager's time). The proper approach, the author argues, is to spend a significant amount of time thinking about how the research will be used to help the manager choose among options and that this should be done long before any attempt is made to collect data. This strict regimen requires the manager and the research supplier (someone in the manager's own organization or an outside supplier) to spend significant time thinking about what is to be done with the data. This conversation leads to a rough outline of the final report and then to decisions about data requirements, possible analysis options, and the presentation format. Only then do questions about how to get the information arise. The result of this careful preplanning process is that when the report arrives, the manager is primed and eager to act on what he or she has already been anticipating.

Thus, this book is not only a primer on how to do research when one has limited resources; it is also a guidebook to how to organize and implement that process in ways that will maximize its value. Great managers thrive on information and insight. If you have fewer dollars and less staff than the corporate and nonprofit giants does not mean that you must act on instinct. The tools are here. The approach is here. It takes only commitment and diligence to turn marketplace fog into acute perceptions that make managerial choices grounded, inevitable, and effective.

July 2002   William A. Smith
Academy for Educational Development
Washington, D.C.

Preface

This book is designed for managers who want to do marketing research but think they cannot afford it. It shows them how to get the information they need to be a better manager and how to do it at low cost.

The basic message of the book is that research need not be expensive, overly complex, or highly statistical to be extremely helpful to managers in a wide range of organizations. The marketing research community is sometimes guilty of making the research process seem so subtle and complicated that it scares off too many people who could make valuable use of low-cost techniques. Anyone can do perfectly decent and useful research without fancy probability samples, complex questionnaires, highly trained interviewers, or the latest in computerized statistical software. This book tells how and gets motivated readers started.

I believe there is a true need for this kind of treatment. Conventional textbooks give only passing reference to the potential of many useful low-cost techniques and seem barely interested in the problems of those who are not working in large corporations or major marketing research agencies. And although there are a few books on practical marketing research techniques, they tend to be how-to-do-it manuals primarily for those who want to do field surveys.

This book, then, is a heartfelt response to the cries for help I have heard from practicing and would-be marketing managers of small and medium-sized organizations in the business, government, and nonprofit sectors—a group I call *low-budget researchers*. For them, the pages that follow are designed to achieve four basic objectives:

1. Demythologize marketing research and do away with misconceptions that keep too many managers from doing any kind of marketing research

2. Offer a basic approach that will ensure that any research that is done is needed and useful to the managers for whom it is designed

3. Describe in a systematic fashion a wide variety of specific research techniques that are low cost and, if carried out with care and appropriate attention to issues of bias, can provide management with crucial market insights to improve marketing decision making

4. Motivate readers to get started—to begin to do the research outlined here and see how it can lead to better and better decisions

This book is also written for students. The techniques discussed typically take up only a brief chapter or so of most basic marketing research texts. The treatment is usually cursory, and one senses that many textbook writers see these topics as preliminary approaches before getting on to a really serious study: the major field study or the complex experiment. They seldom recognize that many of the students who read such books or take marketing research courses will go on to hold jobs or to advise organizations where they will be able to carry out only low-cost studies. This book is also addressed to these future managers and advisers and to those who would teach them.

Outline of the Book

Consonant with its twin objectives of motivating and tutoring, the book is divided into four parts. The first and last parts focus on the larger issues of getting started, adopting appropriate philosophies, and setting up the appropriate organization and systems to ensure the gathering of both low-cost and useful marketing research. The middle two parts deal more with the nitty-gritty of specific low-cost research techniques.

Part One is concerned with getting off on the right foot. This may mean sweeping aside some inhibiting misconceptions about research that many people have harbored over the years—for example, that good research is inevitably expensive, that research must always involve fancy sampling techniques, complex statistics, and elaborate computer programs, and that too much research is academic and off-target and therefore of little use to busy, budget-minded managers. Chapter One indicates why these myths are incorrect. Chapter Two then turns to problems of deciding how to set up a marketing research program, that is, how to recognize needs and opportunities for research within individual organizations and how to set in motion both individual studies and a long-term program of information development. The chapter emphasizes the need to be systematic about the task of developing a program of low-cost research and offers a general procedure for doing so.

Chapter Three continues the discussion of planning by offering an approach to the crucial decision of specifically when it is justified to do research and how much to spend on it. The chapter introduces both formal and rule-of-thumb approaches to the task of estimating the cost and value of research.

Chapter Four tackles what is perhaps the most important issue in low-cost research: how to make sure that every dollar spent on marketing research yields information that is unquestionably useful to managers. The chapter outlines a specific procedure, *backward research design*, that can help both beginning and more experienced researchers achieve the elusive goal of maximal managerial usefulness.

Part Two turns to detailing the major alternative approaches to gathering low-cost data for marketing decisions. These chapters cover uses of existing internal and external archives including the Internet (Chapter Five), systematic observation (Chapter Six), low-cost experimentation (Chapter Seven), and low-cost survey design (Chapter Eight).

Part Three takes up issues of quality. For research to be helpful to managers on limited budgets, it needs to be not only low cost but good. For the research to be good, the researcher must ensure that the data are valid and that the conclusions reached are valid. In a sense, the researcher must ensure that there is not "garbage in/ garbage out." Chapter Nine deals with the problems of achieving valid measurements, particularly when asking questions in field surveys. Chapter Ten then discusses the often dreaded topic of statistics from the standpoint of its role in making sure that the output of a study properly summarizes the major findings, reports only those differences and relationships that are truly present, and milks the most information out of the data. The treatment here is commonsensical and not highly quantitative.

Researchers with low budgets could obviously use as much low-cost help as they can get. Thus the final chapter, Chapter Eleven, focuses on the problems of acquiring the financial, physical, intellectual, and human resources needed to carry out low-cost research projects. The chapter offers a number of approaches to using libraries, colleges, advertising agencies, and commercial research services by researchers with very restricted budgets.

What the Book Is Not

Before leaving the reader to plunge into the exciting possibilities of the world of marketing research that will not break the bank, it is important to keep one's expectations within reason. This is *not* a basic marketing research text or a detailed handbook of low-cost techniques. A number of the traditional subjects that one ought to think about to be a really accomplished, sophisticated marketing researcher are not covered here.

The reader will not find in these pages detailed suggestions on how to design a questionnaire, or how to word questions, or how to draw a probability sample. The more routine aspects of research administration, data reduction, data analysis, and report writing are also absent.

This is a book about a particular, neglected subset of all marketing research. It chooses not to dwell on what other authors cover well but on what they do not. I hope that readers find that this book provides the raw material and the incentive to begin an innovative program of market research that, even though constrained by limited resources, will prove a significant boon to the organization and to the manager wanting to make more informed and less risky marketing decisions.

July 2002

Alan R. Andreasen
Georgetown University
Washington, D.C.

Acknowledgments

This book is a revision and updating of a volume first published by Dow Jones-Irwin in 1988. The book was out of print until two years ago, when colleagues encouraged me to update it. Bill Smith of the Academy for Educational Development was instrumental in launching the project. However, without the exceptional—nay, *heroic*—work of his assistant, Olivia Marinescu, in preparing the manuscript, the task would have been impossible, and you would not have this edition before you. She worked from original preparation carried out by the support staff that I had at the University of California at Los Angeles in the mid-1980s and editing by Dow Jones-Irwin.

The original book was suggested by Bill Matassoni, then of McKinsey & Company, and benefited from a wide range of inputs from both practitioners and scholars. They have been followed by many others who have contributed to my education in this special domain. Among those deserving of special thanks are Bill Smith, Bill Novelli of the AARP, Bill Wells formerly of DDB Needham and more recently the University of Minnesota, Craig Lefebvre of the Prospect Center, Susan Middlestadt of the Academy for Educational Development, and academic colleagues, including Michael Rothschild, Martin Fishbein, Bob Hornik, Paul Bloom, James Prochaska, Philip Kotler, Russell Belk, and Marvin Goldberg. Special thanks must go to my former colleague, the late Seymour Sudman of the University of Illinois. Seymour taught me a great deal of what

I think I know about field research over the years and provided me with several opportunities to test and improve those skills. He also gave the original manuscript a careful reading and offered many valuable suggestions.

The original book and this revision would not have appeared without the encouragement and contributions of my wife, Jean Manning. Jean provided many of the ideas contained here and throughout has been supportive and a constant inspiration.

A.R.A.

The Author

Alan R. Andreasen is professor of marketing at the McDonough School of Business at Georgetown University and executive director of the Social Marketing Institute. He is the author or editor of fifteen books and numerous monographs and reports. His most recent books are *Ethics and Social Marketing* (2001), *Strategic Marketing in Nonprofit Organizations* (6th ed.), coauthored with Philip Kotler (2003), and *Marketing Social Change* (Jossey-Bass, 1995). He has published over one hundred articles and conference papers on a variety of topics and serves on the editorial boards of several major journals. He is a past president of the Association for Consumer Research.

PART ONE

Planning a Low-Cost
Research Program

1

Myths of Marketing Research

Successful marketers are knowledgeable marketers. The world has many intuitively brilliant and sometimes lucky marketers, but the most successful marketers I know are the best informed. They know their target audiences, know their partners, and know which marketing tactics work and which ones don't. They know what their competitors are doing almost as soon as they do it. Most important, they are aware of what they don't know and resolve to find it out. They crave information. They devour it on the job and off the job. They always want to know more, and when they acquire new information, they use it effectively.

Other managers intuitively know this. They know they need more information and ought to be doing marketing research in order to be better marketers. Managers in large enterprises have access to many types of information services and usually a healthy budget for their own research. Managers in small and medium-sized organizations in all three sectors—business, nonprofit, and government—do not have such opportunities. They say:

"We know we need marketing information to be good marketers, but how can we undertake it when we have virtually no budgets?"

"If I did have the money to do research, how can I do it when I really don't know much about statistics and sampling and computers?"

"How dare I risk limited resources, not to mention my credibility with my boss, by doing research that I'm told all too often turns out to be a waste of time and effort?"

"If I decide to go ahead, how can I work effectively with a market research professional when I don't really know what I want, what the researcher can do for me, or how I can tell good research from bad when it gets done?"

This book responds to these cries for help. It is a book about low-cost marketing research designed for both present and future marketing practitioners with limited research budgets and limited experience in carrying out specific research studies or extensive research programs. It offers a rich catalogue of techniques for keeping costs down while maintaining acceptable, and sometimes high, standards of quality. The book's ultimate goal is to make those who use these techniques better managers through timely acquisition of relevant, useful marketing information.

The book is not simply a guide for carrying out a specific set of low-cost research approaches. It also is designed to motivate readers to become active researchers, to take the first steps toward becoming frequent, savvy beneficiaries of the rich possibilities of research. Two barriers keep managers from being active researchers. First, wrong notions about research keep many from even thinking about the topic. Second, many managers simply aren't aware of the wide array of simple, low-cost marketing research techniques that are available.

This book tackles both issues by confronting the myths and outlining step-by-step procedures for setting up a research program and carrying out specific, useful studies. It also describes in detail many techniques for doing low-cost but high-quality research.

We begin by tackling some of the myths that are keeping many managers (consciously or unconsciously) from considering or undertaking marketing research.

Research Priests and the Low-Budget Manager

Many managers with limited research experience hold misperceptions about marketing research. These misperceptions can be traced to the marketing research community, which has created a forbidding mystique about its own profession and its products. Marketing researchers have developed their own jargon, their own reverence for the most sophisticated approaches, and their own propaganda that implies that only those who are properly trained—the research priests—can conduct valid, reliable marketing research.

In some cases, they are correct. Professionals should be the prime sources of research on such sensitive topics as drugs and sex or of research designed to tap complex or deeply rooted mental processes. Professionals must also be used when results have to be projected with a high degree of accuracy to a general population base or to some distant future period. They must also be used where the research is likely to be subject to close outside scrutiny, for example, by the government or the courts. And when a lot is riding on the outcome of a decision or set of decisions that must be based on research, paying for the very best professional work is clearly justified.

But many, many marketing decisions could benefit significantly from marketing research that would not involve a high level of sophistication or expenditure levels that mortgage the organization's future. There are a great many research alternatives that can easily be designed and implemented by any minimally knowledgeable manager or his or her staff. This book is designed to encourage and instruct these people to try their hand at marketing research. It is designed to give the neophyte manager-researcher the basic knowledge necessary to permit frequent and sensible use of a wide range of low-cost marketing research tools.

Many managers are intimidated about carrying out their own marketing research because of myths that have developed over the years. If this book is really to be helpful to its readers, we must first bring these myths into the open and confront them directly.

Myth 1: "I'm Already Doing Enough Research"

Many managers believe they already have enough marketing research information as a by-product of their organization's accounting and control activities. They point to stacks of performance data, profitability analyses, and so forth as proof of their contention. Although such information may be useful as research, the odds are very good that it is both too much and too little. The problem typically is that no one has ever really sat down and tried to specify just what kind of information the manager should have for day-to-day marketing decisions or long-range strategic planning. Thus, the manager is offered only what is available and often in overwhelming abundance. Too much of the wrong kind of data can swamp what is really important. The manager is often left to find the proverbial needle in the haystack.

Data overkill, by its sheer bulk, can intimidate many managers from looking for these needles, while at the same time convincing them that the company is already doing enough marketing research. Certainly the prospect of going into the field and generating even more new and different data will seem highly unpalatable to the overwhelmed manager.

And, of course, the available data may also be too little. As long as the manager keeps making decisions that could have been significantly helped by a few modest additional research projects, we must conclude that the existing information is clearly inadequate. It is Gresham's Law applied to marketing research: bad data drive out good data. An overabundance of useless data is bound to quash any modest ambitions to collect more.

The only way to deal with the problem of data overkill is to systematically identify the organization's long-run research needs and ask whether existing data meet these needs. In most cases, they will not, and the researcher will have to build a research program to meet those needs and find ways of turning off the supply of useless, inhibiting data. Simply hoping that existing data will be adequate is not enough. If existing data are not carefully designed to help make both short- and long-term decisions, they are probably just accounting or output data and should not be classified as research.

Myth 2: "Research Is Only for Big Decisions"

Many managers in small businesses or nonprofit organizations suffer from misplaced modesty. They feel that their decisions are small potatoes compared to those of Procter & Gamble or General Motors. They feel they cannot justify the level of expenditures they think any serious marketing research undertaking will require. This kind of thinking has two major flaws. First, there are many circumstances in both small and large companies where relatively trivial decisions can be significantly improved by a little bit of marketing research and where the research is well worth doing because of its modest cost.

Second, despite what many managers think, there are many situations, even in very large organizations, where marketing research is not justified, even though substantial amounts of resources are at risk. The reason a lot of big decisions do not require research expenditures is that management already has little uncertainty about what to do. By contrast, as we will see in Chapter Three, it is in cases where managers simply do not know which way to turn (even where the stakes are relatively modest) that research can be most helpful. The dollars at risk will, of course, determine the upper limit of the research budget, and therefore, other things equal, bigger decisions will permit more research. But even where relatively modest amounts are involved, if the situation is one of high uncertainty as to what to do, there is usually some level of research expenditure that a manager should accept because it is very likely to tip the balance one way or another.

In many situations with large amounts of money at risk, managers will order research even though it is not justified rationally. Managers often want to feel better about a major decision they are about to make. They may want backup in case the decision is later questioned. In both cases, the manager should recognize that funds allocated to unjustified self-protection are funds that probably should be used to provide information in other contexts that now require management by the seat of the pants.

Myth 3: "Losing Control"

The lost-control myth in part reflects the deeply rooted perceptions of many managers that marketing research is really some arcane religion to which only a very few priests are admitted. They believe that they cannot acquire the level of sophistication needed to do the research alone or specify what research needs to be bought from outside sources. If managers feel they must go outside for any research, many will refrain from going ahead because they feel that they dare not rely on others to gather and analyze data about their decisions. They feel they will have committed a part of their organization's destiny to an outsider who may or may not understand the situation or the realities of its unique political and market environment. In a sense, the managers feel they have lost control.

This would explain why many managers who recognize possibilities for research do not simply hire smart M.B.A.s to do in-house studies or hire outside contractors to fill in critical information gaps. The manager fears losing control. If new information is allowed to become important to decision making and only certain people (not the manager) have access to this specialized information, then they, not the manager, may really have the control. The manager will be beholden to them.

This fear keeps managers from engaging in research and then from using the results of research when it is (grudgingly) carried out. This is especially the case if the research results run counter to the manager's own views. Most of us are reluctant to accept new information, and the problem is significantly exaggerated when managers feel that agreeing with unexpected research results and acting on them means giving up real control of their function.

Understandably, this fear of loss of control is a particular problem for middle managers and those in small or nonprofit businesses.

Personal survival is very important to them, and they often feel they dare not give others the control of their personal organizational fate.

They may also feel that the entire organization is at risk. Organizational fragility is a real and understandable concern of small businesses. If one believes that research is hard to understand and requires a translation to be used effectively, certainly one will be reluctant to delegate one's very livelihood to outside specialists. The outside researcher may not work as hard on the project or on the analysis and interpretation as the manager would like. Worse still, busy outsiders may unwittingly bias the results, understate or neglect key issues, or suppress important reservations.

Finally, many managers worry that outside researchers will be on some theoretical or academic plateau far above the practical realities facing the organization. This will be especially so if the manager has glanced recently at specialized journals in the marketing research field with their articles talking of "part-worths" "canonical coefficients," "Cronbach's Alpha," or "Durbin-Watson statistics."

These fears are not easily reduced. However, this book is designed to make the manager a more savvy research user, one who knows when to hire outsiders and when to go it alone. It introduces a number of very good but not fancy research techniques that the cautious manager can order from outside or do in-house without fear of being unknowledgeable or unprepared. Should the manager have to go outside, the book also describes (in Chapter Four) an excellent technique that can ensure that what is done is on target and highly useful.

Myth 4: "Market Research Is Survey Research"

Just as many nonmarketing people tend to think that marketing is just advertising, so do many managers tend to think of survey research and marketing research as being virtually the same thing. There is a great range of research techniques that use simple observation, archival analysis, and low-cost experimentation rather than surveys.

Myth 5: "Market Research Is Too Expensive"

This is the major straw-man myth that this book is designed to knock down. It exists, in part, because of myth 4. If one equates marketing research with surveys with their large samples, substantial field costs, complicated computer analyses, and so on, it is inevitable to assume that research has to be expensive. Surveys based on careful probability sampling are expensive, but there are many alternatives to survey research that can adequately meet management's information needs at low cost. Furthermore, there are many ways in which the cost of survey research itself can be significantly reduced.

Myth 6: "Most Research Is a Waste"

Research can turn out to be wasteful for many reasons. This book is expressly designed to make sure managers avoid such a fate.

There can be many culprits behind wasted research. Sometimes research is wasted because the manager has personal motives for not effectively using the research after it is done. Inexperience, time pressure, or relying too much on the research supplier can also lead to miscommunication that will virtually ensure that the research cannot be useful.

Often the researcher is an equally guilty culprit. Some research specialists keep a distance from management simply to protect their own special status. Sometimes the researcher, whether by training or inclination, is not adequately concerned about making the research project managerially relevant. This is especially common among academics and freshly graduated Ph.D.s. The researcher may be so caught up in the world of research sophistication that he or she may not really understand, or may have strange ideas about, managerial relevance. It is not uncommon to hear researchers talk about the quality of the design itself or the statistical significance of the results as the true test of whether research was good, rather than how relevant it was to the manager who asked for it.

Finally, the problem may simply not be the fault of anybody or caused by a lack of trying. In many cases where both sides really want to make the research managerially useful, the parties do not have a procedure that can make a piece of research managerially relevant and useful. Chapter Four specifically sets out a procedure that can go a long way toward ensuring a productive manager-researcher collaboration.

Moving Forward

Low-budget managers should not be put off from doing research for any of the following reasons:

- They think they already have enough data; almost always, they don't. I suggest a procedure in Chapter Two for determining what information they really need.
- They don't face enough big decisions. Research is not only for big decisions, and sometimes big decisions do not need it. In Chapter Three, I explain how to determine when to do research and when not to.
- They fear loss of control of their destinies because they are not sophisticated enough to be good research users. But most of the research discussed in this book requires only common sense. Even the discussion of analysis techniques and statistics in Chapter Ten is in simple terms.
- They think research is simply conducting surveys and surveys are expensive. But as I demonstrate in the later chapters, all research is not surveys, and even surveys can be done inexpensively.
- They fear it will be a waste of time and resources. Research can be a waste, but it need not be, especially if the approach outlined in Chapter Four is carefully followed.

Research is essential for management success. Probably nowhere is this more obvious than when an organization is planning a new venture. In such cases, too many managers enamored over an idea that can't miss neglect to do the simplest basic research. For example, Polygon, a New York software company, developed a new product, Easy Path, that would increase the efficiency of hard drives. Despite the product's relatively low cost and obvious usefulness, Polygon neglected to find out whether information technology professionals knew they had a need or problem that the software could address. It turned out they were unwilling to pay $99 for something that wasn't apparently needed. For its next product launch, Polygon decided to spend $20,000 on marketing research.[1]

Even those who believe research may be valuable in launching a new venture may still not embrace it enthusiastically. Take the case of an entrepreneur who had developed a new coated-peanut snack food and hired a researcher to help with initial marketing decisions. But he was "very suspicious of the whole thing. It all seemed like a lot of talk." Yet when the researcher got the entrepreneur directly involved in the research process (an approach we advocate fervently), he became a believer. He was recruited to survey his patrons himself and found a large number of unexpected comments, including one likening the product to dog food. He subsequently reformulated the product and used research to decide on a distribution channel (supermarkets were not a good idea as this would require major advertising to build brand recognition), the most effective packaging (stackable bags), and the price ($3.25 for an eight-ounce bag). Despite a considerable outlay, the entrepreneur felt that the research ultimately "changed my mind about how to sell the product."[2]

This perception is now much more widely shared. Research on new ventures such as this is deemed so crucial that venture capitalists typically no longer consider proposals that are not backed by solid market research.

This book is designed to make not only willing but eager users out of all those attempting new ventures, whether they are products, services, social change campaigns, or new ways to raise funds. It is also for managers in organizations with simpler decisions, such as whether to change an offering, revise a Web site, raise or lower a

price, or run with a new communications theme for an existing venture. Research is essential in most of these cases. In a surprising number of cases, it is not only essential but also affordable. The pages that
follow will make that point crystal clear.

Organization of the Book

I assume that readers are at least willing to suspend major reservations
about the prospect of doing more research and want to move ahead.

This book shows readers how to decide when to use marketing
research even when the budget is small and the stakes are not very
high; describes an approach that can ensure that research that is
undertaken is as useful as possible; and describes and evaluates a
representative range of techniques for carrying out relatively inexpensive research that is still of high quality—or at least of a quality
level commensurate with the decisions management faces.

The next two chapters address two sides of the issue of when to
do research. First, we consider the opportunity for research. Many
managers do not see the myriad chances for conducting relatively
simple investigations that would significantly improve their decision-
making capabilities. They just don't "think research." In part, this is
because too many managers are unaware of the diversity of uses to
which research can be put. Furthermore, they may be unaware of the
diversity of approaches that research can take. Research can consist
of something as simple and straightforward as planned, systematic observation of facts and events around us. It can be a simple market experiment or a controlled case study. It can be analysis of secondary
data that already exist or a survey study of a convenient sample. All
are legitimate research approaches that can prove to be extremely
valuable to open-minded managers if they are done right and fit the
circumstances.

But managers must be prepared to gather information, not just
hope to recognize chances for research when they appear. Chapter
Two has as its major objective showing managers how to organize
to ensure that data are there when they are needed. Research is

much better if it is planned. Anyone who is serious about research must be systematic about it. A serious manager should prepare an annual plan for research just as one prepares an annual plan for advertising or research and development.

Merely recognizing opportunities to do research does not mean that managers should plunge forward heedlessly. There are many times when the opportunity to do research ought to be passed by. Sometimes this is because the state of the research art is not up to the challenge of providing the needed information at a reasonable cost. This is especially the case with research designed to explore customers' psyches—their attitudes, perceptions, motivations, and intentions.

And no one should do research when the economics of the decision situation argue against it. Chapter Three takes up the general question of when it is economically sensible to go ahead with research and, if so, how much to spend on it. This chapter introduces the concept of decision theory, showing how this formal approach leads to reasonable rules of thumb that will help a manager decide whether to do projects A, B, or C or all of them or none of them. It also shows how to determine the total budget.

If research is to meet its promise, the end product must meet the specific needs that management sets out to fulfill. In Chapter Four, therefore, we will assume that both the manager and the researcher want to make the research as relevant and useful as possible but do not know how. The chapter offers a relatively simple approach called *backward research design* that makes it much more likely that the research will be as useful as it can be. But both the manager and the researcher must be willing to devote considerable time to thinking through the research problem in advance, and both must have realistic expectations about what research can do. Research cannot effectively tackle many topics, and it can be only partially helpful in a great many others. If this book is to create satisfied users of research, it must ensure that they are not oversold users, especially when the overselling is something they unwittingly do to themselves.

Chapters Five through Eight get down to the nitty-gritty of the book by spelling out alternative ways of doing low-cost, good research. Each of these chapters introduces a set of techniques and discusses ways in which they should and should not be carried out. Chapter Nine then considers the problems of collecting valid data, especially when using a questionnaire. Chapter Ten follows with an introduction to statistics designed to make a little less formidable a potentially intimidating topic by showing how statistics can serve rather than confuse neophyte researchers. Chapter Eleven concludes the discussion by outlining ways in which managers with a limited budget can acquire outside help and other resources to keep the overall costs of a research program as low as possible.

Concluding Comments

It is important to emphasize two key cautions at this point. First, the low-cost research approaches I am advocating here must be carried out with the highest standards possible (commensurate with the decisions and with the dollars involved). Second, slovenly, low-cost research is the most expensive kind since it can lead to worse decisions than those made without the research. The tragedy of much inexpensive research carried out by the untrained and the unsuspecting is that it is really cheap and dirty research and worse still—dirty often in ways that are hidden from management. It is always possible that bad research by chance will yield correct insights—sometimes because only a dunce would miss the obvious. But in the long run, the only way a manager can be sure that the research has a pretty good chance of being right (and, if the procedure outlined in Chapter Four is followed, on target) is if it is done with as high a level of research standards as the technique and the circumstances permit.

Only if managers are satisfied with the research—only if they feel that they got as close to the truth as possible under the circumstances—are they likely to be repeat users of research themselves and be vocal advocates of the idea of research to business colleagues, coworkers, and employees. Only then will this book achieve its goal of being itself an effective marketing tool.

I believe strongly that a product or an idea (such as the concept of low-cost marketing research) will be accepted only if it meets customers' needs and wants. In this first chapter, I have sought to expose many of the irrational barriers and mystifications that have kept managers with limited budgets from seeing how research can meet their real needs. The following pages provide the tools to achieve this end. But I have only opened the door. It will be up to the reader to make the first daring steps in what can be an extremely rewarding effort.

2

Planning a Research Program

Marketing research opportunities are much more numerous than the typical limited-budget manager thinks. In many cases, a simple, relatively cheap research study can help the manager make a better decision. As with any other important managerial activity, it cannot be left to chance but must be planned. And planning for research requires both an appreciation of the many ways research can help and a systematic approach to specifying and carrying out both continuing and special-purpose studies. The low-budget manager must first learn to recognize research opportunities in the day-to-day work environment. For those not trained in research, this may take some time and conscious effort.

Consider the case of Phil Brady, the vice president for development of a public television station in the Midwest:

Brady's principal marketing objective was to secure listener and corporate donations to finance the station's day-to-day programming and its long-run capital expenditures. Once or twice a year, he designed and conducted an on-the-air pledge drive, a highly successful marketing technique now almost universally employed in public television funding. Despite the overall success of the technique, Brady felt he could do better in one important respect. Every year, 5 to 15 percent of the viewers who called to volunteer a pledge would neglect to make good on their commitment (bogus or prank pledges were rarely a serious problem), requiring the station to undertake some additional follow-up marketing. As a result of these efforts (or perhaps independent of them), about half of the outstanding pledges were fulfilled.

This was a frustrating situation for Brady. Because the typical pledge week can generate $250,000 to $350,000 in potential donations on each drive, even 6 percent nonfulfillment can mean a substantial loss of revenues. But Brady did not really know why the majority did not fulfill their pledges or exactly how to approach these donors. Most development managers simply send out reminder notices that treat nonfulfillers as if they fully intended to pledge and had simply let the matter slip their minds. This follow-up note is typically warm and friendly, thanking nonfulfillers for their pledges, welcoming them to the station's "listener family," and then gently reminding them that the pledged amount has not been received. It is assumed that nonfulfillers fall into three groups: those who had forgotten, those who were about to pledge anyway, and those who had changed their minds. It was assumed that those who truly had let the pledge slip their minds would be thankful for the reminder and that those who were about to mail the pledge anyway would not be offended by the letter's tone. Finally, it was hoped that those who had changed their minds about pledging would either respond positively to the warm note or be embarrassed by the fact that the station was counting on them. Brady had no idea what proportion of the no-shows fit into the third category and whether a stronger letter would be more effective in motivating them to fulfill their pledge.

Brady was also uncertain about whether a mail follow-up strategy was the best way to contact these nonfulfillers. He wondered whether there would be any merit in marketing to the recalcitrant pledgers by telephone. This could be easily done by keeping on some of the volunteer telephone operators who worked during pledge week and having them do the follow-up. Brady didn't know whether this modest expense would be worth it.

Here we have an example of the classic problem that this book addresses: not a great deal was at stake, but it was enough to worry about. At the same time, the manager had some important areas of ignorance. He did not know whether to change the follow-up message to offer a stronger motivation and whether to change the form of that communication. Both represent opportunities for research. The manager had two decisions to make, but in the absence of specific research, he was inclined to go along with intuition and "what we've always done": a mailed, friendly follow-up letter.

Brady did not see this as a research opportunity. Mainly, he did not think it was worth the expense. He saw the potential gain from any kind of study as modest and the mental and financial costs of conducting the research to be significant. Part of the problem was that he also did not really know what research technique might be appropriate and feasible, and certainly not one that would also be low cost.

Framing the Research Problem

In thinking about this modest research opportunity, we must first ask just what might be meant by "low cost" in this case. While formal consideration of the question of research budgets will be taken up in the next chapter, a sense of how a manager might proceed may be offered by attempting to make a rough estimate of the maximum the manager might budget in this case. Assume the following:

- The typical pledge drive runs twice a year and collects an average $300,000 each time.
- Those who need to be contacted for not fulfilling their pledges represent 5 percent of all pledges.

- One-third of those who need to be contacted would have fulfilled their pledges without a follow-up message, one-third needed to be reminded, and one-third had changed their minds about making a gift.

- The usual mailed message is effective with most of those in the first two groups and only partly effective with the latter.

Given these assumptions, designing a better follow-up strategy could at best increase the station's revenues only by bringing in more of the $5,000 in pledges in each drive represented by the nonfulfillers who had not changed their minds (this figure is one-third of 5 percent of $300,000). Assuming the marketing strategy used now motivates payment of $1,000 worth of these pledges and that the absolute most the station would get with a new tougher message and using a telephone follow-up is $2,500, then any improvement in marketing strategy could yield at maximum $1,500 more per pledge drive if there was no additional cost to implementing the new strategy suggested by the research. In the case of a new message, the cost of changing to a stronger wording would be close to zero. If any research project recommended contacting nonfulfillers by telephone, there would be the added cost of this different approach. The $1,500 gain would be extended over several pledge drives, however.

Two studies are possible. One could focus on learning about motivations and figuring out how to design a better approach to those who had changed their minds. The other could focus on which medium is better, telephone or mail. Or the two could be combined. If the two studies had payoffs that were realized over, say, two years (that is, four pledge drives), the maximum one might invest is $6,000 (4 x $1,500) in one or both studies. However, given that the research will inevitably be less than perfect, clearly a manager would want to risk considerably less than this amount, say, $1,000 to $1,500.

You might conclude that a telephone study is probably not worth it because even if telephone solicitation was found to yield more revenue, it would also incur more cost. On the other hand, you might feel that even an imperfect motivational study would be worthwhile because the cost of implementation would be so low. Both of these conclusions are wrong. The motivation study represents an opportunity that should probably be passed up. On the other hand, the telephone study is a good, managerially useful research project that can be carried out for several hundred dollars of out-of-pocket cost.

The Motivation Study

In the case of pledger motivations, discussions with any fundraiser will make it clear that even if a different set of pledger motives was discovered in a future research project, most managers would be reluctant to use this information to change the follow-up message. One reason was implicit in the discussion about the target audiences. Although there are three segments within the set of pledgers who do not initially fulfill their commitments, the motivational message would be directed at only those who had changed their minds. The manager will be legitimately worried that the other two groups may react negatively to a stronger, more insistent new message that is perceived as more irritating than the warm and friendly one already being used. The manager's fear is that for every newly motivated individual converted by a stronger letter, one or more of the others will decide not to pledge because of the more forceful tone. Thus, even if the research did discover the motivations of those who had changed their minds that could be worked on, most managers would probably not be willing to take the risks involved in changing the existing approach. For this reason, the research should not be done because it will not affect a marketing decision. This is an important point, and we will return to it in Chapter Four.

A reasonable alternative approach might be to recommend that the manager continue the existing mailing, wait several weeks, and then send out the new, tougher motivational appeal to those who have not still fulfilled their pleased, The manager might, quite legitimately, express two reservations about this approach. First, a second mailing means additional costs; bookkeeping to keep track of every late nonfulfiller; designing, preparing, and mailing a second letter; and using a new set of stamped return envelopes. Second, the manager might suggest that a message delivered several weeks after the initial pledge drive may be too late. Attitudes may have hardened by then, the excitement of the pledge week will have worn off, and other economic priorities will have intervened in the pledger's household. The likely payoff from this second mailing will be much smaller than if nonpledgers were reached soon after the pledge drive. Furthermore, one may also question whether a research study presumably designed to discover short-term barriers to pledging will prove valid for barriers remaining after several weeks.

There is another problem with the proposed motivational study: whether the findings could be trusted. Without a relatively heavy investment in sophisticated methodology, there is a serious question of whether one could really learn why those in the third group changed their minds. If many are embarrassed by their change of mind, there is good reason to believe that this same embarrassment would also cause many of them to be less than candid in an interview designed to get at the real reasons for their change of mind. This is clearly a research opportunity that should be passed by.

The Telephone Study

The case for a low-cost research study on the telephone versus mail follow-up approach is much more encouraging. The hypothesis to test is clear: the net revenues generated in response to a telephone follow-up with nonfulfilling pledgers will be greater than the net revenues generated by a mail follow-up. In both cases, net revenue is calculated as the return after the cost of the particular method of solicitation is deducted. The research that the hypothesis suggests is a rather simple experiment: take all of those who have not fulfilled their pledges at a particular point (say, after fourteen days), randomly assign them to a telephone and a mail treatment group, contact them as the treatment indicates, keep track of the full costs of each treatment, and wait for the returns. The allocation of subjects to the two treatments need not be equal. Since telephone solicitation is more costly, one way to keep research expenses in check is to allocate less than 50 percent of the sample to the telephone condition. Whatever the proportion, the allocation must be random for the experiment to be valid.

The proposed experiment is really one that virtually anyone can design and implement with the prospect of a relatively high-quality outcome. The secret is to make sure that the assignment of pledgers to treatment groups is random and that those doing the telephone solicitation do not behave (perhaps due to the fact that they know they are part of an experiment) in ways that will influence the study such that one cannot realistically project the results to normal future telephone solicitations.

Just such a study was done for Mr. Brady. The study came about because two students in the communications degree program at the local university were looking for a term project. After talking with Brady, they recognized the research opportunity and went ahead and designed and carried out the required experiment. The only costs to the station were modest additional telephone charges. Although the researchers' services were free, net revenues for the telephone treatment were calculated after estimating what it would have cost to acquire enough telephone lines to handle all the needed calls in the experiment and to pay full-time operators to make the contacts. Even with these costs included and even though the sample was small, the research clearly demonstrated (in statistically supportable fashion) the superiority of telephone solicitation. The station has since implemented the recommendations as part of a broader telemarketing campaign.

It should be emphasized here that this was a student-initiated project and thus reinforces the central thesis of this chapter: that most managers do not easily perceive research opportunities that routinely come up in their daily marketing activities. A second point is that there is a surprising array of free or low-cost resources in the outside world that can keep research within manageable budgets. In this case, the students found the station. It could have been the other way around if the station had looked for the opportunity. Students are a good free resource and can be particularly helpful if the project is of the relatively straightforward type described here. Indeed, Chapter Eleven identifies a wide range of sources of such relatively low-cost or free, and sometimes relatively sophisticated, market research help.

Looking for Opportunity

The extended example of the television station points out two key features of the problem of looking for and recognizing research opportunities. The first lesson is that if managers are to recognize and take advantage of research opportunities, they must learn to suppress the mental barriers to research that they have acquired over the years. As predicted in Chapter One, the development vice president in the preceding case automatically reacted to the two research possibilities by saying:

> "The decision isn't really important enough to merit research. The dollars involved just aren't great enough!"

> "It is impossible to get any reasonably good research done for the few dollars that can be afforded. I can't afford a survey!"

> "Even if the research is affordable, it is impossible to imagine how to go about getting the research done without spending an arm and a leg for assistance."

As we have seen, all three arguments are myths, the kind that can get in the way of a systematic program of marketing research.

The second lesson to be learned from the example is that research opportunities do not usually reach out and tap one on the shoulder as was the case when the students came to Brady. For cheap but good research to become common practice in any organization, managers constantly have to look for these possibilities. This involves two changes in typical management practice. First, managers must cultivate a sixth sense for the serendipitous research opportunity. From time to time in most organizations, there will appear not only needs for research but also chances for research, and managers must train themselves to be alert to both. Second, management must develop an annual research plan as part of its annual planning cycle. The research plan requires that once a year, the manager set out a research want list and then either expressly budget to fill it in or fill it in with serendipitous projects as the occasions arise. We will consider the problem of research planning first.

Research Planning

An appropriate framework for beginning research planning on an annual basis is to start by cataloguing the major types of marketing decisions that managers in the researcher's organization will face within a typical year's time, including decisions to maintain the status quo. These can be the basis for determining what information is needed to help make each decision better and should yield a list of potential research projects that can be prioritized and implemented. In each succeeding year, the planning task then becomes one of determining whether any new decisions are to be made and whether the research programs already in place need to be modified in any obvious ways. This process is outlined in Figure 2.1.

The Decision Framework

Although the decisions for each individual manager will be to some extent idiosyncratic, the kinds of marketing decisions most managers face will require information differing along three broad dimensions.[1] First, decisions will be either long run or short run. Managers often must look ahead several planning periods in order to decide

FIGURE 2.1 Research Planning Process.

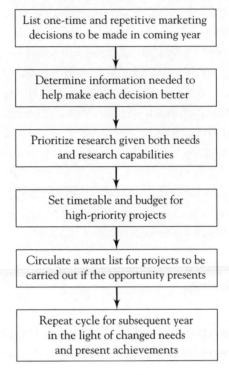

whether to make investments that would put the organization in the best possible position to exploit that future environment. Contrasted to these decisions are those short-term decisions that relate to this year's, this month's, or even this week's activities.

The second dimension is the distinction between strategy and tactics. In the main, long-run decisions will involve broad issues of strategy: what groups to be influenced, what products or services to offer or behaviors to promote, what general approaches to use to motivate key behaviors, and what organizational structure, systems, and personnel to employ to carry out these strategies. Short-run decisions, although often focusing on strategic questions, usually involve tactical issues, such as choosing between audience segments

A and B or moving a service outlet to meet sudden shifts in population or economic conditions.

The third dimension for research planning is whether the decisions are about elements of the marketing mix, such as products, channels, prices, and promotion (advertising, personal influence, promotion, public relations), or about the resources and structures needed to ensure that the mix is effectively implemented.

The three dimensions yield a basic framework for assessing marketing research needs at the start of the annual planning process. The framework is reproduced in Exhibit 2.1.

The manager can begin the marketing research planning cycle by listing the kinds of recurring decisions to be made in each of the six major sectors of Exhibit 2.1 over the course of the year. The next step in the research planning process is to ask what kinds of information are necessary and desirable to help make those decisions better. These information needs can then be translated into a funded program of future research and a list of projects to be carried out if the occasion arises.

A suggested list of the kinds of research projects that may evolve is included in Table 2.1. Although this table reports the experiences of relatively large and sophisticated organizations, it nevertheless suggests the kinds of marketing research that an aggressive low-budget researcher might contemplate.

It turns out that the information management will need in a given year will be descriptive, explanatory, or predictive.

Descriptive Information. Management is seeking to learn the state of its present market environment. One approach to specifying these *descriptive* needs is to conduct a marketing audit.[2] The market environment comprises the following major dimensions:

- Customers: Who is currently responding positively to your strategy, and who is not? What are their preferences, attitudes, and intentions with respect to your offerings?

EXHIBIT 2.1 Decision Checklist for Market Research Planning.

Subject Area	Long-Run Strategy	Short-Run Strategy	Short-Run Tactics
Segments to emphasize			
Behaviors to emphasize			
Positioning			
Marketing mix			
Benefits offered			
Services offered			
Consumer prices			
Channels for distribution			
Promotion levels			
Promotion channels			
Promotion messages			
Web strategy			
Public relations			
Resources and systems			
Partnerships			
Management staff			
Line staff			
Support staff			
Reporting systems			
Analysis capabilities			
Databases			

- Competition: What alternatives are your target audience members considering? What strategy and tactics do competitors currently employ, what marketing mix, what spending levels, and with what audience focus?

- Channels: Where do target audience members encounter your offerings and those of competitors? What partners are you using, and how satisfied are they with the relationship? How costly is the distribution system? Can the Internet be used to deliver options?

TABLE 2.1 Research Activities of 435 Companies in 1988 and 1997.

Research Activity	Percentage of Companies That Perform This Activity	
	1988	1997
Business/Economic and Corporate Research		
Industry/market characteristics and trends	83%	92%
Acquisition/diversification	50	50
Market share analysis	79	85
Internal employee studies	54	72
Pricing		
Cost analysis	60	57
Profit analysis	59	55
Price elasticity	45	56
Demand analysis		
Market potential	74	78
Sales potential	69	75
Sales forecast	67	71
Product		
Concept development and testing	63	78
Brand-name testing	38	55
Test markets	45	55
Existing product tests	47	63
Packaging studies	31	48
Competitive product studies	58	54
Distribution		
Location studies	23	25
Performance studies	29	
Coverage studies	26	
International studies	19	
Promotion		
Motivation research	37	56
Media research	57	70
Copy research	50	68
Advertising effectiveness	65	67

TABLE 2.1 (*Continued*)

	Percentage of Companies That Perform This Activity	
Research Activity	*1988*	*1997*
Competitive advertising studies	47	43
Public image studies	60	65
Sales Force Research		
Compensation	30	34
Quotas	26	28
Territory structure	31	32
Sales promotion	36	47
Buyer Behavior		
Brand preferences	54	78
Brand attitudes	53	76
Satisfaction	68	87
Purchase behavior	61	80
Purchase intentions	60	79
Brand awareness	59	80
Segmentation	60	84

Sources: Reprinted with permission from Thomas C. Kinnear and Ann R. Rott, *1988 Survey of Marketing Research* (Chicago: American Marketing Association, 1988), p. 43; Thomas C. Kinnear and Ann R. Rott, *1997 Survey of Marketing Research* (Chicago: American Marketing Association, 1997), p. 9.

- Marketing system performance: How well are your various offerings performing? Are they self-sufficient? What are the trends?

- Economic and social conditions: What is the status of general social approval or disapproval of the organization's offerings or marketing tactics? What is the state of social and economic health for each of the major audiences served?

Explanatory Information. Management typically seeks cause-and-effect linkages among the bits of descriptive information so that decisions can be made as to whether to continue or change any elements of the marketing mix. This means eventually getting answers to several questions:

- Factors outside management's control: Do changes in social and economic conditions or consumers' and system partners' goals, attitudes, and preferences significantly influence the organization's marketing effectiveness, and how?
- Factors within management's control: Does the nature and level of the marketing mix directed at target audiences significantly influence marketing effectiveness? If so, how?
- Changing market factors: What factors make today's explanations consistent or inconsistent with those of the past, that is, in what ways, if any, are the dynamics of the program environment changing?

Predictive Information. The descriptive and explanatory information can help to define what is most essential to effective management: predictions about the future. Since the actions that the manager will take in the next year will have their consequences in the future, it becomes essential to know what that future will be like and what will work in that future. Any descriptive and explanatory information gathered may or may not fill this role. It is up to management to determine which of its current assumptions will hold true for the future.[3]

Additional kinds of predictive information that management may also feel the need for include the following:

- What are partners' likely future strategies and tactics as they might affect the organization's operations?
- Are there important developments in the political and social

environment of which the manager should be aware that will pose critical opportunities or threats?

- What will the future technological environment be? Are there developments in communications systems or the Internet that the manager ought to be prepared to adapt to?

- Are significant shifts in target audience attitudes and behavior likely to arise in the future that are not simply extensions of the past?

- What of the manager's own organization? If it stays on the same course, are its financial resources, personnel, and systems going to be up to the tasks they will face?

Predictive information is mainly useful for strategic decisions with implications for the longer run. Explanatory and descriptive information, on the other hand, is most valuable in shorter-run strategic and tactical decisions.

Getting Started

At this point, the reader may well be reeling from the apparent depth and complexity of the research planning process, especially when several products or divisions are involved. But three points must be made. First, because something is challenging doesn't mean that it should not be done. Who said planning was easy? If a manager is to be effective, sacrifices are going to have to be made. The hallmark of modern managers is that they do not run the organization, or their part of it, by the seat of the pants. Careful soundings must be taken of the environment and then just as carefully merged into thoughtful plans. A manager must be organized and methodical, as well as creative and daring, to be a success. There are, of course, times when a manager must make decisions on the basis of intuition because there is no other course. This means going ahead without research or with only partly successful research because either the situation doesn't justify the expenditure or the state of the art in research technology cannot provide the information needed. Still, a good manager must be systematic in making sure that seat-of-the-pants judgments are made only after, not instead of, the possibility of collecting research information has been carefully and systematically considered. This is the role of the annual research plan.

The second point to be made with respect to the planning process is that many of the possibilities enumerated may not be relevant. Topics within a category may simply not be important to the manager and others who may be consulted in the research planning process.

Finally, the first time this planning task is carried out, it may prove formidable, but the manager should take comfort in the fact that in subsequent planning cycles, the task will be much more tractable, and maybe even easy.

Preparing the First Research Plan

The procedure recommended for the first cycling of this research planning task should have several characteristics that have proven to be important to virtually all kinds of serious planning efforts. To start, all of the key management personnel who can usefully contribute to the planning process should be brought in on it—not only key marketing staff members but others who may be expected to use the information generated.

Also, if possible, an adviser from the outside market research community should be included in the initial planning steps. The adviser can offer creative ideas for research projects based on technology with which management may not be familiar and can introduce some realistic caution to the more ambitious or off-the-wall management suggestions.

It is critical to set aside a specific time for the research planning task early in the organization's planning cycle. Allow enough time to get the job done right. The time blocked off should, at least on the first iteration, be free of other obligations. A good approach is often to undertake the research planning activity away from the office.

Research categories should be covered one at a time starting with longer-range strategic needs in Exhibit 2.1 and then moving on to short-range strategy and then to short-range tactics. The first time, the manager must be dogged in insisting that each category be covered thoroughly.

Those participating should be instructed that the major objective of the planning activity is to construct what is in effect a research want list. This should make the exercise more enjoyable than many other annual planning tasks. Staff should be urged to be uninhibited, stating what they would ideally like to know to make better marketing decisions. At this step, they should be discouraged from arbitrarily censoring certain research wants as foolish or impossible. The realities of the organization's budget and its research capabilities can be introduced at a later stage.

Prioritizing

The next stage (preferably after a good pause and perhaps a night's sleep) is to take each of the projects on the want list and group them into categories (see Table 2.2):

• Category A: Projects that are doable, essential, and merit specific funding during the planning year.

• Category B: Projects that are doable but not so essential as to merit immediate commitment of funds. These projects are still high on the want list, and management must constantly seek opportunities and funds over the year to carry them out.

• Category C: Projects that are doable but represent information it would be nice to have. Management should be alert to serendipitous opportunities to acquire the information free or at very low cost (for example, using some of the secondary sources or cooperative data collection strategies mentioned in Chapters Five and Eleven).

• Category D: Projects that would have fit into category A but appear not to be feasible now because of gaps in research knowledge or because the organization does not have access to the necessary

TABLE 2.2 Ranking of Annual Research Projects.

Managerial Relevance	Doable	Not Doable
Highly important	Category A: Fund this year.	Category D: Seek outside suggestions on feasible methodology.
Somewhat important	Category B: Do not fund. Look for opportunities to fund small studies.	Category E: Remain vigilant for new methodology that can make study feasible.
Not important	Category C: Acquire only if free or very low cost.	Category F: Ignore.

skills. Because they are potentially category A projects, that is, proj-ects to which management would clearly commit funds if they could bring the study off, some amount of managerial effort should be expended to ascertain whether the assumption about the infea-sibility of these project is indeed valid. To achieve this end, a sim-ple Request for Proposal (RFP) for a low-cost study on the topic could be sent out to several creative local research suppliers or individual consultants to see if they can come up with ways of researching the problem.

• Category E: There are currently nonfeasible projects that might fit category B. Here, almost all that management should do is maintain the vigilance suggested in the last paragraph. As in the case of category B projects, learning that a project is now doable still does not mean that the research should be done, only that it be put on hold until the opportunity presents itself.

• Category F: Nonfeasible projects that are both unimportant and not feasible given existing methodology. They should be ignored.

The final stage in the research planning process is a time-table and specific budget for undertaking category A projects and putting into motion activities needed to carry them out. At the same time, the manager should begin any steps that can be undertaken to explore the feasibility of deferred category D projects. A list of category B projects can be circulated to other managers with suggestions as to the kinds of occasions on which serendipitous data gathering might be undertaken.

Future Planning Cycles

Something like this procedure can then be repeated each subsequent planning year with important modifications. Taking the previous year's research plan, the manager need simply ask:

- Which of last year's research projects have been completed that now do not need to be done again, at least for a while?
- Which of those projects can be deleted as now irrelevant or otherwise unjustifiable?
- What new projects need to be added either because over the year management has become conscious of the need for them or because circumstances have changed?
- Which of the projects to be repeated will take the same form, and which projects need to be updated to take account of new knowledge or new circumstances?

An additional step should be added after the first year: a review of the process itself. Management, or perhaps an outsider, should look at the research decisions that were taken on the basis of the first-year plan and ask whether the planning process needs to be improved. This would involve investigating at least the following questions:

- Was the categorizing system appropriate? Were projects in various categories recategorized over the year? Was there anything that could have been done in the planning process that could have anticipated these reassignments and that could be built into the next cycle?

- What new wants were added to the list over the year, and could these have been anticipated?
- What category D and E projects were shifted to categories A and B, and why? Does this suggest any systematic ignorance in the organization about the world of research that would recommend some sort of future management training or the greater use of outside experts?
- Which category B projects were actually carried out, if any? What precipitated them, and can these precipitants be introduced in the future to ensure that more low-cost research is carried out serendipitously?

All of this involves an evaluation of the research planning process. In the next chapter, we will address more directly the question of evaluating each individual research project in terms of its own specific criteria.

Finding Research Opportunities

Many managers do not do good low-cost research because they do not see the opportunity for it. Not recognizing opportunities is the result of three often understandable gaps in the knowledge of the low-budget manager. First, opportunities may not be perceived because the manager does not know what research can do. Second, they are not perceived because the manager does not want them to be perceived. The manager may fear a loss of control or a revelation of ignorance that is to be avoided at all costs. Finally, many managers do not see research opportunities because they do not systematically look for them.

To overcome this, I have proposed a procedure for systematically identifying research needs and making room for serendipitous research possibilities. Although the task of setting up a research program may be forbidding the first time, recognizing and acting on opportunities for low-cost research over the long run will put the organization in a significantly superior strategic position in relation to its competitors. If nothing else, the research planning process can leave the new researcher-manager with a satisfied feeling that comes from knowing that the organization is making sound, if risky, marketing decisions that have been backed by the best research information that the stakes at issue can justify. These would seem to be adequate rewards for the thinking, evaluating, and planning involved in the research planning process outlined here.

Serendipitous Research: Recognizing Research Opportunities as You Go

Not all research projects can be planned ahead. Some come about because occasions for filling in items on this year's want list make their appearance.

Some years ago, an executive seminar provided me with just such an opportunity. I had been asked by the Public Broadcasting System (PBS) to spend an afternoon with its specialists in audience development to discuss several of the topics raised in this book. In preparation for the session, I read a good deal of the literature on the current turmoil in the telecommunications industry and quickly realized that I had a limited appreciation of which topics in the broad area of marketing and marketing research might be of interest to this particular audience.

At the same time, I was also searching for ways to make my presentation and discussion more realistic and more dramatic. I decided that it would be quite useful to poll the audience development specialists at each of the 170 PBS affiliates around the United States and ask them which marketing problems they would like to see addressed in my presentation. The poll would also ask about their years on the job, their formal education in marketing (if any), and their marketing experience. Since this request for help was to be a mail solicitation much like those that these audience development specialists send out all the time to potential donors and subscribers, I decided to try to demonstrate how this occasion could provide a serendipitous opportunity for research.

Many of the decisions that face those who use the mail for soliciting financial aid involve the positioning of the letter that in-

corporates the request for help. Two of the relatively minor decisions are who signs the letter and how much the mailing should be
personalized. In this study, it was decided to determine whether it
would be more effective to have the mail request signed by someone from PBS or by me. Would recipients of the solicitation respond better if the request came from a familiar source and to whom
they might feel a certain responsibility (PBS), or would the response
be greater if the source was not personally known to the respondents but was an independent individual in a high-status position
(a university professor) with whom they could be more candid and
forthright?

The second issue was whether personalizing the correspondence
would be worth the cost. While many direct mailers routinely use
computers to make cover letters speak more directly to each recip-
ient, many respondents claim that they know when a letter has been
written by a computer. A way to truly personalize the letter would be
to include a handwritten note. This would be time-consuming and
costly, but it might yield a higher payoff.

On the basis of these considerations, the decision was to split
the sample of 170 specialists randomly into four groups. Half of the
sample was to be sent cover letters with a handwritten note at the
bottom stating, "I would very much appreciate your help in this request" (the personalized treatment). The other half had no note.
Half of each of these groups received notes I signed, and half received notes the PBS director signed. One virtue of using this experimental design (formally called a *fully factorial* design) was that
it would permit us to see whether the combination of a personalized
solicitation from a particular source would be even more effective
than the effects of the personalization and the nature of the letter
writer taken separately. The criterion in testing the effects of these
four experimental treatments was to be the overall rate of response
to the request for the questionnaire information.

This project was carried out with high research standards and
was virtually costless since we were going to send the questionnaires
out anyway and did not feel we needed to place a stamp on the return envelopes. (In fact, the overall response rate for this cheap,

good study was 61 percent, a rate achieved with no stamps and no follow-up letters.)

The 170 organizations were assigned to the four treatment groups on a fully random basis. The four basic cover letters were identical in wording. The same handwriting was used for both personalized treatments. The letters were sent out the same day to everyone. All were on PBS letterhead, and all were returned to me at the University of California at Los Angeles (UCLA), where I was teaching at the time. UCLA's computer was used to analyze the results, and care was taken to apply only the appropriate analysis of variance statistics.

The findings were surprising: essentially, there were no effects. This was significant and important to know. Both the program director and I (and much of the audience when I reported the results) expected that there would be a significant effect at least from the personalized note. Given these expectations, the results were very useful. It appears that the added cost of personalizing this kind of mail solicitation, at least in the way we did it, is not at all worth the expense. The research would save managers who send out frequent large mailings considerable amounts of money they might have spent on unnecessary personalization. (Indeed, this is a conclusion of experienced research practitioners.)

One other step in the analysis was taken. When it seemed likely that the overall response rate was not going to show any significant differences between treatments, it was then decided to go back and see whether there was any effect of the treatments on the speed of response as indicated by the postmark on the return envelope. In this case, there did turn out to be a modest, although still not statistically significant, effect here for one treatment combination: personalized letters over my signature got marginally quicker responses. However, further computer analysis showed that a better predictor than the nature of the letter of how fast someone would return the questionnaire was how much formal training in marketing he or she had. The greater was the respondent's background in marketing, the faster was the response. This would suggest that those who will respond quickest to any solicitation will be those who can most closely empathize with the solicitor's needs. This too is a conclusion that can be generalized to other contexts.

This last set of analyses illustrates two other features of a well-designed program of cheap but good research. First, I went back to the database when a new researchable question occurred to me. Although in this case, it was only a matter of a few days before I decided to take a second helping from the data by looking at the postmarks to gauge the speed of response, this could have occurred months, even years, later (assuming the database was still available). Digging into an existing archive can be a productive, virtually free research opportunity (ignoring for the moment the cost of the researcher's own time and effort). Such reworking of an existing data archive, whether already in analyzable form or requiring further modification, can often prove a rich source of low-cost research. And to anticipate a point that will be made later, a nontrivial advantage of using the PBS database was that since it was my own, I knew its flaws and in fact could take pleasure in its relatively high quality. This is often not the case when using someone else's data archives.

A second feature of my follow-up analysis is that the measure of speed of response used was not part of the original design. The postmark data were available for me to use as an archive, but I had to recognize this possibility. Then all I had to do was to go back to each envelope and record its time trace. (In two cases, the cancellation machine missed the entire envelope, so I could not discern the real date, one of the many tribulations of real-world research.) There are a great many traces such as this available in the marketplace that are free for use if we only have the imagination to see them and know how to fold them into our research program.

The last lesson that can be drawn from the PBS example relates to the computer analysis. Although our original interest was in the effects of the four experimental treatments on the quantity and speed of response, an attempt was made to see whether any of the other information that was collected about respondents along the way (their marketing backgrounds) was a predictor of the speed of response, as indeed was the case. Wringing as much information out of existing data sets as possible is a major technique for keeping the cost of research low.

The Decision Opportunity

There are a number of situations in which research can be done to contribute significantly to anticipated decisions that a manager faces in the day-to-day competitive world of marketing. Daily, managers have many chances to act and, therefore, where there is time, many chances to do research. Becoming a more effective decision maker through the use of low-cost but good research requires the proper mind-set. Learning to recognize research opportunities is not just a matter of being more alert for research windows; it is also having research techniques ready to apply. Part Two offers just such an arsenal of techniques available at low cost that can be matched with relative ease to specific decision problems when they arise.

But research should not always be done even when a perfectly good low-cost technique is available. What is needed is the judicious use of research. Even when there is a lot at stake, research should not necessarily be undertaken. But we will say more about this in the next chapter.

3

Evaluating Individual Research Projects

We will assume you are ready to embark on a modest program of preplanned annual research and are much more open than you were to serendipitous research opportunities that might crop up. You and your staff have already set aside a weekend in the woods to hammer out your first research plan.

But now you are beginning to have second thoughts. "Where does it all end?" you say. "How will I know where to draw the line? How can I determine which projects to move ahead on and how much to invest in each? How do I set an annual budget for the entire research program? Basically, how do I figure out just how cheap the research has to be to be worthwhile?"

This chapter addresses these questions. To do so, we will explore some concepts borrowed from what management schools call formal decision theory.

Setting Budgets

Let us begin by reviewing some simplistic—and often wrong-headed—alternative rules of thumb for setting research budgets.

The Percentage-of-Sales Pseudoequity Approach

This approach is based on some managerially divine notion of proportionality. It says, in effect, that there exists some magical percentage rate that ought to be applied to whatever is at stake in a given managerial decision to establish a reasonable budget for research. For the annual budget, it might be a fixed percentage of projected sales. For a specific project, it might also be a percentage of the projected sales or of the capital investment.

The approach has a nice simplicity. It is easy to compute and easy to justify, and it deflects criticism and internal conflict within the organization. For example, suppose your CEO sees that you plan to spend $51,386 on research this year compared to only $36,912 last year and asks about the great increase. You can easily justify the increase by pointing out that last year's expenditure was just one-half of 1 percent of the investment made in new product development and—lo and behold—the current budget is *also* one half of 1 percent of new product investment. Or suppose a division complains that the research budget set aside for its problems has been cut 25 percent, while another division's budget has been increased 12 percent. The apparent inequities can be resolved again by showing that resulting final figures were one-half of 1 percent of sales in both cases.

This approach is like the advertising manager's reliance on percentage of sales as the determinant of the advertising budget. The fallacy in research budgeting is the same as in advertising: the percentage chosen may not be adequate or may be excessive for the tasks at hand. In advertising, the reliance on sales as the basis for the budget calculation leads to the peculiar outcome that when sales are down, competition is toughest, and advertising should be working its hardest, the percentage calculation leads the firm to cut back on its advertising budget. Conversely, when the sales and profit picture is rosiest and customers are falling all over themselves to buy any and every product the firm and its competition can produce, the Iron Law of the Percentage dictates that the firm should spend more on advertising.

In a sense, the same antilogic applies to research expenditures. Managers seem to think that research need is related to the stakes involved in a particular decision. If the stakes are great, you should spend a great deal, and when the stakes are smaller, you should spend less. Of course, what you can spend on research is not independent of what is at stake, and other things being equal, the more dollars that are at stake, the more ought to be spent on research. Nevertheless, a moment's reflection points to an obvious fallacy in all this.

In many cases, management is going to go ahead with a particular course of action in some major sales category unless the research would indicate that management's assumptions were 180 degrees off base. Although the stakes in these projects would allow a significant amount of research, management would not make a different decision because of the results. The same logic would apply to a boom market. If sales are expected to be very strong, management may not be worried about making the right decisions about, say, advertising copy. They may believe that almost anything will work. Again, research is less often justified even though sales are high. Conversely, when sales are down, management may be very worried about making just the right decision. On these occasions, the value of research is much greater despite the smaller stakes.

The illogic of the percentage method for research budgeting can also be seen dramatically when one considers the perfectly performing product line experiencing no major competitive problems and no managerial issues. The Iron Law would suggest still spending the Magic Percentage on this category. Does management hope that the research in these circumstances will come up with strategic insights or undetected weaknesses that will justify the research in the first place? This is the kind of fishing expedition we warned against in the previous chapter.

The Affordable or Residual Approach

One rationale for the percentage-of-sales approach is that it makes sure that the organization can afford the research. If sales are up, it can afford more research. If sales are down, it can afford less.

The affordable philosophy is a little different from that found in the percentage-of-sales approach in that it is based on a calculus

that subtracts from sales or the stakes at issue all other direct justi-
fiable expenditures plus a normal profit and then asks, "What is left
for discretionary items such as research?" Unfortunately, this is a
stance that sees marketing research as a highly discretionary expenditure. In part, this attitude reflects years in which too much research has indeed proved to be less than fully useful, if not totally
irrelevant, to management's needs. Given this history, managers
can easily convince themselves in times of financial stringency that
budgets for research that is likely to be of limited use can be deci-
mated to the immediate benefit of the bottom line with what is assumed are no major long-run negative impacts on the organization.

The affordability approach has the exasperating effect of making
the research budget gyrate even more grotesquely than the company's
sale curve. When sales are off a little, discretionary research budgets
fall quickly to zero, and planned research projects are curtailed dramatically, if not totally. And when sales are up, discretionary budgets
may soar even more rapidly (although one suspects never as high as
the research director would like). This volatility under both the percentage and affordable approaches tends to make a career in marketing research even more fragile than one in advertising.

The fallacy here is the same as that for the percentage-of-sales
approach: there is no logical reason that the affordability calculation will bear anything but the remotest relationship to the need for
this research. It is this latter criterion that should be management's
guide, not some arbitrary, inflexible rule of thumb.

The Free Market or Delegated Approach

This approach usually stems from management's naiveté about
what is needed to solve decision problems. In effect, it throws the
budget problem into the hands of the research supplier by means of
a request for research proposals. In its extreme form, it says in effect,
"I have a rough idea about how much is too much, but I don't really
understand what kind of research I need, and I do know how much
it will have to cost. You educate me, and perhaps I'll buy it."

Ironically, the manager adopting this approach often feels that he or she will not be really at the mercy of the suppliers in determining the research budget if the project is put out for bids. The manager apparently assumes that there is some sort of competitive market out there. If several organizations respond to an RFP for the project, the manager expects to become pretty well educated as to the cost and design implications of doing the research by reading their submissions. Then, by taking one of the lower-priced alternatives, the manager may erroneously believe that everything possible has been done to keep the cost appropriate to the problem.

The key fallacy in this commonly used approach is that the manager expects the bidding cost somehow magically to be in line with the decision. Yet the cost-determining processes the manager has set in motion are really driven by the technology the researchers choose to bring to bear and to some extent by market forces and the suppliers' bidding strategies. It is as if in the days before the motor car, a manager put out requests for bids for a method for moving raw materials over land without relying on fixed railbeds or waterways. Sending this problem out for bids may elicit a lot of very expensive and sometimes strange proposals (reflecting the state of the art). But unless the manager really has thought through what this thing called a truck will do for the company, the budget may end up five, ten, or fifteen times what it ought to be.

So it is with the research RFP. One can spend a great deal more than one ought. Different bidders will quote on different designs using different overhead allocations based on different (often arbitrary) accounting standards and profit rates, with the final total based in part on the supplier's estimate of the requesting organization's naiveté or generosity. Certainly, under this scenario, there is no reason to believe that the amount will be at all appropriate to the management's decision.

Other Factors

A number of other factors will come into play to either expand or contract a budget even where the basic criterion is relatively rational. Budgets may be affected by the following considerations.

Customer Relations. Sometimes questionnaires or depth interviews are intended in part to gather information and in part to allow customers to voice opinions. A much larger sample than is necessary (perhaps the entire population) may be surveyed in part to develop goodwill. One author cites a university study of the opinions of all incoming freshmen as excessive from a sampling theory perspective but desirable from the standpoint of student relations.[1]

External Political Necessity. Sometimes studies are too extensive because of some perceived external requirement to leave no stone unturned. This is typically the case when data are to be used in a legal case or in a regulatory setting.

Internal Political Necessity. When there is fear that a decision is about to be attacked or a department is in some organizational jeopardy, research budgets can become bloated as researchers rush to protect their jobs. This is not unlike the effect of growing malpractice threats on the research budgets of physicians and hospitals.

Rhetorical Necessity. For a researcher or a manager to win specific internal corporate battles, it may be necessary to have a larger study than is statistically essential. There may be some accepted sample size below which those who must be convinced of the results will lack confidence. In a statewide telephone survey for a public health agency, a sample size of five hundred was chosen because "prevailing wisdom, past experiences, and previous reports appeared to have conspired to create the myth about the magic of 500."[2] In a corporate setting, it is not uncommon to hear naive managers say, "How could you possibly conclude that when the sample size is so small?"

Decision-Based Research Budgeting

If the preceding examples outline approaches not to use to budget research, then how should you do it? It will come as no surprise that the answer advocated here *is to begin with the decision or decisions at is-*

sue. This, of course assumes that by the point at which the question of how much to budget is raised, the potential researcher will have framed the basic research issue in terms of one or more decisions to be made by the organization. If this is not the case, then it is essential that they or the managers involved go back and make this determination.

Structuring the Decision

What is it about the decision that will affect what should be spent on the specific research project—indeed, whether to spend anything at all? To answer this question, it will be useful to make a brief detour into the academic world of decision theory, which is simply a structured way of thinking about management problems. It says that all decision situations have five major characteristics:

1. The decision alternatives
2. A decision environment
3. The expected outcomes
4. The probabilities of various future scenarios coming to pass
5. A decision rule

Decision Alternatives. The first step management must take is to set out all the realistic decision alternatives. These alternatives can be very simple, such as whether to leave a price as it is or raise or lower it 6 percent, or relatively complicated, such as whether to (1) introduce product A containing raw materials 1, 2, and 3, at a price of P, an advertising budget of $M, and an advertising theme of Q, or (2) introduce product B with raw materials 1, 4, and 6, at a price of 2P, an advertising budget of $1/2M, and the same advertising theme Q. Nevertheless, the only requirement is that each alternative should be mutually exclusive of every other alternative. The alternatives needn't be exhaustive, but they should cover the major alternatives management is considering.

A Decision Environment. The next step is to specify the major dimensions of the future environment that will affect whether the choice of alternative 1, 2, or 3 is a good or a bad idea. These could be factors outside management's control, such as future interest rates or the proportion of a market already owning a particular electronic appliance or computer software. Alternatively, they could be factors over which management could have some influence through the alternatives it chooses, such as competitors' prices and advertising budgets.

These environmental influences, formally called *states of nature* in the decision theory literature, also can be complex. For example, one future scenario facing a marketer of a new privacy software could be that interest rates will be at 6 percent, 35 percent of the market will own privacy software, competitors' average price will be $312, and their average advertising budget will be $3.5 million. Another future could be an interest rate of 7 percent, 20 percent privacy software penetration, $350 average price, and advertising at $4.5 million. These alternative futures need not be exhaustive, but they do need to cover the major possibilities.

Expected Outcomes. For each combination of decision alternative and future environment, management must estimate an outcome. Typically, this outcome will be a dollars-and-cents estimate of the consequences of taking some action in the face of some particular environment, such as net profits before taxes. For nonprofit organizations, the outcomes may be stated in other terms, such as votes for a candidate or for a referendum or the number of individuals taking up a good health habit or visiting a museum.

Probabilities of Future Scenarios Coming to Pass. Managers are usually not neutral about the future. They have hunches or intuitions, often based on years of experience and sometimes on a recent similar situation, that some futures are more likely than others. Formal decision theory simply requires that management write down these estimates as probabilities, called *prior probabilities*. They must collectively cover the most likely possible futures.

A Decision Rule. This complex mix of alternatives, future environmental states, outcomes, and subjective probabilities must now be combined in order to come up with a final decision. This requires that management decide on a rule that it is going to use to choose among the alternatives. There are several rules that management could use. Two decision rules that are *not* usually recommended are outlined in Exhibit 3.1.

A weighted average rule (called the *expected value rule* in formal decision theory) is somewhere between the two extremes outlined in Exhibit 3.1. It requires that the manager explicitly use the probabilities of the various future environments to weigh the outcomes under each decision alternative. The recommended course of action then becomes the one that yields the best weighted sum of all possible future outcomes, with each outcome weighted by the probability of its occurrence. This doesn't guarantee one will be correct in any specific case. But in the long run, the weighted average rule will yield the best average payoffs. This is likely because in each decision

EXHIBIT 3.1   Decision Rules to Avoid.

Going for Broke. This rule, formally called the maximax criterion in decision theory, advocates that the manager choose that course of action that, across all combinations of actions and future environments, yields the single best outcome. This is a rule expressly made for the high rollers or for those organizations that believe they will stand or fall on the basis of getting one big payoff. The major deficiency of this rule is that it expressly ignores all other (potentially negative) futures that are also possible.

Playing It Safe. The other extreme is to look at the worst outcome under each alternative course of action and choose the action that involves the best worst outcome. This is known formally as the minimax criterion and is advocated for the very conservative organization. This might be one that is so financially strapped that it cannot survive a very bad loss. For most organizations, however, this approach is also faulty in that it does not consider other possible outcomes under the chosen alternative that may greatly affect its overall desirability.

---

instance, use is made of all that management knows about the decision situation. The framework also gives needed direction in deciding when to do research and how much to spend on it.

A Simplified Example

To make this framework more concrete, let us consider a hypothetical, but typical, example of a simple research problem a low-budget manager might face.

Assume that the manager of a university conference center in a woodsy resort area wishes to increase room occupancy on weekends. Weekends are a time with few conferences yet continuing high fixed costs of operation. Traditionally, the manager has promoted weekend vacations at the center through a general-purpose brochure directed at three markets: university faculty, university staff, and alumni. The brochure describes the center's programs and features, trying to offer an incentive for every taste and interest. He is now considering a brochure carefully targeted at families with young children promoting family weekends at the conference center. He believes such a brochure can be narrowly distributed to those likely to have families by developing a mailing list aimed at (1) assistant and associate professors, (2) staff who have been with the university five to fifteen years, and (3) alumni who graduated five to fifteen years ago. Each of these groups can be precisely identified.

The proposed brochure would feature child-centered activities and would cost approximately $2,400 to produce. The manager's principal concern at this point is that he is not sure that his target audience would be interested in family-centered weekends. Perhaps they may prefer childless weekend getaways. If that were the case, his new brochure might actually *decrease* bookings by scaring away those who wish to escape. The key question he now faces is whether to conduct research to assess the target audience's preferences or to proceed with his present best judgment.

Assume that discussions with the manager produce the payoff table outlined in Table 3.1. If he continues to use the existing general brochure, his revenues will be unchanged (except for any trends) from what they are now. He estimates that if he uses the new brochure and is right about the audience being child centered, he will reap $10,800 added revenues from which he would have to deduct the cost of the brochure. If he is wrong, he will lose only $1,200 in revenues, plus the $2,400 for the brochure. At the moment, he thinks there is a 60 percent chance he is right.

Table 3.1 indicates that using the weighted-average criterion, the rational course without research is to go ahead with the new brochure. The expected payoff is $3,600 greater than the payoff with the traditional campaign. What is it worth to him to check out his intuitions through research?

One way to approach the problem is to estimate the *cost of uncertainty,* that is, formally calculate how much he is worse off by not knowing the truth about his market. Let us assume the manager could acquire perfect information from the all-knowing Madame Olga. If Madame Olga found that the market wanted child-free weekends, it would be better to send out the regular brochure and keep the revenue as it is now (zero payoff). If Madame Olga said the market wanted child-centered weekends, the manager would use the new brochure and reap a payoff of $8,400. At the moment, his best guess is that there is a 60 percent chance that Madame Olga will say the market is child centered and a 40 percent chance that

TABLE 3.1 Payoff Decision Table: Gains or Losses from Normal Campaign.

Alternatives	Child-Free Preference	Child-Centered Preference	Weighted-Average Expected Payoff
New brochure	−3,600	+8,400	+3,600
Normal campaign	0	0	0
Probability	.4	.6	

Weighted average expected payoff = .4 (−3,600) + .6 (+8,400) = +3,600 she will say it is child free. Thus, the weighted expected outcome from perfect research (using Madame Olga) is $5,040 ([.6 x $8,400] + [.4 x $0]). The difference between this expected payoff with perfect information and the expected payoff without research is the most he would pay for this perfect study. This amount, $1,440, is a dollar measurement of the cost of uncertainty. This manager is $1,440 worse off by not knowing with certainty what the truth is. It represents the most he should pay for any research study since it is the most that should be paid for a perfect study.

Determinants of the Cost of Uncertainty

Two factors directly affect the cost of uncertainty. The more obvious one is the stakes in the decision. If we were dealing with dollar amounts ten times greater than those entered in Table 3.1, the cost of uncertainty would also be ten times as great.

The other determinant is the manager's uncertainty. But this uncertainty is not what you might think. It is *not* how uncertain the manager is about the state of the current market or what it will be in the future. Rather, it is the manager's uncertainty about the *better course of action to take*. There are times when the manager will not need research in spite of great gaps in knowledge about the market if the organization is already quite committed to a specific program or course of action. Alternatively, research may be very important if the manager has strong feelings about the nature of the market but is quite unsure about what to do. The latter case often comes about when the manager has strong forebodings about the market but still sees a particular venture as worth a try. For these reasons, we will refer to this second determinant of the research budget as *decision uncertainty*.

Imperfect Research

Of course, the manager cannot acquire a perfect study. We are thus still left with the question of what the manager should do about buying a research study that will not be perfect. The first step in the example is to ask whether there is any way to get a reasonable estimate of the truth for less than $1,440. Since this is the upper boundary on research expenditure, it serves as a quick checkpoint for determining whether the study is feasible under any circumstances.

Suppose the manager, after having read through the rest of this book, thinks that there are at least some techniques that might be useful for this problem at a reasonable cost, such as convenience sampling or telephone research using existing center staff. The question now is how much should be budgeted for such research given that it will be imperfect. There is a formal answer to this question using decision theory and a spreadsheet computer program with which experienced decision makers are familiar. However, most managers at this point simply use judgment and experience in the light of the stakes and degree of decision uncertainty involved to decide just how much less than the maximum (perfect study) amount should be committed.

Other Factors

Although dollars and cents of profit have been used as the measure of the stakes in the example, it is possible that the stakes may have some nonmonetary elements, such as risks to a personal career or to a company's Wall Street image or the possibility that a government agency will question a particular action. These consequences are difficult to quantify, and a consideration of techniques to attempt to do so is beyond the scope of this book. However, it is perfectly valid, and indeed sound management practice, to augment or decrease a particular dollars-and-cents outcome to take account of nonquantifiable yet important outcomes in the decision environment. For example, in the example, the manager might wish to add a value of $1,000 to the payoffs under the new brochure option to reflect an imputed value for the positive effects on staff motivation of trying any new approach.

When to Resist Research

This book is premised on the notion that research should be a more frequently used management tool once a wider audience becomes aware that research can be understandable, low cost, and useful.

There are two kinds of danger here. First, if managers become more aware of research approaches that are relatively inexpensive and relatively simple, they may do too much research, arguing, "Since the cost of the research can be kept so low, why don't we go ahead and do the research anyhow?" Such "Why not?" research can lead all too often to wasted research funds. The manager who too often says, "Why not?" may well be one who will eventually shift from a positive attitude toward research to a negative attitude. Since many of the "Why not?" studies will be of little value to the managers, they may well come to conclude that research indeed usually is wasted.

There are two major rules to apply in order to resist the urge to do unnecessary research:

- Resist the research urge if the research is not directly related to some decision to be made.
- Resist the research urge if there is not some reasonable degree of uncertainty as to the correct action to take.

The second danger in too much research is that attempts to do low-cost research will quickly degenerate into the old faithful cheap and questionable research. Later chapters introduce a number of techniques that are relatively simple and straightforward in concept in addition to being low in cost. Each of these chapters contains admonitions to observe standards that will differentiate good from questionable research. I will try to make it difficult for the careful researcher to carry out questionable research unknowingly. Where cost constraints force an easing of quality constraints, however, the researcher must know where the potential biases will creep in and how to make allowance for them in subsequent decision making.

Being able to carry out a quality research program successfully, even a low-cost one, requires considerable training (or at least careful reflection about what is written in this book) and care and conscientiousness. *Resist the research urge if the research is likely to be flawed in ways that cannot be estimated or adjusted for when making a decision.*

There are also a number of other situations to avoid research:

- *Resist doing research if it is really designed to bolster personal insecurities.* A manager who has worked through the decision framework outlined above and come to the clear conclusion that research is not a rational choice should not still go ahead because the research is not too expensive and will make him or her feel better about the risky action about to be taken.

- *Resist research if it is designed only to provide ammunition to justify a decision to others in the organization.* If experience says that the boss or rival managers will insist on research to back up your actions, do the research. This is a rational choice, but costs should be kept within reason. However, the research should not be done on the rare chance it will be politically necessary.

- *Resist research designed just to check up on how things are going.* Unless such checking is part of a consciously designed program of market monitoring or unless there is reason to believe something is up out there, this checking up is just another managerially cowardly act. Keep an ear to the ground informally all the time; however, committing research dollars where an informal ear will suffice is an abuse of fiduciary trust.

- *Resist research that is, at base, a fishing expedition.* Over time, every manager faces spells of corporate malaise and vague uneasiness when someone may say, "Why don't we take a look at . . . ?" If the look can be justified by some concrete suspicions or supporting rationale, then formal research can be justified. A fishing expedition can be pleasurable, and if it is just the manager's own time and money involved, it is not irresponsible. Indeed (like all fishermen, I suspect), the manager may catch fish just often enough to be convinced that the activity is justified by the payoff. However, in research, if the activity is not rationally justified as helping managers make specific decisions now or in the future, avoid it.

• *Resist research that is designed to appeal to the manager's curiosity.* Many wasteful research projects have grown out of the pregnant expression, "Wouldn't it be interesting to know if . . . " (for example) more women used the product than men; corporate ads reached a lot of political bigwigs; the eastern region was more profitable because it had more large accounts; and so forth. Interesting research results are not useful research results unless they affect actions. Whenever the manager hears (or says), "Wouldn't it be interesting . . ." a loud bell should ring. First analyze the decision carefully on paper, asking whether further research information would change the decision materially. If the answer to the question is no, the conclusion should be to suppress curiosity and not waste company resources.

• *Resist research that keeps up with the Joneses.* Rare is the manager who hasn't once in a while come back from a conference, a meeting with the advertising agency, or a telephone call to another company division frustrated that someone else is doing more or different research than he or she is. This is particularly a problem with research fads. Many years ago, I was asked to do a psychographics study for a major eastern bank. (A psychographics study would develop information on customer demographics and lifestyles that would yield recognizable customer segment types; for example, "fearful seniors," "risk-taking Boomers," and so on.) It seems that the marketing director had just returned from a conference where everybody was talking psychographics. The manager felt left out, behind the times. His ego was bruised. And darn it, he was going to have his psychographic study.

A two-hour discussion quickly revealed two things. First, the manager had not at all thought through how he was going to use the psychographic study to affect advertising decisions, product offerings, or, indeed, much of anything else. He apparently expected this to emerge from the results (the fishing expedition problem). Second, our discussions revealed a lot of more important gaps in the bank's marketing knowledge that cried out to be filled before doing a psychographics study. A simple inexpensive research project would analyze internal records to learn which customers used more than one service (had a checking account and a safety deposit box or had a mortgage and certificates of deposit, and so on). This exercise could yield management much valuable information as to which services to sell to customers of other bank services and which to sell to single-service customers. A short survey of multiple-services customers might also be undertaken to assess reasons for heavy use and motivations and barriers that seemed to affect multiple use. Such insights could then suggest how solicitations directed at single-service users could be worded. (The bank manager found someone else who would do his psychographics study.)

• *Resist research for the sport of it.* Research can be seductive. Many times, I have found myself going back to do one more computer run or send out one more particularly complex questionnaire or conduct a simple little experiment just because I was excited about the project. It is challenging to see whether I could do it! But I try hard to avoid these urges, especially when I am spending someone else's money. Research can be fun. It can provide its own momentum. It is absolutely crucial to make sure that this momentum is toward useful research and not toward research for its own sake. To do otherwise will make the researcher in effect an accomplice to misappropriation of corporate resources.

4

Backward Marketing Research

An executive of a performing arts organization company decided that she knew too little about the consumer segments she was serving or hoped to serve. She had been practicing an obvious segmentation strategy aiming some programs at younger audiences, some at older ones, some at families, and some at singles. She needed a more sophisticated strategy, so she commissioned a research agency to analyze the company's market. Despite high hopes, glowing promises, and the production of a glossy report heavy with statistics, the executive was disappointed in the findings. She said, "The research mostly told me things I already know."

Her service operated in an industry whose primary consumers had already been studied more than two hundred times. Each study said virtually the same thing as this one: the audience was largely female, economically upscale, well educated, urban, and mainly on either end of the age distribution scale.

"Even where the results were new," she said, "they didn't tell me what I needed to know so I could use them." The consumer profile relied on demographics as the principal segmentation variable. "Sure," the manager added, I know that men attend less often than women, but why? Do they see fewer benefits than women, or are

Much of the material in this chapter originally appeared as Alan R. Andreasen, "'Backward' Marketing Research," *Harvard Business Review*, May–June 1985, pp. 176–182. Copyright © 1985 by the Harvard Business School Publishing Corp.; all rights reserved. Reprinted with permission.

there barriers to attendance that apply to men and not to women? And what about the age profile? Does the middle-aged group drop out because we don't meet their needs, or are they just focused on things that we can't match, like building a family?" She had learned who her customers were but nothing about how to motivate them.

"When the researcher tried to explain the results, it was obvious he hadn't understood what I wanted. The results were all a bit off the mark." Consider the measurement of loyalty. The researcher assumed his client wanted a behavioral measure, so he sought information on the proportion of recent entertainment purchases that were from each type of performing arts and each location. But his client also wanted an attitudinal measure revealing consumer intentions. She wanted to know less about their past loyalty than about their likely future loyalty.

How Research Goes Wrong

We can sympathize with this executive's complaints, although clearly she must share the blame for poor study design. She neglected to make the undertaking a real collaboration with the researcher, a common fault. Indeed, studies of research successes and failures point again and again to close collaboration between researcher and client as the most important factor predicting a good outcome.

The typical approach of the two parties starts with defining the problem. Then they translate the problem into a research methodology, which leads to the development of research instruments, a sampling plan, coding and interviewing instructions, and other details. The researcher takes to the field, examines the resulting data, and writes a report. This traditional approach is outlined in Figure 4.1.

The executive then steps in to translate the researcher's submissions into action. She has, of course, already devoted some thought to the application of the results. From my observations, however, before the research is undertaken, the intended action is left vague and general. Managers tend to define the research problem as a broad area of ignorance. They say, in effect, "Here are some things I don't

FIGURE 4.1 Forward Research Design.

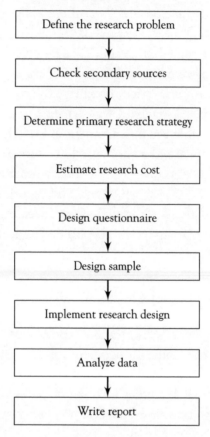

know. When the results come in, I'll know more. And when I know more, then I can figure out what to do!" In my experience, this approach makes it highly likely that the findings will be off-target.

I suggest a proven procedure that turns the traditional approach to research design on its head. This procedure, which stresses close collaboration between researcher and corporate decision makers, markedly raises the odds that the company will come up with findings that are not only interesting but will lead to actionable conclusions.

There are only two cases in which research is not expected to be immediately actionable. The first is when the research is intended to be basic—that is, to lay the groundwork for later investigation or action rather than have any near-term impact. The second occasion is when the research is methodological—that is, designed to improve the organization's ability to ask questions in the future. Except for these two instances, research should be designed to lead to a decision.

Turning the Process on Its Head

The backward approach I advocate rests on the premise that the best way to design usable research is to start where the process usually ends and then work backward. We develop each stage of the process on the basis of what comes after it, not before. This approach is outlined in Figure 4.2. The procedure is as follows:

Step 1: Determine what key decisions are to be made using the research results.

Step 2: Determine what information will help management make the best decisions.

Step 3: Prepare a prototype report and ask management if this is what will best help them make their decisions.

Step 4: Determine the analysis that will be necessary to fill in the report.

Step 5: Determine what questions must be asked to provide the data required by the analysis.

Step 6: Ascertain whether the needed questions have been answered already somewhere.

Step 7: Design the sample.

Step 8: Implement the research design.

Step 9: Write the report.

Step 10: Assist management in implementing the results.

Step 11: Evaluate the research process and its contribution.

As one might expect, the first step is the most important.

FIGURE 4.2 Backward Marketing Research.

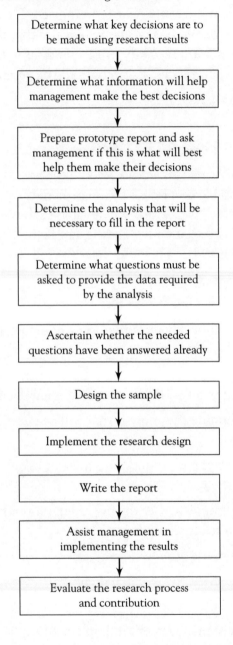

Step 1: Determine What Decisions Are to Be Made

To most managers, the research problem is seen as a lack of important facts about their marketing environment. A manager may say, "The problem is I don't know if service A is preferred over service B," or, "The problem is I don't know if my collaborators are more satisfied with my organization than my major competitor's partners are with them, and if they aren't, what they're unhappy about." By defining the problem, the solution is simply a reduction in the level of ignorance. The data elicited may be very interesting and may give managers a great deal of satisfaction in revealing things they didn't know, but satisfaction can quickly turn to frustration and disappointment when the executive tries to use the results.

Consider a lifestyle study done not long ago on over-the-counter drugs. Some respondents who claimed they were always getting colds and the flu were very pessimistic about their health. They frequently went to doctors, but the doctors were never much help. The respondents thought that over-the-counter drugs were often beneficial but weren't sure why. This information, together with other details, caused the researchers to label this group the *hypochondriacs*.

What to do with these results? As is usually the case with segmentation strategies, there are quantity and quality decisions to make. The company has to decide whether to pump more marketing resources into the hypochondriac group than its proportion of the population would justify. The marketing vice president might first say yes because the hypochondriacs are heavy over-the-counter drug users, but the picture is more complicated than that. Perhaps hypochondriacs are sophisticated buyers, set in their purchase patterns and loyal to favorite brands. If so, money aimed at them would have little impact on market share. Light users, on the other hand, may have fragile loyalties, and throwing money at them could entice them to switch brands. Of course, just the opposite might be true: the hypochondriacs, being heavy users, might prove highly impressionable and responsive to compelling ads.

On the qualitative side, lifestyle research could be much more helpful. Since it generates a rich profile describing each group's jobs, families, values, and preferences, this research could tell the company what to say. But the frustrated manager is likely not to know where to say these things. There is no *Hypochondriac's Journal* in which to advertise, and there may be no viewing or reading patterns that don't apply to heavy users in general, hypochondriacs or not.

A self-selection strategy could be tried: the company develops an ad speaking to hypochondriacs' fears and worries in the hope that they will see the message and say to themselves, "Ah, they're talking about me!" But nonhypochondriac heavy users who read the ad might say, "Well, if this product is really for those wimpy worrywarts, it certainly is not for sensible, rational me! I'll take my patronage elsewhere." In this case, the research will be very interesting (fine fodder for cocktail party banter) but not actionable.

Suppose that the company had first laid out all the action alternatives it might take after the study. If the marketing vice president had made it clear that his problems were whether to allocate marketing dollars differently and whether to develop marketing campaigns aimed at particular, newly discovered segments, he would have set the project in a more appropriate direction. In the first case, discussions with the researcher would help the vice president determine the criteria that would justify a different budget allocation. Naturally, before he can reach a decision, the vice president needs research on the likely responses of different segments to advertising and promotional money spent on them. In the second case, the manager needs to know whether there are indeed channels for best reaching these segments. Only by management's first thinking through the decisions to be made with the research results will the project be started with high likelihood of action.

Step 2: Determine Information Needed for Decision

Conversations with management will reveal the kinds of answers that will allow the choice among the courses of actions being considered. These can often be multiple answers to increase chances that the right course will be chosen.

Step 3: Prepare a Prototype Report

Management should ask itself, "What should the final report look like so that we'll know exactly what moves to make when the report is in?" The collaboration between the researcher and the manager should intensify and prove dynamic and exceedingly creative.

Scenario writing is a good technique for developing ideas for the contents of the report. The initiative here lies with the researcher who generates elements of a hypothetical report and then confronts management with tough questions like, "If I came up with this cross-tabulation with these numbers in it, what would you do?"

The first payoff from this exercise arises from improvement of the research itself. These prototype tables can take the project forward by sharpening the decision alternatives and backward by indicating the best design for the questionnaire or pointing out how the analysis of the findings should be carried out. (See Table 4.1 for an example prototype table.) The forward effect is evident in the following case:

> A manager marketing a high-priced service is considering cancelling a discount for multiple purchases because she thinks that most people taking advantage of it are loyal customers who are already heavy users, are upscale, and are largely price inelastic. Therefore, she speculates, the discount is just lost revenue. She is seriously considering dropping the discount altogether. To determine whether this is a sound decision, she needs to predict the responses of both old and new customers to the elimination of the discounts.

Suppose the researcher hypothesizes that long-time customers will be price inelastic and new customers will be price elastic. Results from such an outcome would be like those in Table 4.1. Here,

TABLE 4.1 Hypothetical Sales Results Before and After Discount.

	Sales at Discounted Price	Sales at Nondiscounted Price	Number of Respondents
New customers	100	53	40
Old customers	100	92	460

we see that only 8 percent of her sales represents new customers and that eliminating the discount will have little effect on old customers. These results confirm the manager's decision to drop the discounts. However, reflecting on the results in Table 4.1 showing that new customers do respond to the discount, the manager thinks, "What if we offered a one-time discount to consumers who have never tried the service?" In considering this alternative, the manager realizes that before she can reach this decision, she needs to know whether potential new customers can be reached with the special offer in a way that will minimize (or, better, foreclose) purchases at a discount by long-time customers.

This new formulation of the decision leads to a discussion of the results that indicates that the study *really* needs to ask not only about the permanent discount but also about a one-time discount. The results of these questions can be captured in another dummy table showing responsiveness to the one-time discount by past patronage behavior, as in Table 4.2. This table suggests that it does make sense to go ahead with the one-time discount.

As the manager reflects on this table, she realizes that she still needs a way of minimizing the chance that old customers will take advantage of the one-time discount. One way this could be accomplished is by avoiding announcing the offer in media that old customers read or listen to. This indicates to the manager (and the researcher) that the questionnaire should also contain some questions on media habits. And so it goes.

This pattern of presenting possible results and rethinking design needs can be very productive. The process can sometimes have unan-

TABLE 4.2 Hypothetical Sales Results Under Three Pricing Strategies.

	Sales at Discounted Price	Sales at Nondiscounted Price	Sales at One-Time Discount	Number of Respondents
New customers	100	53	76	40
Old customers	100	92	97	460

ticipated consequences. Sometimes the researcher will present contrasting tables pointing to exactly opposite conclusions, only to discover that management is most likely to take the same course of action despite the results. This is usually a case for doing away with that part of the research design altogether.

Participation by the manager in this step of the backward research process has other advantages:

- It serves to co-opt managers into supporting the research work should it be criticized later.

- It deepens their understanding of many of the details of the research itself and their appreciation of both its strengths and its weaknesses.

- Working with hypothetical tables can make the manager eager for the findings when they do appear and ready to implement them.

- Working with contrasting tables makes it unlikely that the manager will be startled by surprising results, an outcome that sometimes causes manager to reject an entire study.

- Participation will reveal to management any limitations of the study. In my experience, managers are often tempted to go far beyond research truth when implementing the results, especially if the reported truth supports the course of action they prefer anyway.

Step 4: Determine the Analysis Needed

The form of the report will clearly dictate the nature of the analysis. If management proves to be leery of analysis more complex than cross-tabulations in the earlier interactions, the researcher can design a series of step-by-step tabulations for the report that can make a complex argument. If management is comfortable with the higher reaches of statistics, the researcher can draw out some of the more advanced analytic procedures. In general, however, the analysis phase should be straightforward. If the exercise of hypothetical table writing has gone well, the analysis should amount to little more than filling in the blanks.

Step 5: Decide on the Questions to Be Asked in the Study

The backward approach is very helpful in the data-gathering stage in indicating what kinds of data to gather. It can also help in wording questions. One large electronics manufacturer wanted to gauge young consumers' knowledge of and preferences for stereo components. Not until the researcher had prepared mock tables showing preference data by age and sex did the client's wishes become clear. By "young," the client meant children as young as ten years old. Moreover, the client believed that preteens, being a very volatile group, undergo radical changes from year to year, especially as they approach puberty.

Original research design plans had set a lower age cutoff for the sample at age thirteen and grouped respondents by relatively broad age categories, such as thirteen to sixteen and seventeen to twenty. This design went out the window. If the researcher had been following the usual design approach, the client's expectations may not have surfaced until the study was well under way.

Step 6: See If the Data Already Exist Somewhere

This exploration of existing secondary sources is now much easier than it was a decade ago because of the Internet and because there is simply much more marketing research going on.

Step 7: Design the Sample

Backward design can also help determine the appropriateness of using careful probability sampling techniques. If, for example, management wants to project certain findings to some universe, the research must employ precise probability methods. On the other hand, if the client is chiefly interested in frequency counts (say, of words that consumers use to describe the organization's major brands or of complaints voiced about its frontline people), sampling restrictions need not be so tight. In my experience, researchers often build either too much or too little sampling quality for the uses the company has in mind. Similarly, scenario writing will usually also reveal that management wants more breakdowns of the results than the researcher anticipates, requiring larger sample sizes or more precise stratification procedures than initially planned. Through simulating the application of the findings, the final research design is much more likely to meet management's needs and permit low field costs.

Steps 8 Through 11

The first seven steps encompass the major advantages of the backward technique. Steps 8 through 9 revert to a traditional forward approach that applies the research decisions and judgments made earlier. If all parties have collaborated well in the early stages, these steps will carry through what has already been largely determined. Note, however, that in this approach, the process does not stop with writing the report. It is important to complete the research follow through, help management implement the results, and then evaluate the research process itself (steps 10 and 11).

Conclusion

You can use the traditional approach and hope that careful thinking about the problem will lead to the needed design improvements. However, the backward approach gives management and the researcher a specific step-by-step technique for ensuring that these improvements will emerge. The approach has the additional advantages of making management able to understand the results once they do appear, unsurprised by some outcomes, and eager and ready to put the findings to use immediately. More widespread adoption of this approach will go a long way toward eliminating the perception of too many managers that research all too often is obvious, off-target, or unimplementable.

Low-budget researchers cannot afford to fund projects that are obviously off-target or unimplementable. The backward approach takes time, but in the long run, it is time well spent for both researcher and management. It guarantees the research the best possible chance of being truly useful and used.

PART TWO

Alternative Low-Cost
Research Techniques

5

Using Available Data

In this chapter, we begin our consideration of techniques for providing low-cost marketing research information. As we have seen, many managers think that producing market information means going into the field to collect data themselves. Field research can be done relatively inexpensively. However, it is always more costly to gather new data than to analyze existing data. There is almost always a gold mine of data in every organization simply lying about as archives waiting to be milked for their marketing and managerial insights. The primary goal of this and the next chapter is to alert low-budget researchers to the possibilities of discovering rich mother lodes of information already available (often on the Internet) that are usually ignored, or at least greatly underused, by inexperienced marketing managers.

One of the solutions is to get more information out of primary data that you have already collected and superficially analyzed. It is my experience that most primary commercial research data are sadly underanalyzed. Researchers sometimes lack the sophistication to take a deep cut into a study's meaning. Sometimes they avoid such sophistication because they believe that the managers for whom they work would not understand the more complex results if they gave them to them. Most often, underanalysis is simply a matter of not having enough time. In the commercial world, often one study is just barely done before it is time to move on to the next one.

We will delay a consideration of advanced analytical techniques that could be applied to existing data (if time were available) to Chapter Ten. We turn here to considering all of the other existing sources of data that often have never been thought of as a source of marketing research.

Archives

Existing data ready to be gathered and analyzed at a relatively modest cost represent an extremely diverse array. To put some order on this diversity, it will be helpful to develop a classification scheme. This scheme not only helps organize the material in this and the next chapter, but also offers a checklist for using the possibilities for this kind of cheap in-house research.

There are two basic sources of existing information that are readily accessible to conscientious low-budget researchers. First, there are existing records or documents that enumerate events, actions, and outcomes that have already taken place. These records and documents, usually referred to as *archives,* include such running records as billing invoices, fundraisers' expense accounts, target audience complaint letters, and Web site hits. Archives can be further partitioned into records that are generated by your own organization and records that are generated by somebody else. We will refer to data collected in-house and by others as internal and external archives, respectively.

The second class of readily accessible data is phenomena that are not already recorded but can be simply observed. Obvious examples in marketing are observations of traffic flows of visitors to a museum, license plates in a parking lot that can indicate geographic profiles of customers, or conversations between contact people and customers. In the case of observation, some preliminary effort will have to be made to record the data systematically before they can be analyzed.

These two types of sources, archives and observations, have an important feature in common: they do not involve questioning respondents or otherwise intruding on the subjects of the research. This helps keep the cost down. They also have another very important benefit in improving research quality. A study conducted thirty years ago pointed out that research that is intrusive can have major distorting effects on the phenomena it is attempting to study.[1] Asking people questions makes them wonder about the researcher's motives, makes them cautious about what they reveal, and makes them concerned about how they portray themselves, all of which can distort the answers they give. Overtly observing people as they shop or watch television or talk to a salesperson can make them behave more cautiously or rationally than they would otherwise. In both cases, the process of measurement alters that which is measured. The advantage of the techniques that we will discuss here and in the next chapter is that they can eliminate this potentially major source of bias. Of course, if not systematically carried out, unobtrusive observation or archival studies can have their own biases. But at least they are not compromised by distortions that the techniques themselves create.

In this chapter, we consider internal and external archives. In Chapter Six, we explore the possibilities of using unobtrusive observations.

Internal Archives

Most organizations are rich storehouses of data. These data can be separated into two broad categories. First, there are records that represent measurements of some kind—for example, sales records. An excellent cheap, good research project would be one that simply organizes and analyzes such records in imaginative ways. The other kind of internal record is what might be called measurable records: data that are transcribed in some nonnumerical form and so require as a first step attaching numerical values to them. Examples of measurable archives that come most readily to mind are customer complaint letters, narrative reports of customer contacts, and reports of visits to competitive locations.

A simple enumeration or coding of the data in measured or measurable records can provide intriguing new insights to a marketing manager. Even in the rare case where the records are biased (as is the case with complaint letters), they can still be managerially useful.

Internal Measured Records

Modern organizations collect and keep a great deal of data in numerical form. Such data are potential sources of rich insights to the person who sets out to wring meaning from them.

Sales Reports. Sales reports are often a rich source of undetected research insights. For example, magazine publishers routinely use newsstand sales to judge the popularity of cover subjects and individuals.

Consider the following example:

In the fall of 1997, Fran Herzog, the manager of a performing arts facility at a major midwestern university, was concerned about the informal way she forecast attendance at various events. Forecasts were used to determine seating configurations for the facility and the number of ushers and concessionaires to hire and to estimate the likely revenues and profits (or losses). She was concerned that most of her forecasts were seat-of-the-pants guesses based on her own experience and that of her staff. She was eager to develop a better, more scientific approach, particularly if such a forecast could also serve as the starting point for "What if?" speculations about the probable effects of changing prices, increasing (or decreasing) advertising, or spending more for publicity.

Preliminary investigation into the problem by a senior staff member, Ardeth McKenzie, revealed that buried in the drawers of the facility's main office was a wealth of detailed data in the form of sales records on performances over the past eleven years. Information for most, although not all, of the 264 events over the period had been recorded on individual sheets of paper on the following performance characteristics:

- Prices charged in each of three seating categories
- Size of the total house
- Number of seats assigned to each price category
- Number of tickets sold at each price level
- Dollars spent on advertising
- Costs of the performance (for example, overhead, operating expenses, performers' fees)
- Date and time of performance
- Weather on the day of the performance

McKenzie, a student in the university's M.B.A. program, entered this rich trove of archival data into her personal computer and proceeded to apply multiple regression statistical analysis to it. The resulting equation showed management the extent to which sales were affected by price, advertising expenditures, time of year, and weather within each of several event categories, holding all the other factors constant. Although Herzog was hampered by small numbers of cases in some categories, the data gave her the more scientific platform she desired from which to make her future predictions. The new model, of course, provided only ballpark figures. Herzog and her staff still added to the prediction base their own experiences and intuitions about the likely popularity of various groups and events they were thinking of booking. Still, the new forecasting results were considered a major enhancement to what had been heretofore a seat-of-the-pants decision-making process. The forecasts were particularly useful at the beginning of the planning year in helping management estimate the effects on annual revenue of different mixes of events. Further use of the equations to explore alternative marketing mixes was contemplated for the future.

A similar study some years ago analyzed season ticket preferences of theater subscribers to the Mark Taper Forum in downtown Los Angeles. It analyzed sales data archives for 108 choices made by subscribers each year from 1970 to 1976 using a complex multiple regression model. The model was very successful in explaining 79.2 percent of the variation in sales. The researchers were able to tell management that with other variables held constant:

- Saturday was the best day for performances, followed by Thursday.
- Matinees were a bit more popular than evenings (other things equal, which they are usually not).
- Seating in section A was less preferred to section B, suggesting a possible price reduction for the former.
- Having a discussion after the performance had a positive motivating effect and should be continued.
- Subscribers preferred early weeks in the run of a particular show. For this reason, they deserve particular attention as they will have crucial word-of-mouth influence on later individual ticket buyers.[2]

Pseudoexperiments. Attendance records can be the basis for tracking the effects of unexpected occurrences in the organization's environment. Because attendance data comprise a continuing record, one can monitor the effect of some event or events by looking at performance measures before and after that event. The occurrence of unexpected events, like a blizzard or a strike at a major area employer, is sometimes referred to as a pseudoexperiment. True experiments involve the random assignment of subjects (such as cities, outlets, or target audience members) to various treatment or control conditions so that effects due to factors other than the treatment (for example, a new communication theme or the addition of a new behavioral incentive) can be measured and eliminated. In a pseudoexperiment, the manager has not exerted such quality control. This often means that the researcher will have difficulty separating out the effects of the event under study from other things going on at the same time.

In a pseudoexperiment, the researcher can dig back into the performance archives to look at the effects of the uncontrolled event on attendance. For example, compared to the previous period, did the four-week factory strike reduce attendance a little, a lot, or not at all? A problem of interpretation occurs if the researcher has no comparative contemporary situation in which the event did not occur (in this situation, data from a similar operation in a similar community with no factory strike). There is always the possibility that the change in attendance would have occurred without the strike.

Even where there is a comparison site with no strike, the researcher may still have problems. The comparison site community may be enjoying a long-term economic upturn (or downturn), or the comparison institution may have recently changed its own offerings. Performance effects from the comparison site therefore may not be generalizable to any other market. Consider a case where one city raises its sales taxes and the researcher wishes to observe its effect on performance. It may be that the taxes were increased only because other city revenues, such as corporate or property taxes, were very low or declining. The performance archives may show a decline after the increase in city taxes compared to the period before the sales tax increase. But the real (or major) cause may be a general decline in the local economy.

Pseudoexperiments using performance archives, however, can be very helpful as a research approach, provided careful attention is paid to thinking through (and discounting) all other possible causes of the effects observed. An example will be illuminating:

In a project in which I was involved, a sales contest was held among three salespeople of a distributor of contraceptive products in a developing country. Analysis of sales archives for the contest period during a three-month period indicated that (1) sales for the three salespeople overall had risen compared to the year-earlier period, (2) the sales increase had been greater for only one of the two product lines, and (3) only one of the three salespeople had exceeded expected sales.

Management wanted to know whether such contests should be used in future. A first problem was to see whether the contest *did* have an impact on sales as total sales had risen over the year-earlier period. The real question was, What would have happened to these sales had there not been the sales contest? The year-earlier figures were the best benchmark assuming there were no major year-to-year increases in overall sales. Unfortunately, the latter was not true. There had been a major increase in sales over the previous year.

Reanalysis of the sales data archives showed that the increase over the year-earlier sales achieved in the three-month contest period almost exactly equaled the increase in sales for both products for the other nine months of the same year. Thus, it was tentatively concluded that the sales contest's overall effects were due to a general upward trend in sales, not to any special sales efforts on the part of the contest participants.

But that did not explain why one salesperson exceeded the others. One possibility was that the winner was able personally to increase sales as the contest intended. However, the winner had a territory that contained the largest retail outlets in the country's capital city, which contained half the country's population. This fact suggested that the higher level of sales was made possible by the fact that the salesperson's large accounts could more easily load up inventory under pressure from a persuasive salesperson who was trying to win a contest. The smaller retail stores served by the other salespeople presumably would less often have the financial strength to be so accommodating.

A few telephone calls to the larger outlets in the winner's territory could reveal the truth. If the results of the calls showed no loading up, one would not be able to rule out such behavior. First, it is possible that the retailers might not have recalled their behavior for one or two minor products in one specific three-month period (in this country, one could not rely on their store records). Alternatively, the retailers might simply lie, not wanting to admit that they had been coerced into excessive inventory accumulation.

Since this obtrusive procedure seemed likely to be unsatisfying, an obvious use of another archive, invoices of sales to the individual outlets, seemed a reasonable and potentially unbiased alternative. Although the database was small, the overall indications from this analysis were that excessive loading up by the large retailers was not a factor. It was concluded that sales in this one territory had benefited from the contest. However, the fact that two markets showed no effects led management to conclude that contests were probably not a good way to increase sales.

Individual Transaction Records. Sales invoices can give important insight into what is going on in a particular market and can be analyzed in other ways too. For example, fundraising records can allow calculation of average donation per transaction. When compared to the cost of each transaction, figures can indicate whether some donors are not worth visiting or some proposals not worth making.

Dates on transactions can be used to calculate how often contact people visit customers or donors and the average length of time between visits (assuming that most contacts result in transactions). An analysis of transaction proceeds can show whether contact people allocate their visit frequencies proportional to the expected returns. They can also reveal which contact people have favorite customers they seem to like to visit regardless of potential.

Separate analysis of refund slips can provide early warnings of weak products or services. Also, the analysis of the number of voided invoices or of the thoroughness with which invoices are filled out can help evaluate the quality of individual staff members.

Sales invoices can be used to double-check other data collected in primary studies, for example, to validate a survey respondent's reported purchases. A study of the family planning product distribution system in Bangladesh made detailed use of distributor's call records to help verify data on purchases reported by retailers in a retail audit. These archival data gave the researchers confidence in the primary field data that could not be obtained in any other way.

Postal code locations of customers can be analyzed. Is greater attention suggested for a particular area? Should additional personnel be assigned? When new products or services are introduced, invoices can lead to the discovery of target markets by showing whether some kinds of customers or some postal code areas are more likely to try the offering than others.

Contact Reports.   Many organizations have personnel prepare verbal reports of customer comments, trade show gossip, and other significant market behavior. Evaluation of the quality of such reports can be used as one measure of staff performance.

Mileage per day, when controlled for territory size, can suggest the extent to which contact people such as fundraisers are using their time efficiently. And mileage data uncontrolled for territory size can support a fundraiser's claim that territories are too large and cause too much driving time.

Miscellaneous Records.   In some service businesses, purchase orders for various supplies (such as soaps or shampoos for clinics or children's game cards in child care centers) can be good indicators of demand for particular services. In addition, the number and length of long-distance calls or Internet "conversations" can be monitored to indicate staff activity and pattern of contacts.

When the organization markets services to its own staff, accounting records can often identify important sales opportunities. Several years ago, a major university's transportation department was seeking new opportunities for renting its cars and trucks to faculty and staff. A computer analysis of accounting archives pinpointed departments that were heavy users of outside auto and truck rental agencies. These departments were then targeted for direct personal and telephone selling by the transportation division's staff.

Internal Measurable Data

Many kinds of archives are not in numerical form. Someone has to quantify the data to make them usable for research purposes. Some archives of this type are complaint records and inquiries and comments.

Complaint Records. Virtually all organizations receive letters and telephone calls from irate target audience members. Surprisingly, though, few organizations routinely record the data in these potential archives or analyze them. What is required is some relatively simple master coding scheme that sets categories for (1) the organizational activity or offering involved, (2) the nature of the complaint, (3) the original contact person, (4) the date and location of problem, and (5) complainer characteristics (plus whatever other data the organization may wish to track). Someone then must code each complaint letter or telephone call according to the preestablished categories so that the results can be added up and analyzed.

These data are potentially very rich, but they are biased in two important ways. First, many studies suggest that those who voluntarily complain are not fully representative of all of those with complaints. For one thing, someone with a problem who wants to contact the organization must know *how* to complain and be somewhat assertive and articulate, traits associated with higher education and higher social status. Poorer, less educated, more timid customers are less likely to speak up. And in many categories, the latter group of customers can represent a major target audience, and their unrelieved frustration may be the source of significant negative word-of-mouth against the organization and its offerings in certain communities. To tap the concerns of these noncomplainers, it will be important from time to time to elicit their complaints using some other supplementary research technique, such as a limited telephone survey. For organizations with a more upscale clientele, the Internet might be used for the follow-up study.

The other source of bias in complaint data is that the complaints received are not necessarily representative of all types of complaints. Not surprisingly, people are more likely to speak up when large costs or inconvenience are involved. They are also more likely to speak up about things that are manifestly wrong and clearly the marketer's fault. If they are not sure that there really is a problem (for example, they left the clinic with a headache they did not have when they came) or if they think they might be partly or wholly to blame ("Maybe I should not have had so much coffee on an empty stomach"), they are less likely to speak up and register their complaints. But these unvoiced complaints have the potential to be important problems for an organization because minor problems can silently destroy a well-developed reputation. Perhaps more important, these subtle dissatisfactions are just the kind of thing that cause unhappy clients to decide not to come back or use a service again without telling anyone about their distress. Again, direct telephone or Internet studies from time to time may be needed to make sure that there are not whole classes of problems lurking undetected in the community.

Although complaint data are flawed, they can still be very useful in identifying potentially serious organizational problems. This is particularly the case if complaint data are analyzed repeatedly over time. One may choose not to trust the absolute level of complaints of various kinds at a single time because of the biases already noted. However, changes in the number and types of complaints over time may be a significant signal of either growing problems or (when they decline) improved performance. Even if the data are not to be used over time, statistically large numbers of complaints may not be needed at all. A few cases may be enough to alert a manager to a problem that must be fixed before it sabotages a carefully wrought marketing strategy.

A good example of the latter is an observant analysis by the U.S. Consumer Product Safety Commission (CPSC). Many years ago, the CPSC noted that among the medical complaints it was receiving routinely from a small sample of hospital emergency rooms was a noticeable number of cases involving young boys who reported injuring their genitals while bike riding, This small number of unusual cases led to investigation and eventually to the commission's recommending major changes in the placement and design of gear levers on boys' bicycles sold in the United States. What the commission discovered was that on many models, these levers were still located on the crossbar, and boys in minor accidents were being thrown painfully into the protruding gearshift levers. Only a few entries in these medical archives were needed for the CPSC to discover and correct a serious product design problem. This was possible only because the CPSC had set up a system to assemble and track the complaints that hospitals had. Without a system, no one, except by chance, would have put together all the unique occurrences to come up with such an important conclusion.

Finally, analysis of complaint data may have an important secondary value in helping to evaluate personnel or partners who contribute to the organization's mission. Many organizations seek out complaints through field surveys as a way of getting independent assessments of how their staff or partners are performing.

Inquiries and Comments. Consumers often write to or call organizations to complain. But they also write to and call to raise questions and offer praise. When properly analyzed, these communications can give management a good notion of what is on people's minds and what might be emphasized in future. An imaginative use of such records is the practice of magazines to carry out a yearly analysis of its letters to the editor. Such analyses reveal significant shifts in reader interest. For example, letters about domestic news issues may have dropped, while letters on foreign issues have increased significantly. The letters also can reveal shifts to and away from supporting particular groups or positions.

Miscellaneous Internal Measurable Records. Other sources of unobtrusive internal measurements are notations on desk calendars or appointment books or data in personal computer files (where organizational policy permits such inspections) that, when collated with expense records and telephone bills, can help a manager evaluate how effectively he or she is allocating personal time between meetings, customer contacts, sales supervision, and other duties. Also, computers can be programmed to collect data on how people use the system, what software routines they use most, and where visitors go on the organization's Web site (and where they come from).

Information Centers

One approach that relatively large organizations are using to synthesize and process these internal data is to establish an information technology (IT) center. It is, in effect, an internal consulting and service unit that creates software and networks linked to the company's server so that computer users around a organization can have access to the organization's own internal databases. It helps train managers in what databases are available and how to use them. It guides managers in using the Web to mine data sources outside the organization.

IT staff members are responsible for setting up the system and choosing the software and hardware. They then spend many hours consulting and coaching early users to get them effectively on-line. Consulting begins in person and graduates to the telephone and eventually e-mail. Word-of-mouth spreads, and users typically tend to be highly satisfied with what is now really decentralized data processing.

IT systems are not cheap. The low-budget researcher should pursue the IT idea only when other company departments will share the cost and where there is an overall organization commitment to the concept.

External Archives

It is possible to divide data produced by others (that is, external archives or, as they are sometimes called, secondary data) into data that are either measured or measurable. Obvious examples in the first case are the major marketing research data sources one could purchase or in an increasing number of cases acquire free on the Web (examples are census data and journal articles). In the case of measurable secondary data, the most obvious examples that come to mind are public evidence of donor interests, organizations, and potential partners' strategies.

External Measured Records

Many sets of data, such as Census files, are already in numerical form. They may be in the form of raw data or already digested data.

Raw Data in Secondary Sources. The marketing world in developed countries contains an extremely diverse and growing array of secondary data that a marketer can acquire at anywhere from virtually no cost to rather hefty one-time or yearly fees. These data can be separated into two broad categories depending on whether they are raw data or data that have already been analyzed by others to some greater or lesser degree. Raw data include census data tapes, purchased panel records, and academic researchers' raw data, which can often be acquired at the cost of a few CD-ROM disks and a few hours of programmer time. They can then be subject to the purchaser's own analysis. However, when using someone else's raw data, it is crucial to understand the potential biases in the data and, if necessary, adjust for them. This is always possible with one's own data, but sometimes it is difficult to learn from external sources. On the other hand, available raw data from outside sources have the distinct advantage that they can be manipulated, categorized, summarized, or otherwise analyzed in any way the researcher wishes.

Predigested Secondary Sources. Sometimes the low-budget researcher may not have the time, equipment, or sophistication to analyze someone else's raw data. On such occasions, predigested external data may be an excellent, and often superior, substitute.

An excellent source of predigested information for marketing managers is state, federal, and local government studies and reports, widely available in libraries, from government agencies, and on the Web in increasingly accessible form. They are inexpensive and usually very accurate. Marketers generally find particularly valuable the following:

U.S. Bureau of the Census (*www.census.gov*)

- Decennial census of the population
- Census of housing
- Censuses of various industries (for example, retailing, wholesaling, services, manufacturing, transportation, agriculture, and minerals)
- Current population reports
- County business patterns
- Current business reports
- Selected characteristics of foreign-owned U.S. firms
- Quarterly financial reports for manufacturing, mining, and trade corporations

Other Federal Government Sources

- *Federal Reserve Bulletin* (monthly)
- *Monthly Labor Review*
- *Commerce Business Daily*

- *Overseas Business Reports* (annual)
- *Statistics of Income Bulletin* (quarterly)
- *U.S. Industrial Outlook* (annual)
- *Business Cycles: Handbook of Indicators* (monthly)
- *Survey of Current Business* (monthly)
- *Business Conditions Digest* (monthly)
- *Agricultural Outlook* (monthly)
- *Consumer Expenditure Survey* (decennial)
- *Council of Economic Advisors Economic Indicators* (monthly)
- *Current Construction Reports* (various series)
- *Current Housing Reports* (various series)
- *Consumer Price Index Detailed Report* (monthly)
- *Highlights of U.S. Export and Import Trade* (monthly and cumulative)

These data serve several important research purposes. They can describe the existing state of various populations and trends in those populations over time. These data, in turn, can help determine desirable opportunities, set quotas for future activities, and help evaluate performance. They are also often used as bases against which to compare the characteristics of customers or the profile of respondents in a specific research study.

A growing use of government data sources is in prospecting for opportunities in foreign societies. The costs of gathering original data in other countries is usually prohibitive for low-budget researchers, and U.S. government agencies can provide information on the population and economic and social characteristics of most foreign countries. These data can often be supplemented by information from foreign embassies and various Web sites. Both local and foreign sources can also provide critical information on how to access desirable foreign markets.

In the United States, a number of regional and local sources can be used as the marketer narrows the focus to specific sites. State agencies, banks, chambers of commerce, and local media produce considerable information to attract enterprises to their area. These data are usually free and sometimes can be customized for the user. However, since some of these sources have a vested interest in influencing others' marketing decisions, the marketer should be cautious about the completeness and interpretations of data from these sources.

Syndicated Services. Increasingly useful secondary sources for marketers are various regular series of data provided for a fee by syndicated services. One place to start is with the search engines available on the Web. In addition to the general engines like Yahoo! and Google, there are what are called market research aggregator Web sites, which have their own search capabilities and contain information on research reports from a wide selection of sources—for example:

www.AllNetResearch.Com

www.Bitpipe.com

www.MarketResearch.com

www.Profound.com

www.USADATA.com

After this, one can use a range of general-purpose and specialized sources—for example:

- *American Demographics* magazine (www.marketingtools. com)—texts of the magazine's publications
- Dow Jones and Company (www.dowjones.com)—Web links to a wide range of financial and company data
- Mead Data Central—LEXIS-NEXIS databases (www. lexis-nexis.com) that provide full-text information on legal, business, and general news (fee for subscription)

- Find/SVP (www.findsvp.com)—provides fee-based information searches
- USA Data (www.usadata.com)—reports on industries, geographical locations, and brands (available for a fee)
- The Dialog Company (www.dialog.com)—over 450 databases with millions of documents
- Forrester (www.forrester.com)—information on the Web and other business issues
- allnetresearch.internet.com—a wide range of data sources

There is a great deal of economic information from brokerage services such as these:

- Ameritrade (www.ameritrade.com)
- Charles Schwab (www.schwab.com)
- Fidelity Investments (www.fidelity.com)
- E-Trade (www.etrade.com)
- CNN Financial News Network (www.cjjfn.com)
- Dun & Bradstreet (www.dnb.com)

In addition, there are a number of discussion sites where one can ask others for help. A general-purpose site is USENET, which has thousands of discussion sites. Some of these groups have been aggregated by other services—for example:

- Egroups (www.egroups.com)
- ForumOne (www.forumone.com)
- Topica (www.topica.com)

In addition, many academic and trade associations maintain listservs that can be queried.

Predigested syndicated sources are well exemplified by the PRIZM system. For PRIZM, the Claritas Corporation collects a huge amount of primary data on the 35,600 postal code areas in the United States and then clusters these areas into sixty-two categories, which are given such colorful names as "Money and Brains," "Shotguns and Pickups," and "Norma Rae-Ville" (see Table 5.1). Marketers can use these data to help locate new markets or learn what sells in existing markets. They can acquire a list of all the postal codes in a selected area in the lifestyle categories that are deemed to be the best targets for their organization's goods and services. Alternatively, PRIZM can help define markets. A marketer can learn from PRIZM just which markets are the best prospects for particular products or services. PRIZM can

> tell you more than you probably ever wanted to know about [an] area's typical residents: what they like to eat; which cars they like to drive; whether they prefer scotch or sangria, tuna extender or yogurt, hunting or tennis . . . which magazines they read, which TV shows they watch, whether they are more likely to buy calculators or laxatives, whether they're single or are potential customers for a diaper service.[3]

Similar services are provided by the ACORN and MOSAIC systems. MOSAIC provides geoclustering data in several non-U.S. markets. These systems offer several advantages. A much broader and richer database (for example, product purchases, demographic and economic data, television watching, magazine readership, and other relevant behavior for each postal code in the United States) can be brought to bear on a research problem than any individual low-budget marketer could possibly afford. The data are subjected to much more sophisticated analysis by the research supplier than most low-budget researchers can afford. Finally, purchase of some part or all of these kinds of services usually includes some amount of consulting help from the database supplier that can materially supplement the low-budget researcher's own skills. The disadvantage, of

TABLE 5.1 PRIZM Cluster Categories and Percentage of Population, 2000.

	Label	Description	Percentage of Population
01	Blue Blood Estates	Elite Super-Rich Families	1.35
02	Winner's Circle	Executive Urban Families	2.45
03	Executive Suites	Upscale White-Collar Couples	1.15
04	Pools and Patios	Established Empty Nesters	1.89
05	Kids and Cul-de-Sacs	Upscale Suburban Families	3.48
06	Urban Gold Coast	Elite Urban Singles and Couples	.37
07	Money and Brains	Sophisticated Townhouse Couples	1.1
08	Young Literati	Upscale Urban Singles and Couples	.76
09	American Dreams	Established Urban Immigrant Families	1.74
10	Bohemian Mix	Bohemian Singles and Couples	1.02
11	Second City Elite	Upscale Executive Families	1.96
12	Upward Bound	Young Upscale White-Collar Families	1.94
13	Gray Power	Affluent Retirees in Sunbelt Cities	1.67
14	Country Squires	Elite Exurban Families	1.53
15	God's Country	Executive Exurban Families	2.96
16	Big Fish, Small Pond	Small Town Executive Families	1.41
17	Greenbelt Families	Young, Middle-Class Town Families	1.59
18	Young Influentials	Upwardly Mobile Singles and Couples	1.08
19	New Empty Nests	Upscale Suburban Fringe Couple	2.12
20	Boomers and Babies	Young White-Collar Suburban Families	1.13
21	Suburban Sprawl	Young Suburban Townhouse Couples	1.34
22	Blue-Chip Blues	Upscale Blue-Collar Families	2.21
23	Upstarts and Seniors	Middle Income Empty Nesters	1.12

TABLE 5.1 (Continued)

	Label	Description	Percentage of Population
24	New Beginnings	Young Mobile City Singles	.92
25	Mobility Blues	Young Blue Collar/Service Families	1.54
26	Gray Collars	Aging Couples in Inner Suburbs	1.95
27	Urban Achievers	Mid-level, White-Collar Urban Couples	1.40
28	Big City Blend	Middle-Income Immigrant Families	1.16
29	Old Yankee Rows	Empty-Nest, Middle-Class Families	1.26
30	Mid-City Mix	African-American Singles and Families	1.21
31	Latino America	Hispanic Middle-Class Families	1.58
32	Middleburg Managers	Mid-Level White-Collar Couples	1.65
33	Boomtown Singles	Middle Income Young Singles	.73
34	Starter Families	Young Middle-Class Families	1.59
35	Sunset City Blues	Empty Nests in Aging Industrial Cities	1.65
36	Towns and Gowns	College Town Singles	1.34
37	New Homesteaders	Young Middle-Class Families	1.64
38	Middle America	Midscale Families in Midsize Towns	2.34
39	Red, White and Blues	Small Town Blue-Collar Families	1.85
40	Military Quarters	GIs and Surrounding Off-Base Families	.67
41	Big Sky Families	Midscale Couples, Kids and Farmland	1.63
42	New Eco-Topia	Rural White/Blue-Collar/Farm Families	.87
43	River City, USA	Middle-Class, Rural Families	1.90
44	Shotguns and Pickups	Rural Blue-Collar Workers and Families	2.03

45	Single City Blues	Ethnically-Mixed Urban Singles	1.4
46	Hispanic Mix	Urban Hispanic Singles and Families	1.74
47	Inner Cities	Inner City, Solo-Parent Families	1.99
48	Smalltown Downtown	Older Renters and Young Families	1.51
49	Hometown Retired	Low-Income, Older Singles and Families	.93
50	Family Scramble	Low-Income Hispanic Families	2.28
51	Southside City	African-American Service Workers	1.94
52	Golden Ponds	Retirement Town Seniors	1.47
53	Rural Industrial	Low-Income, Blue-Collar Families	1.75
54	Norma Rae–Ville	Young Families, Bi-Racial Mill Towns	1.37
55	Mines and Mills	Older Families, Mine and Mill Towns	1.96
56	Agri-Business	Rural Farm-Town and Ranch Families	1.56
57	Grain Belt	Farm Owners and Tenants	2.36
58	Blue Highways	Moderate Blue-Collar/Farm Families	2.02
59	Rustic Elders	Low-Income, Older, Rural Couples	1.77
60	Back Country Folks	Remote Rural/Town Families	2.18
61	Scrub Pine Flats	Older African-American Farm Families	1.58
62	Hard Scrabble	Older Families in Poor Isolated Areas	1.92

Source: Copyright 2001, Claritas Inc. Reprinted with permission.

course, is that predigested results may not be exactly what the marketer needs since someone else has done the analysis according to that person's specifications or according to what that person thinks the average client would want.

Thus, the summaries may not be the ones the marketer needs, critical details may be left out, and so on. It also means that the data will likely be more expensive than the raw data since one must buy the analysis also. Nevertheless, the low-budget manager may choose to accept these limitations and the likely higher cost because he or she doesn't have the time or expertise to carry out the needed analysis.

On-Line Databases. A major source of external data is now available on-line. These external databases include such diverse information as:

- Newspaper and magazine stories
- Market characteristics for specific geographical areas
- Economic time series
- Stock quotes
- Company profiles
- Regulation, legislation, and legal cases
- Yellow Page listings in four thousand places
- Patents and trademarks
- Newspaper, radio, and television audiences
- Public relations releases
- Biographies
- Bibliographies and citations
- Ad placements by competitors

Many of these data are available for both the United States and other countries and can be accessed as full texts, data files, and indexes. Using different data files on-line, a low-budget researcher can define a specific geographical area to be targeted; develop a demographic profile of the market for today and five years into the future; develop psychographic profiles, audience preferences, and media behavior patterns for individuals in the target area; get Yellow Pages listings of possible partners; learn if similar organizations are headquartered or have branches nearby; access recent articles on organizations to learn if they have any plans for a particular market; and review general articles on the geographical area indicating whether there are important economic or political trends that may affect the organization's prospects.

All that is necessary to have access to this rich treasure trove of data is a computer terminal and a password to each needed database or database vendor. The password will be provided once the researcher has signed up with the system and sometimes paid an initial or monthly subscription fee.

It is possible in most cases to go directly to the original sources of the data. However, most experienced on-line database users go direct or sign up with one or more intermediary vendors or information brokers. For one fee, a subscriber can have access to a range of databases. Among the best-known and widely used vendors are the following:

- BRS (BRS Wormation Technologies, Latham, N.Y.): Bibliographical citations, abstracts, and (sometimes) full texts from a wide range of sources.
- CompuServe, Inc. (CompuServe, Columbus, Ohio), a division of H&R Block: Wide range of business data, including Standard & Poor's ratings, electronic clipping services, travel information, computer shopping, and a base of technical report information.
- DIALOG (DIALOG Information Services, Palo Alto, Calif.): The Business Connection service can provide corporate intelligence, financial screening, sales prospecting, and product and market analysis.

- Dow Jones News/Retrieval (Dow Jones News/Retrieval, Princeton, N.J.): Databases support two categories of services: Business and Investor Services (business data, news, stock quotes) and General Services (world news, travel, shopping).

- Mead Data Central: LEXIS, NEXIS and MEDIS (Mead Data Control, Dayton, Ohio): Full-text databases of legal, news, business, and general information, including medical references and financial and accounting information.

- SDC/ORBIT (SDC Information Services, Santa Monica, Calif.): Databases primarily in science and technology, although also patents and accounting,

- I.P. Sharp Associates: InfoService, InfoMagic (I.P. Sharp Associates Limited, Toronto, Canada): Primarily numeric databases weighted toward aviation, economics, energy, finance, and news, with the data often in time series.

- The Source (Source Telecomputing Corporation, McLean, Va.): Business and financial information plus electronic networking.

- NewsNet (NewsNet Inc., Bryn Mawr, Pa.): News and information from newsletters, wire services, and specialty publications on industries and professions.

Costs for these services vary by supplier. In some cases, there may be a sign-up fee. Beyond this, there may be a basic connect-time cost, usually varying by time of day or week (for example, prime time versus non–prime time) and by the speed with which data are transmitted.

There may be additional costs for specific kinds of database specific information. At first, the costs may seem relatively low. However, considerable time can be eaten up with unproductive searches. Many of these systems are relatively difficult to use. Indeed, in many communities, there exist independent search specialists who can make searching more efficient by thinking the problem through off-line. Finally, even when the search is done, additional costs will be incurred in downloading or printing the accessed information. To the extent possible, on-line researchers prefer to copy information onto a hard drive or floppy disc and then print it off-line, since the files can be very large.

The data can be extremely valuable, as suggested by one commercial company's experience:

> The company had learned that a competitor might be planning an attack on one of its personal care products. The firm considered cutting price to meet the challenge, but first contacted the Helicon Group Ltd., a consulting firm specializing in competitive intelligence, to learn what it could from secondary sources. Helicon developed the following information from on-line sources:

- The competitor had been purchased several years earlier by a conglomerate.
- Local business newspaper databases did *not* report the competitor's hiring an ad agency for a new product.
- The parent company had once tried to sell the unprofitable subsidiary.
- The parent's commercial debentures were being downgraded, and a lawsuit was being filed by a debenture holder.
- A business news database indicated that a senior executive had recently retired with no successor named, and two other executives had left.

> The company realized from Helicon's data gathering that the competitor posed no threat at all. A hasty price cut would have been a very foolish action.[4]

Measurable External Archives

Some external archives are not in numeric form.

Competitors' Advertising Expenditures. It is critical that managers know about important social and economic characteristics of their target audience and their industry and how they are changing over time. Many archives can provide this information: newspapers, magazines, the trade press, and even television and radio.

Managers may wish more detail, or they may find press reports nonexistent. In such cases, they may wish to access an on-line database or collect the data themselves. If the marketer proceeds alone (for example, if the database does not include key communities or groups), it will be difficult to assemble all of the newspapers or magazines that will give a full picture. Still, if the typical span of media is relatively narrow (for example, if print media are the major vehicles in the sector), the manager may select a few representative print media and set an assistant to sampling such media routinely on a monthly or quarterly basis to assess trends. Assuming the major media are covered, the manager's repeated measures, although biased, can reveal changes in important social and economic indexes. Alternatively, commercial clipping services can be engaged for this task.

Communication Behavior. There are numerous possibilities for collecting and analyzing the content of communications of key players in the organization's environment. For example, an antitobacco organization can assemble sample communications of tobacco marketers and conduct an analysis to identify major themes, differences in strategy across target markets, and, perhaps most important, subtle shifts in strategies over time. Managers may believe that a careful reading or viewing of these communications is enough. However, one person's perceptions may be faulty or idiosyncratic. Worse, they may change over time so that changes that seem to be taking place in the real world are really changes in the manager's interests and orientation.

Systematic content analysis is required to provide objective recorded evidence. It is a technique that can be applied to advertising and several other measurable external archives, like competitors' annual reports, publicity releases, direct mail messages, product packages, and inserts. The content analysis should observe some important precautions:

- The selection of the materials to be analyzed must be objective and randomized in some fashion.
- Characteristics of the content to be measured should be defined in advance so that what the analyst sees does not unduly influence the determination of what should be seen. This set of characteristics can be modified subsequently if the analysis scheme is found to be incomplete in some important respect.
- Trial analyses of a subset of the materials should be conducted and rules established for ambiguous cases. (Is a goldfish a pet? Is the headline "greater-than-ever value" an indication of an emphasis on price or an emphasis on quality?)
- If at all possible, more than one individual should analyze the materials, and at least some documents should be assigned to more than one person simultaneously to establish interanalyst consistency and indirectly test the logic and consistency of the coding scheme.

Content measures will not tell management anything about which competitors' messages work and which do not. However, in some rare cases, the anti-tobacco manager may notice effects on his or her firm's own performance (such as receptivity among policymakers) following some measured change in tobacco company advertising. This represents another example of a pseudoexperiment that may yield some insight into what does and does not seem to work well in the organization's environment.

Publicity. How the world views an organization and its performance is often clearly reflected in various public and semipublic archival records. Two important sources here are (1) articles about the organization and its offerings in newspapers, popular magazines, and the trade press, and (2) evaluations by rating agencies. Clearly, management will be interested in what is said about the organization and about its partners and competitors and undoubtedly will notice such publicity when it chances across the desk. This casual reading can be turned into true research if the details of these public comments are routinely and objectively evaluated and recorded. On-line databases can be very valuable here.

Other Intelligence Gathering. Repetitive archival records of the activities of key players in the organization's environment can tell managers a lot about systematic changes in their strategies and tactics over time. One-time critical changes are equally important, but they may be harder to detect. Fortunately, there are a number of archives that can be accessed to provide important intelligence about what is going on within other organizations' management suites. Among the documents that would serve this function from on-line databases are these:

- Publicity releases (for example, from the PR Newswire database).

- Speeches by organization personnel, including nonmarketers such as treasurers and lawyers, who often do not realize the value to a marketer of what they are saying.

- Articles by organization personnel in the trade press, academic journals, and popular periodicals.

- Any internal organization communication that may be acquired ethically.

- Patents applied for.

- Court records if the organization has been sued lately. These are rich sources of data on past practices and sometimes reveal strategy. (This is a reason that many firms avoid public trials.)

- Biographies of key executives whose past may give a good indication of future strategies. This can be particularly valuable when the leadership at a major organization or political institution changes.

In addition to on-line databases, managers can do the following:

- Subscribe to all of the periodicals, trade magazines, academic journals, and conference proceedings where valuable comments by key players might appear.
- Subscribe to an independent clipping service (some on-line electronic database vendors do this automatically).

  If business information is needed, subscribe to the *Wall Street Transcript*, which reports details of corporate presentations to security analysts or brokerage firms.
- Require someone to consult search engines like Google regularly for references to key players (and to yourself).
- Require all organization personnel to routinely submit any documents acquired on visits to customers, attendance at conferences, and reading on airplanes that contain even the smallest snippet of intelligence about other important organizations and institutions (and your own firm too).
- Purchase a few shares of business stock if you need to secure insiders' data on company plans and past performance.
- Send periodic letters of inquiry to industry or country analysts at the U.S. Department of Commerce, the Department of Agriculture, the Department of State, or the National Reference Center on industry topics.

Conclusion

Whatever the source, it is important to make the data flow routinely into a low-cost competitive intelligence data bank. For this purpose, a summary report of each secondary document should be recorded and put into a carefully indexed, preferably electronic file to be collated and reviewed periodically. As the examples in this chapter indicate, even the slightest advance warning of changes in the organization's environment can have major benefits for the alert and rapidly responding marketer.

6

Systematic Observation

We saw in the previous chapter that archival data are all around us. We just need to find them and, in some cases, apply measurements to them to change them from inert data into managerially useful information. What sets the truly superior manager apart is not leaving these insights to chance. The superior manager realizes that a systematic application of low-budget research techniques directed in the right places can make rare insights routine.

Knowing where to look and being systematic about looking are the two keys of effective and efficient use of archives. These same two principles apply equally well to mining information from other features of the environment that are not written records. In this chapter, we are concerned with the use of observations of the physical, human, and electronic environment as a means of conducting low-cost marketing research.

The chapter focuses on each step of the observing process. First, researchers must create the opportunity to observe. These opportunities can be classified as episodic or repeated observation and divided into natural and contrived occasions. Contrived observations are episodes where the researcher intervenes in natural events and watches what happens. They are usually found in formally designed experiments, which are considered in the next chapter.

Setting up the opportunity to observe is not enough. The effective researcher needs to know how to observe. Thus, the chapter considers briefly the kinds of observations that can be made and procedures for doing so.

Systematic observation represents the ultimate in cheap but good research. Observations represent free goods. Marketers already use these free goods daily. They watch customers. They look at and evaluate other organizations' advertising and their own. They visit other service establishments or eat in their restaurants. They sign up for a service to see how a competitor treats a customer. And they try new approaches and see how they work. They try calling clients by their first names for a while and see if they warm up faster or seem to buy more. They reshuffle their displays or change their room arrangements and see if these make a difference in traffic patterns. Good marketers are doing this kind of free research all the time, but most of it is neither systematic nor purposeful.

Too often, marketers treat casual observation as if it were truly a free good. They shouldn't. Good observational research is not costless at all. It must be systematic and objective. This can be hard work. It requires that systems be put in place, that at least moderate preplanning be undertaken, and that observers be trained to be objective and thorough in what they observe. It is only when these investments are made that chance voyeurism turns into serious research.

Collecting Natural Observations

Observations and archives can be episodic or continuing. An episodic observation is a one-time look at a phenomenon of interest. This can come about as a result of a particular one-time research interest. For example, a manager considering a relocation may observe the ages and types of automobiles passing a proposed new site or parked at nearby shopping centers to gather information to help decide how much volume to anticipate, what price level might be appropriate, and how fancy the premises should be. A social service agency might observe what waiting room brochures are most often thrown in the wastebasket to learn what topics or content are least appealing. The manager of a cafeteria might observe the number of orders placed for a new menu item and then how much of each serving is left on plates to decide whether to keep the item on the menu.

Observations in both episodic and continuing situations typically comprise one or more of three activities: counting, measuring, or seeking patterns. They can be carried out both obtrusively, as when one visits a competitor's fundraising event and takes notes, or unobtrusively, as when a child care center uses two-way mirrors to observe how children play with the toys and how they interact. These observations can be done by people or by mechanical or electronic devices.

Counting

This research typically involves quantifying objects (including people) or behaviors of special interest. Counting typically has as its goal either estimating demand for something or assessing response to some marketing tactic. Web sites can be equipped with software to do such counting automatically.

Counting was the principal research method DioLight Technology used to decide which markets to target for its new long-lasting light bulb. DioLight's marketing director, Kevin Callaghan, visited office buildings and counted the average number of exit signs that would need long-lasting bulbs. He also developed secondary data to learn the number of hospitals in the United States that would need twenty-four-hour-a-day lighting. Based on these observational and archival data, Callaghan concluded that industrial buyers would be a better market than consumer households. In its first year of operations, the firm had $1 million in revenue from its new bulbs, 95 percent of which came from industrial sources.[1]

Other examples of counts of natural phenomena made at very low cost that are helpful for marketing purposes include the following:

- Counting the number of pedestrians or automobiles passing a proposed site

- Counting the number of competitors within various distances of a proposed service location
- Counting the incidence of some correlate of potential product or service use, such as the number of homeless people living near a proposed shelter or the number of youngsters loitering on street corners after school who might need special programs
- Estimating the proportion of men, women, or children at particular fundraising events
- Counting the number of out-of-state license plates from specific states passing through a specific tourist town

Counting is often the only means of assessing the effects of competitors' actions or unexpected events. Empty spaces in the parking lot can suggest the effects of a competitor's promotions or a sudden snowstorm. So can counts of people entering nearby sites. One can count people stopping at specific new museum displays or showing interest in a new poster.

A major virtue of simple counting is that it can be carried out by unskilled researchers. For example, one or two teenagers could be hired and sent out to make observations at other museums or other competitive forms of entertainment. Careful training is still necessary and procedures must be carefully specified, but costs can be kept low.

Measuring

Rather than simply counting people or objects or behaviors, observation is more useful if it involves some sort of measurement. This can prove particularly fruitful in the measurement of physical traces. Often an environmental characteristic of interest leaves behind a residue that we can observe and measure. The researchers who use these *physical traces* are in a sense modern-day archaeologists.

Physical traces may be divided into three broad groupings: accretion, erosion, and traces. They were all the stock-in-trade of perhaps the best low-budget researcher of all time, Sherlock Holmes. In fact, reading the collected works of Arthur Conan Doyle provides innumerable excellent examples of the powers of a keen observer who routinely used accretions, erosions, and physical traces to solve crimes. Holmes was always astonishing the less observant Watson with the leaps of insight he could derive from observing such things as the type of mud on the shoes of a seemingly innocent houseguest (an accretion) or the size of the footprint near the trellis in the garden (a physical trace) or the missing matches on the left side of the matchbook of the left-handed smoker (an erosion).

In marketing, a good example of the use of accretion data is in the observance of litter. City managers can analyze the amount and type of litter on selected downtown streets for clues as to which areas should be the focus of antilitter campaigns. Garbage counts of liquor bottles can be used to estimate the need for alcohol reduction programs in communities where interview data would be unreliable or package stores do not exist. It is particularly valuable in subject areas where consumers may be reluctant to reveal true behavior.

Other physical measures that have been used by marketers are wear on particular magazines in physician waiting rooms that suggests popularity and thus potential value of different media for advertising and radio settings of car radios in cars parked by staff at a fundraising event that suggest stations to use for the future advertising.

Mechanical or Electronic Observation

An obvious problem with even such a simple technique as counting is human error. Even the best-intentioned individual researcher can be distracted or fatigued or can count the wrong thing. Such failings need not be fatal to studies. Debriefing the researcher or comparing results among researchers can usually detect large systematic mistakes. Distraction and fatigue can also be accommodated if they are essentially random. However, they may not be. Noisy teenagers at a site may easily distract a researcher (especially another teenager), leading to an undercount of those teenagers and their behavior. Fatigue often sets in late in the day or just before meals. If researchers are not scheduled to work at different times over the course of the study, data on late-afternoon shoppers or the lunchtime crowd may be systematically distorted.

There may be other problems using human observers. Researchers may not want to work late at night or early in the morning, leaving a major potential bias. A more serious problem is that the presence of a human observer during the observation process may itself be obtrusive. A researcher hovering around a particular display or doorway with a clipboard or mechanical counter may discourage customers from looking over the goods on the display or visiting a particular service outlet.

Nevertheless, biases may not be fatal if the manager's interest is in comparison or trend data and the biases are relatively similar between observations. Although all data are biased, the differences can be assumed to be meaningful.

A low-cost alternative is to eliminate the potential for human error or bias by using electronic or mechanical observation techniques. Indeed, several major commercial research services are based on just such mechanical or electronic observation. Nielsen's television rating service electronically records (observes) the stations to which its sample households are tuned with a "people-meter." Eye cameras are used by some advertising researchers to study how people look over an ad.

A significant development in marketing research in the packaged consumer goods industry (scanner research) is the use of electronic scanning of the purchases of a preselected sample of households as they check out in supermarkets. In sophisticated scanner research systems, advertising input into sample households by cable is experimentally manipulated and the effects on supermarket purchases selectively observed. Any item with a bar code is potentially susceptible to measuring electronically

All of these techniques require great cost and levels of sophistication beyond the low-budget researcher. Other options are available, however:

- *Pneumatic traffic counters.* These are the rubber hoses stretched across highways or streets to count automobiles. Although subject to certain errors (for example, three-axle trucks or playful teenagers re-crossing a counter), these counters can monitor traffic passing po-tential outlet locations or cars entering a shopping mall before and after specific promotional events.

- *Electronic eyes.* These devices count bodies breaking a beam of light and can be used to note unobtrusively the number of peo-ple passing a display or entering a room or building.

- *Digital cameras.* Photographs can provide important observa-tional data. For example, a marketer in a performing arts center could photograph an audience at a preconcert lecture and note the gender and possibly age distribution. If repeated, this technique could help measure the popularity of different performances or per-formers for different segments.

- *Videotape recorders.* Customers in many outlets are accus-tomed to video cameras. Recorded images can provide useful obser-vations of the types of clothing attendees wear, the relative number of males and females, and the number of elderly attending a partic-ular event. They can also indicate movement patterns, such as where patrons spend their time before a concert or play. Cameras can re-cord how quickly service staff approach clients, how long clients stay on the premises, which direction they move as they circulate through-out the store, and so on.

- *Computer software.* Web sites can be programmed to record items considered on a Web page or the length of time a visitor spent viewing a particular page.

Seeking Patterns in Natural Observations

Using electronic or mechanical devices to count and measure ig-nores one of the most important human faculties: the ability to find patterns in what we see. In the field of anthropology, observation is the principal research tool. For the anthropologist, the key concern is finding patterns, getting a full, rich sense of what it is that makes opera audiences in Houston different from theatergoers in Seattle. While anthropologists count and use physical traces, more often, cultural and social anthropologists simply go into the field, watch what people do, and try to synthesize their observations by detecting the patterns that seem to be there.

A good example of the kind of insight that can be gained from seeking patterns through low-cost, relatively unobtrusive observation of naturally occurring consumer behavior is in supermarket observations. Several years ago, two university researchers explored the potential for direct observation of supermarket shoppers in three product categories: cereal, detergent, and candy. Fifteen hundred observations were made by three students in supermarkets in northern New Jersey. The students observed any shopper entering the aisle where the products in question were offered who appeared intent on making a purchase.

The kinds of questions this study methodology could answer are:

- Who actually chooses the products, and who or what influences the choice at the point of sale?
- To what extent are the brand choices made before the shopper enters the store versus at the point of purchase?
- How many people check price?
- Do shoppers check the package before purchase?

The first major finding of the study was that the observations were easy to make. The only problems occurred at the training stage, when it was discovered that the observers were not getting sufficient detail into their records. In practice trials, the students were inclined to record only the bare bones of each transaction, omitting the detail that is the essence of the method. A second problem was in getting the researchers to record their observations immediately after the episode. Thorough training overcame both problems.

The study sought both to count behavior (for example, how many cereal shoppers had children with them) and to seek patterns.

The difficulty in trying to see patterns was exemplified when the researchers attempted to estimate the proportion of shoppers who knew what they wanted when they approached the cereal counter. It is difficult to infer a state of mind. When the shopper marches right up to a specific spot at the display and grabs a box, the evidence suggesting a preformed choice is all but conclusive. But when a shopper hesitates, searches, and physically inspects several packages, it is hard to guess whether the shopper doesn't know what he or she wants or knows what he or she wants and can't find it. In cases such as these, the students learned to make judgments based on the overall patterns they observed.

Although the study was only a pilot venture, the following patterns were suggested:

- Women do more of the family shopping than men, but men do enough to warrant a marketer's attention.

- Husbands who accompany wives and try to influence purchase decisions almost always succeed.

- Children, especially urban children, are also influential, although this varies by product class.

- Urban shoppers show more concern with price than suburban shoppers. This also varies by type of product and by sex.

- Many shoppers of all types inspect packages before they buy. The tactile dimension therefore deserves more attention than it usually receives in most package research.

Another example of anthropological research in marketing is a study by consumer researchers of a swap meet in Arizona. A team of three professionals with diverse skills in consumer research took a minivan, a set of tape recorders and television cameras, computers, and large notebooks to a small town and over several days talked, filmed, and recorded buyers and sellers at a permanent local swap meet. They observed people buying and selling and asked them questions about their activities and the meanings the transactions had for them personally. The researchers found that such naturalistic inquiry can yield thick data on important market phenomena. The technique is labor intensive, but the researchers found that their odyssey was relatively low cost yet richly insightful.[2]

Controlling the Quality of Natural Observations

While it is easy to look at phenomena, there are many dangers in efforts to draw meaning from them.

Problems of Inference

Some observations, such as garbage counts or observations of clothing preferences or client gender, require a considerable leap of inference before the implications for marketing strategy are clear. For instance, if there is an increase in the proportion of symphony attendees who dress casually, does this indicate that the orchestra is attracting a more downscale or younger audiences, or is this simply an indication of broad changes in clothing styles? The research manager must make strong assumptions before allowing the data to affect marketing strategy. In many such situations, it will be desirable to back up the observations with other measurement methods. For example, in the case of clothing preferences, a few discrete interviews might quickly resolve some of the ambiguities in the observations.

Indeed, when using low-budget techniques, it is always excellent strategy to attempt to assess key phenomena in many different ways, that is, to practice triangulation (get several different readings of the phenomenon of interest). Many of the techniques proposed in this book must make some compromises in methodology in order to keep costs down. As a consequence, the results of any given low-cost study must always be viewed with at least some skepticism. However, if the researcher can develop multiple measures of several aspects or traits of the same phenomena, preferably using different kinds of research methods, the unique biases of each technique may often cancel each other out. If the same conclusion emerges from several different approaches (for example, focus groups plus a few interviews plus observations), the researcher can have much more confidence in what is found. I am a strong advocate of what researchers have come to call the *multimeasure multitrait technique*. This means measuring many facets of some important market characteristic using many measurement approaches.

Problems of Collection

Observation should be systematic and objective if it is to be trusted by management and reliable. The goal is to secure a representative, accurate sample of the phenomena to be observed. Two steps must be taken to achieve this goal: (1) a sampling procedure must be carefully developed to ensure that each potential observation that one could make has a known (perhaps equal) chance of being recorded, and (2) the field observer has as little freedom as possible in what is observed when the observation is made.

Making observations is a method of collecting data, just like asking questions with a questionnaire. Yet many researchers who would be very systematic in designing a careful sampling plan before sending interviewers into the field are often extremely casual about sending individuals out to observe phenomena. Of course, it isn't always the case that a sampling plan is needed for an observational study. Just as with a questionnaire survey, the research objectives may require only a limited number of typical contacts (for example, to help develop hypotheses or to detect serious problems with a new toy or appliance). However, if one wishes to project the results to a broader population or to conduct statistical tests, the usual rules of sampling (discussed in Chapter Nine) need to be followed. Typically, this requires procedures for three kinds of observational sampling:

• *Places*. If one is to observe a phenomenon at different locations, then observations must be taken with either equal observations at each site or observations proportional to expected occurrence. In

both cases, the researcher must first estimate how many events, phenomena, or potential observations will occur at each location. This will
permit the results at each location to be postweighted by the expected
number of observations. Alternatively, the prior estimates may be used
for assigning quotas for the number of observations at each site.

• *Times*. All possible times for observations should be sampled.
Results can be severely biased if observers always go at the same time,
for example, when it is convenient for them or when there are few
people at the site. Again, one must estimate in advance the likely
distribution of events over time and assign observations to cover
the spectrum. The time allocations can be proportional, or they can
be equal and then postweighted.

• *Individual events*. Even if places and times are randomly selected, interviewers should be given some guidance in event sampling. The simplest approach is systematic sampling. The observer
can be told to observe every nth event, for example, every fifth person passing on the north side of the ficus tree just inside the Children's Museum's southeast entrance. If this is problematic, an
alternative rule could be to take the fifth person after the last observation is completed. Whatever the procedure, the objective is to
give the observer a firm rule so that he or she will not just observe
what seems interesting or easy.

Observing Accurately

Field researchers can be attentive, objective observers or sloppy and
casual. The secret to ensuring the former is to follow four guidelines:

1. Recruit a potential set of field observers who are likely to be
   attentive and objective.

2. Give them an observation test to screen out the poorer
   prospects.

3. Establish clear written guidelines specifying what and how
   to observe.

4. Have the observers practice, practice, practice.

7

Low-Cost Experimentation

In the previous chapter, we took the world as it is, doing our best to observe and record what it had to tell us. An obvious restriction on observed data is that we must accept reality. This is often desirable because it means the data are not contaminated by our intrusions. On the other hand, we cannot observe something that has not taken place, such as a marketing tactic never tried. Marketers are doers, and it is their mission in the corporate or nonprofit worlds to make changes rather than to respond to them. Thus, when managers look to research for help, it is almost always to tell them what to do in the future. (As I noted in Chapters Three and Four, this is the only time they should ask for research help.) Managers are typically very suspicious of research that tells them only what worked in the past or (worse still) that requires great feats of inference and analysis to tell them even that. What managers really want to know is what will work tomorrow. Trying things out on a pilot basis is a very good way to gain just this kind of insight.

This is the role of experimentation: trying things out. Experimentation is immediate. It will help managers learn whether implementing tactic A will lead to result X. And assuming the rest of the world holds still, it can suggest pretty strongly that doing A tomorrow will lead to X the day after. Experimentation is intentionally intrusive. But the cost in potential bias is often well compensated by four major virtues important to managerial applications:

1. It permits the experimenter to control the intervention so that it closely parallels just what management's strategic options are likely to be.

2. By careful design, experimenters can control a large part of the natural world's chaos, factors that tend to foul up other naturally occurring pseudoexperiments.

3. Experimentation often can prove cause and effect; it can say that since everything else was held constant, the result X must have been caused by A.

4. Since experimenters can dictate the timing of the intervention, experiments are often speedier and more efficient than many other approaches, especially field observation, which has to wait for events to occur naturally.

Most major marketers in the private sector routinely use experimentation. Test marketing, a form of real-world experimentation, is a standard technique in most new-product and service development processes. Market tests are used to assess such things as likely demand levels, responses to alternative advertising budgets, and the desirability of changes in building design and ambience or signage.

In a classic market study, a major brand marketer systematically varied its advertising budgets in different markets over several months. Historically, the company had changed advertising in only small increments and so did not have any experience with big changes. In some of its market tests, it doubled its advertising budget; in others, it halved it. As a result of the study, the firm gained precise knowledge of the responsiveness of sales to significant changes in advertising and concluded that in general, it could cut its budgets significantly and reap substantial rewards in improved profitability.

Experimentation is not a research approach that naturally comes to the mind of the limited-budget manager. Yet it can be a very effective and often very cheap research technique. Experimentation can have an extremely favorable benefit-cost ratio. Yet it is all too rarely used. Why is this? The answer, I believe, lies in what I have come to call the *one-best-strategy* mentality of many managers. The manager feels under a great deal of pressure to produce and to do so without spending much money. To accomplish this goal, the manager typically tries to be as cautious as possible. The limited-budget manager is usually very risk averse. This means that he or she changes the status quo only when the case for the change is convincing. And, typically, to reduce the insecurity when such a change is made, the manager settles on the one best alternative and, once the decision is made, avoids thinking about any option that is assumed to be less than best. This approach tends to inhibit experimentation. The manager thinks, "Why try anything that is less than my best choice, even on an experimental basis, since almost by definition, it is very likely to reduce my revenues?"

There are fatal flaws in this reasoning. Most important, it assumes that the manager is really correct: that the best strategy has indeed been chosen. But if the cost of an experiment can be kept low, it may well be worth it if there is some probability of a major gain in knowing what really is best—for example, if the best strategy is substantially off-target. To see why this is so, recall the approach to analyzing the costs and benefits of research outlined in Chapter Four.

Suppose a fundraiser is planning to send 10,000 letters to potential donors at a cost of $8,200. The best strategy is expected to yield 500 replies, generating an estimated $25,000 in donations and, allowing 25 percent for other related expenditures, net proceeds of $10,550 after deducting the cost of the mailing. Suppose further that for an extra $1,000, a second mailer could be prepared using a strategy that is thought to be second best but *could* be better in the long run. Suppose that the manager predicts that if this second-best mailer is sent to 20 percent of the mailing list, only 80 replies instead of 100 would be received (because it is second best). At an average return of $50 per response and proceeds after other costs of $37.50, the experiment would cost $1,750, including the cost of the second mailer and the lost profits.

Now suppose the manager is willing to admit that perhaps the second-best mailer could really be better and could increase returns at maximum by 15 percent. In this case, the better strategy would yield 575 replies at an average donation of $50 and an average profit of $37.50, for a total increase in proceeds of $2,812.50 per mailing. If a strategy lasts, say, four mailings to 10,000 potential donors, this is an overall $11,250 gain in future proceeds. Furthermore, if the second strategy was better, there would be no loss from this mailing, and returns would rise from 100 to 115, meaning that the experiment would really cost only $562.50, so overall, management would be $10,687.50 ahead.

If the manager concedes there is a 20 percent chance the second strategy will turn out to be better, there are two possible payoffs associated with experimenting when compared to the strategy of just continuing with the present one-best-strategy: (1) a 20 percent chance of being better off by $10,687.50 and (2) an 80 percent chance of being worse off by $1,750. The weighted expected value then is a positive $737.50. Management, on average, would gain this amount by conducting experiments like this even if there was only a relatively modest chance (20 percent) that the one best strategy really wasn't best.

Although this example is hypothetical and the amounts are small, it clearly demonstrates why the very best managers are always experimenting. First, experimental managers tend to be less risk averse and are not quite so fearful that a risky second strategy would turn out to be a big disaster, that is, that expected losses from forgone returns would be very high. At the same time, they are more likely to entertain the possibility that they are wrong. Furthermore, their marketing aggressiveness leads them constantly to look for ways of doing things better. And so they often conclude that even if a careful estimate of the expected value from experimentation is negative, it is still worth the research because something will be learned, even if it is only that this second-best alternative can be eliminated in future.

The sophisticated manager is also more likely to think strategically about the long run. That is, the manager will be willing to accept quite a number of failures in experimentation in the short run recognizing that if experiments are done in series, over time he or she can accumulate a sharp sense of what does and does not work in a particular market environment. Experimentation for these managers is really systematic wisdom building.

Experimental Design

The opportunities for experimentation are almost boundless, limited for the most part only by the imagination of the researcher. The object of experimentation is to try something different and, by following a few simple rules of proper experimental design, learn what the effect of this difference is, if any, on a result of interest to management, such as brand awareness or product preference. The rules are very important, however, because there are many things that can go wrong with experimentation.

Experimentation can apply to almost any aspect of the marketing mix. New-product and service offerings can be tried out, prices can be manipulated, new benefits promoted, or changes made in hours of operation or in organization logos or mission statements. Different communications options can be exposed to different target audiences alone or in various combinations. Experimentation can address large and small issues. For example, for print communications, one can learn whether to use pictures or no pictures, whether to show people or show statistics, whether the copy should be long or short, or whether the organization logo should go on the left side or the right side. One can also study the effect of totally withdrawing communications from a Web site or doubling it. Experimentation can help explore alternative client presentations, media combinations, timing of messages, and approaches to services. New outlets can be tried, as can new types of staff contact people and even new salary incentive schemes.

Experiments can be done in the real world or in the laboratory. The real world has the virtue of being like the eventual environment the organization will face. But a lot of other events will be going on (such as a change in economic conditions or actions of other organizations) that can cloud a result. In the laboratory, all else can be held constant. But what one gains in control of the experimental setting, one obviously loses in realism.

Results of experiments can be measured in terms of cognitions or actual behavior, or both. Cognitions include measures of awareness, perception of various communication features, preferences, attitudes toward future patronage, and potential favorable word-of-mouth. Behavioral measures include customer responses, staff behavior, and behavior of various organizational partners or potential partners.

To be most useful to a manager, an experiment should ideally possess three characteristics. First, there should be random assignments of different experimental treatments (for example, different communications) to different groups of subjects (for example, locations or individuals). Second, the experiment should be designed such that (ideally), nothing else could have caused the results observed. Third, the results of the experiment should be projectable to the future real-world marketing situation the organization will face, with few doubts as to its applicability. The major variations in experimental design discussed in this chapter are simply different ways of controlling one or more of the major kinds of threats to these last two characteristics, sometimes called *internal* or *external validity*.

These requirements help us distinguish between a true experiment and research that seems like an experiment but isn't. The following hypothetical cases look like experiments but are not:

- One month after a major plant layoff, the local theater manager notices a 20 percent decline in attendance.

- A national wildlife organization observes that when a rival California environmental group reduced its membership fees by 10 percent while no other local group in the United States did so, membership applications for the national organization fell 20 percent in California with no changes elsewhere.

- A government health clinic is shut down, and client visits to three of your own clinics rise significantly.

These all look like experiments in the sense that something is changed and there appear to be consequences that the something caused. But these situations are really what we call *pseudoexperiments*. Can an analysis of the impact of these natural events meet the test of internal validity? That is, can one eliminate the possibility that the observed results are due to something entirely different from the factor thought to have caused it? In each of the cases, at least one reasonable alternative hypothesis can be offered.

In the theater case, suppose the plant layoff occurred at the same time as a new state-of-the-art movie complex was opened, attendance in the previous three months was 30 percent *above* average, the local college basketball team was in the NCAA finals, or the current production saw a change of two key cast members. All of these might have been the real cause of the decline.

In the California case, the competitors have cut membership fees because they sensed a decline in interest in wildlife issues in California. Your sales may have declined anyway, not as a result of their actions.

In the clinic case, there may have been a major residential shift in population that made the government clinic not cost-effective. At the same time, the population may have moved to new low-income housing near your clinics, and so demand would have risen even if the government clinic had not closed.

In all three cases, the problem with the experiment was that there was no control for other possible explanations. The reasons were threefold. First, since we didn't systematically control the cause, there was no random assignment of the subjects of the experiment to the conditions. In the theater and clinic cases, everybody was exposed to the condition. In the other case, although residents in California, and not other states, were the target of the intervention, many other local factors may have led to the fee reduction.

Second, all three cases have the additional problem that because the change affected everyone, we had no comparison or control group. We don't know what would have happened in the absence of the treatment.

Third, in the California case, since we didn't control the timing of the treatments, we cannot even say that the fee reduction preceded our membership decline rather than appeared at the same time, thus confusing association with causation.

This then leads us to define three requirements of a true experiment:

1. The experimental treatment must precede the effects it is designed to cause.
2. There must be a comparison group that did not receive the treatment or received a different treatment.
3. There must be random assignment of treatments (or the absence of a treatment) to groups.

The last point is especially crucial. Unless one randomly assigns treatments to targets, there is always the danger that those exposed to the treatment (for example, those who volunteer for it) will be different from those not exposed. Unless there is random assignment, we cannot by definition rule out the possibility that any differences that show up are due to the fact that the two groups are different to begin with.

This is not to deny that pseudoexperiments can be informative. Sometimes they are the only way to observe an effect such as the market's responses to some sudden action by a rival organization or an environmental shock like a plant closing. In such instances, low-cost researchers should attempt to learn as much as possible from the pseudoexperiment, making every effort to consider and adjust for whatever biases may be present. Often, there is no reason to believe that the occurrence of the natural event was not randomly distributed. If the results from the pseudoexperiment are believable, this may be quite adequate as a basis for a risk-taking manager to take action.

Types of Experiments

True experiments can take many forms and can be complicated. We will restrict our attention here to relatively simple experiments. The experiments discussed here differ in two respects; (1) whether measures were taken before and after the treatment or only before, and (2) whether there was a control group with which to compare the group receiving the treatment. In this framework, pseudo-experiments would be classified as after-only experiments with no control.

The Simplest Designs

We will consider two of the simplest and most commonly used designs first and then introduce some more complex alternatives for those who have more difficult decision problems to investigate.

After Measure with Control. The simplest experiment to design and administer is called the *after measure with control* design. It requires that the researcher randomly assign subjects to two or more groups, leaving one group alone as a control and applying a treatment to each of the remaining groups. The effects of each treatment are then measured and compared with the untouched control group. The difference provides a measure of treatment effect that eliminates any systematic bias between the groups (as when subjects self-select the treatment they will expose themselves to) although there can still be random differences between the groups.

Let us consider an example. Suppose the manager of twenty child care centers for low-income families in a major urban area is curious as to whether a modest direct mail campaign aimed at residents near a center would have an effect on enrollments for the coming season. A simple after-measure-with-control experiment could be used with two or more centers assigned to each group:

Group	Treatment	After Measure
1	Yes	Yes
2	No	Yes

To ensure that this is a true experiment, the manager must randomly assign centers to the two conditions and not, for example, conduct the mailing around centers nearest headquarters (so someone can keep an eye on traffic in the centers). Random assignment has the advantage of eliminating systematic bias, and the presence of the control group not only gives a basis for comparison but helps monitor another harsh reality of real-world market experiments: the world does not stand still, and other events, such as an economic downturn, may affect outcomes. But such potentially contaminating events will affect the control sites just as much as the treatment sites, so that the differences in results will still indicate treatment effects.

This approach has one other feature to recommend it. Because measurements are taken only after the treatment, one does not risk the possibility of unduly influencing a treatment group before applying the treatment. Let us, however, consider why we might want to measure a group before a treatment.

Before and After Measures with Control. Suppose the results of the above experiment turned out as in Table 7.1. The question the researcher must now ask is, Are there any explanations for the effects other than the treatment? One possibility is that the after measures simply reflect differences in the groups (centers) that existed before the study and that the treatment had no effect. This is possible even though the centers were assigned randomly.

Suppose the center owner in our example had only four locations to assign to the two conditions described. Suppose further that the centers ranged in size from very small to very large. The problem quickly becomes obvious. If the larger centers by chance were assigned to the direct mail treatment condition, enrollments will be very high and the treatment will appear to be more effective. But if

TABLE 7.1 Hypothetical Experimental Research Results: After-Only with Control.

	Average Enrollments
Direct mail	227
No direct mail	198

the larger centers end up in the control group, no treatment would appear to be effective. The explanation of the after results then would be confounded by the unmeasured before conditions.

If it is feared that random assignment may leave the groups greatly different even without any systematic bias (for example, where one is using a small sample), an obvious precaution would be to take a reading on the groups before the treatment as well as after. One could then proceed to compute before-and-after differences for each of the groups and compare the difference for the treatment group with the difference for the control group. This would have the effect of eliminating the effects of differences in starting position across the groups. (An alternative way of handling this problem is called blocking. It can be used if one already has a measure of some important prior difference or some characteristic that is believed to be highly associated with it. Blocking in this case would put large stores in one block and small stores in the other. Assignment is random within blocks, ensuring that each treatment has one randomly chosen small store and one randomly chosen large store.)

A hypothetical result is reproduced in Table 7.2. Here, we can see that the effects of the mailing were much less dramatic than Table 7.1 suggested.

So why not do this all the time? Certainly, where it is easy to take a before measure in an unobtrusive fashion (as when records can be collected or retrieved), this should be done. However, in other cases, there are two reasons that a researcher might not want to take

TABLE 7.2 Hypothetical Experimental Research Results: Before-After with Control.

	Average Enrollments		
	Before Mailing	After Mailing	Difference
Direct mail	201	227	+16
No direct mail	190	196	+6

a before measure. One is cost; the more measurements that are taken, the greater the cost. The other is the danger of contaminating the groups. If someone takes a prior measure, it is not inconceivable that either (1) the before measure itself will cause a change or (2) the before measure will cause the treatment to have more impact than it would have if the before measure was not taken.

These two possibilities can most easily be seen in the context of communication research. Suppose our child care center manager wishes to test the effectiveness of a new poster theme on reenrollment intentions of parents of children now in their centers.

Premeasures are taken in both treatment and control centers asking a sample of mothers about their intentions to enroll their children in the next season. Scores for each center are computed. The posters are displayed in the treatment centers, and after six weeks, the same parents in both areas are reinterviewed. The before-and-after results are shown in Table 7.3.

It appears from the results that the posters in the treatment group were a great success. They increased enrollments more than in the control group. But a closer look will reveal three problems with the results:

1. The before measures in the two sets of centers are not the same. This would suggest a nonrandom factor in the selection of treatment and control centers, such as putting the posters in centers that already have higher reenrollment rates.

TABLE 7.3 Hypothetical Results of Enrollment (percentage indicating reenrollment).

	Treatment		Control	
	Before	After	Before	After
Reenrollment	55	73	46	58

2. Intentions rose in the control group as well as the treatment group. Since there were no posters there, the only plausible explanation is that the first interview spurred some respondents to think more carefully about their reenrollment plans, and some changed their minds. This could be an example of a pretest effect.

3. Because we suspect that the pretest influenced the parents, it is possible that the pretest could also have caused the parents to notice and be influenced by the new posters to a greater degree than they would have without the pretest effect. This is called a potential interaction between the premeasure and the experimental treatment.

The bottom line is that we do not know whether the "poster effect" is due to differences in starting conditions, a pretest effect, an interaction between the pretest and the treatment (the posters), or the treatment. Because of all of these problems, we must reluctantly conclude that the experiment is inconclusive.

Most studies involving cognitive changes are very susceptible to premeasure contamination. In such cases, after-only measures are preferable. But in many studies, the need for a premeasure will be important, and the researcher will have to make a judgment as to which set of potential problems is more worrisome: not having a premeasure or having a premeasure that confounds the results. In general, the larger the number of cases one can assign to each condition, the less one has to worry about prior differences across groups and can choose the after-only approach. But contaminating premeasures could be used if one is looking only at differences among various treatments, and there is reason to believe that premeasures will inflate postmeasures for all groups alike and will not exaggerate the effect of any one treatment. In such cases, the assumption is that the difference scores are all biased to the same degree, and the researcher can proceed to compare the (biased) treatment differences to the (biased) control group differences. (This is another case of learning to live with bias.)

If a premeasure is crucial—for example, where one is worried about important differences across groups, such as in neighborhoods—and if a premeasure may inflate only the treatment effect (that is, the biases will not be constant), there is sometimes another option: to measure different samples of people before and after the treatments. This could have been done in the poster study. Someone could have interviewed one group before the posters went up and a different group after. However, the conclusions of the study would rely on the assumption that the sample group studied after the posters went up would have shown the same prior status as the premeasure group, that is, there are no differences in starting position between the pre- and posttreatment groups. But this is not always reasonable, especially when the sample is small. Remember that the reason for the premeasure in the first place was to take into account just such sampling differences between groups. A second problem with using two different samples is that the researcher would not be able to learn which households were affected by the treatment. For example, in the poster study, the child care center manager would not know if the increased awareness came from young or old, large or small households, or different ethnic groups.

Other Biases. Even where the researcher can safely assume that there are no premeasure effects or interactions, other possible sources of bias can appear. Subjects of many experiments may realize they are part of a study. In so-called laboratory studies, this is always a problem. Subjects in laboratory settings *know* they are part of a study and may not behave as they ordinarily would in the situation. For example, if they are watching slides of advertisements or packaging, they will likely examine the image much more carefully than they usually would. If a control group is subject to the same effect due to being part of a lab experiment, then the researcher may safely use the "constant bias" assumption. Even in the real world, the experimentation bias is a possibility. For example, suppose a clinic manager wishes to experiment with a new clinic poster. It is possible that personnel in the clinics with the new posters will simply try harder to get reenrollments because they know they are part of a study. Higher enrollments, then, cannot be attributed to the new posters but may be due to the hothouse effects of the study itself.

This effect may sometimes apply to the control group as well. In MRFIT, a famous $40 million heart-risk study, the researchers had to inform doctors in the control group that they were part of the study, in part because the researchers needed careful records on patients of all physicians. Ironically, the researchers found that there was a greater control of heart problems in the control group than in the group practicing the approved regimen, exercising more, and reducing salt intake. They attributed this to the fact that doctors in the control group were more diligent with their patients because they knew they were being watched.[1]

More Complex Experimental Designs

In the examples so far, we have considered only one treatment. In many marketing situations, management will wish to know which of several alternatives is best. In such cases, a simple solution is to increase the number of randomly selected treatment groups and have one control sample that remains touched. Alternatively, if there is no intention to leave the market as it is now and the managerial decision is to choose among several new alternatives, then there is no need for a control group. That is, for management's purposes, one does not need to know whether there is any effect, but only which treatment (if any) has the most effect.

Suppose management is considering new tactics that are not simply substitutes for each other (such as, different posters) but might be used in combination (such as different reenrollment fees)? Here, managers typically want to know *main effects* (Did any of the tactics by itself have a differential effect?) and *interaction effects* (Did some combination of tactics yield greater effects than predicted by the separate main effects)?

To make this point clear, consider the case of a nonprofit fundraiser. The fundraiser wishes to know whether she should recommend a minimum donation of $30, $50, or $75 and whether to include an annual report in the mailing or a specially crafted flyer. The criterion is dollars donated per response. The fundraiser might think that considered alone, the $30 donation level and the special flyer would get higher average returns. However, it may be that the combination of a $50 donation level and the annual report would do the best. From an experimental standpoint, the manager is asking:

- Is there a main effect due to donation level? That is, do returns differ significantly depending on what level of donation is suggested?
- Is there a main effect due to communication piece? That is, are significantly more revenues generated with the flyer or the annual report?
- Is there an interaction effect between donation level and communications piece?

To answer these questions, we must have a much more complicated design. Here we need to use six experimental treatments: one for each combination of donation level and communications piece. Without all possible combinations, we cannot estimate the interaction effects. In each of the six conditions, or cells, we will want a significant number of mailings so that a good measure of random variation within the cells can be secured. Suppose the results over several weeks turned out as in Table 7.4.

Although we must apply statistical tests to each of the three possible effects (see Chapter Ten), the following results are suggested:

TABLE 7.4 Average Returns for Direct Mail Experiment.

| Mail Piece | Suggested Donation Level | | | |
	$30	$50	$75	Average
Flyer	$30,000	$19,000	$17,000	$22,000
Annual report	5,000	17,000	20,000	14,000
Average	17,500	18,000	18,500	18,000

- There is no main effect due to donation level. That is, if nothing else were changed, management should not care what it suggests as a minimum donation.

- There is a main effect due to communications piece. The fancy flyer does much better than the usual annual report.

- Most important, there is an interaction effect. Clearly, the best strategy is to set a donation level of $30 and use the special flyer.

Although this experiment is complex, with many mailings the cost of the study is very low, and the potential returns can be high. Compared to the average strategy return of $180,000 the optimal combination yields $120,000 more. Assuming no great differences in the number of responses, the added payoff can be in the thousands of dollars, even after the cost of developing, testing, and preparing the flyer.

There are a great many possibilities for this more complex kind of low-cost experimentation through direct mail. A great many organizations spend a lot of effort mailing letters, brochures, publicity releases, advocacy letters, volunteer recruitment solicitations, and other pieces, all designed to generate responses. Clearly, learning how to increase the response would be very valuable.

Experimentation is the obvious approach here. There are a number of reasons that direct mail experiments are popular:

- It is easy to assign subjects to treatments randomly.
- Because large numbers can be assigned to each treatment, the need for a premeasure is virtually nonexistent.
- It is easy to keep track of which responses are associated with which treatments. Slightly modified layouts of return envelopes can be used to indicate different treatments. Code numbers can be incorporated on the mail response form itself or on the return envelope. Different post office box numbers can be assigned to different treatments (at a slight added cost), or the return envelope can be

addressed to different people or to one person with different middle initials corresponding to different treatments. For telephone responses (for example, in catalogue sales or public service announcements), callers can be asked to identify the mailing material (treatment) number to which they are responding.

- The treatment conditions can be carefully controlled as to the precise character and timing of the stimulus and all irrelevant factors that must be held constant.

- The private nature of the mail system makes it unlikely that competitors will learn of the experiment. (Of course, if they too have learned to use low-cost competitive intelligence techniques, they or their employees may already be on several of your mailing lists.)

- External validity is great because usually what is tried out in a mail experiment is what the marketer will use over the long term.

- Because mail pieces are relatively complicated and because most recipients are on only one mailing list, subjects are unlikely to realize that they are part of an experiment. In this sense, mail studies are unobtrusive.

- Complete combinations of treatments that can assess interactions are possible because of large sample bases.

Direct mail experimentation should be a routine part of any low-budget researcher's arsenal. Similar possibilities are now becoming possible with e-mail campaigns.

Laboratory Experiments

Despite their problems, laboratory experiments can be valuable alternatives to field experiments. They can be carried out in hotel rooms, trailers in shopping center malls, university classrooms, or the researcher's or the marketer's offices. The advantage of laboratory studies is that a great many factors can be controlled in these cases. Participants can be carefully assigned to treatments, stimuli precisely introduced, and extraneous factors totally eliminated. For such reasons, laboratory experiments are popular for taste, touch, or sniff tests, communications copy studies, pricing studies, and new-product or service concept tests. In the laboratory, mechanical or electronic measuring devices can be used that would be cumbersome in the field. These could include measures of responses to marketing stimuli in the form of changes in heartbeat, eye movement, conductivity of sweat, and pupil diameter or delay times on a computer.

An example of a simple laboratory study was one conducted by a group of my students at UCLA. At the time of the introduction of New Coke, the students were curious about the effects of the new product's advertising on perceptions of its taste. They set up a table on a campus quadrangle and poured subjects drinks in random order from three cola bottles labeled "New Coke," "Old Coke," and "Pepsi." They asked respondents to rate the three drinks on a number of dimensions, including traits emphasized in early New Coke advertising and their preference among the three samples. They also asked each subject for their favorite cola in the past and whether they recalled seeing or hearing any ads for New Coke in recent days. Comparisons across subjects showed:

- There were no significant differences in perceptions of the three drinks on all dimensions for all subjects.

- There were significant differences for those who reported recalling the New Coke ads, and the differences were in the direction emphasized in the advertising copy.

- Most respondents had little difficulty indicating a clear preference among the three drinks.

What was most interesting about this laboratory study was that unlike the real world, the researchers could control what was in the bottles. And the colas were all the same: they were all old Coke. The study could clearly demonstrate that what advertising leads one to expect is what one thinks one gets. Advertising, even in such a simple product category, is much more powerful than many people suspect. No wonder we are inundated with ads calling colas "the real thing" or part of a "new generation."

However, laboratory experiments give up a lot for what they gain. Subjects who know they are guinea pigs have been known to behave in ways that would be out of character for them. Many will try to guess what the researchers want them to do (sometimes called the experimental *demand effect*) and try to please them.

Still, lab experiments are usually inexpensive to set up and can be done quickly. Often there is little need for representativeness in the samples as long as the participants are members of the target market and, where appropriate, randomly assigned. As a consequence, simple lab experiments are usually a good first step in testing new ideas or alternative strategies. One can recruit friends, church members, or sometimes employees, randomly assign them to groups and see which treatment works best, taking care to control the other sources of explanation outlined earlier in this chapter.

Making Experimentation Easy

In the course of exploring these approaches to experimental design, the reader should have begun to appreciate both the potential benefits and the potential problems of the basic technique. There are a great many circumstances, perhaps the majority of cases, where elaborate controls and close checking of outside contamination are not really needed. Here are some instances in which experimentation should be relatively easy to accomplish:

• Often in experimental situations, premeasures already exist. For example, in studies where markets or outlets are the experimental unit, sales are often the measurement of primary interest. Since sales data usually are already available (although not always in the form one wants), premeasures can be avoided. If samples within cells must be small due to cost considerations, blocking on past revenues or customer responses can be used to control for potential bias due to size differences across cells that could occur by chance if there was random assignment.

- Even where no premeasure exists, it may be possible and realistic to record premeasures unobtrusively, again eliminating possible negative premeasure effects. For instance, the effect of specific selections of toys in a preschool might be tracked by visual counts of the number of children handling the toys observed unobtrusively before and after an experiment, for example, by a television camera.

- Often the time interval involved between a treatment and a measurement is so short that no external environmental effects are likely to confound a field study. Thus, one need not worry about trying to monitor these potential contaminants. The same would be true in longer-term studies if the competitive environment was normally highly stable or if the researcher could easily disguise an experiment (for example, with mail studies or in subtle advertising or service facility changes).

- The population may be very homogeneous, and if randomization is carefully done, a premeasure may be unnecessary.

- Multiple measures of experimental outcomes can be used if there is a concern that one or two could be biased. Their individual biases may cancel each other out.

- As the researcher accumulates experience in experimentation, it will often be possible to make a confident estimate of possible biasing effects. Even using experiments without estimates may be better than doing no experimentation at all if it can be assumed the biases are reasonably constant or proportional across groups.

- Given an appropriate opportunity (as in the case where human beings are the guinea pigs), there is nothing at all wrong with asking the subjects of an experiment after the study whether they were in fact biased by some aspect of the study design and, if so, how. This is usually called *debriefing*. Debriefing is routine in most professional and academic experiments involving human subjects. Codes of ethics require that subjects be informed of their rights not to participate and that they be told after the fact in the debriefing, except under unusual circumstances, what the aim of the study really was and who was its sponsor.

Conclusion

Before leaving the subject, let us recall several key points to keep in mind even when doing relatively inexpensive, simple experiments:

- Always be sure that the experiment is designed to help management make decisions. The researcher should get management to think through the uses of a set of hypothetical experimental results to make sure that future actions will be taken. Try out a different but plausible set of results, and make sure management is clear that it will accept and act on surprising outcomes, and you know what those actions would be.

- Plan to make multiple measures of the experiment's outcomes to ensure that detected effects are real and that measurement peculiarities and biases do not either cover up something important or suggest something that isn't important. Also, it is important to randomize the sample population across treatment groups.

- In field studies, always monitor potential outside influences by competitors or in the socioeconomic environment in which the study is done that may contaminate the outcomes.

- Allow enough time after the treatment for the effects to show up. Make sure that if lasting effects are wanted, the researcher does not settle for a quick, favorable response. For example, humorous communications always get quick, favorable reactions from subjects, but the effects tend to fade rather quickly. Less lively communications often have much more substantial lasting effects.

- Consider the possibility of using multiple treatments in the experiment. The incremental costs of added complexity are often relatively low.

- Be careful that employees or other accomplices do not bias the findings. For example, make sure that if a new in-house experiment is tried, the staff do not act in ways such that the real results are due to their actions, not the experimental treatments themselves.

- If possible, debrief the subjects after the study to see if any biases were introduced (this applies to the staff members too).

- After the experiment is all over, write a brief methodological note about what was learned about how to do experiments that you will be sure to incorporate (or avoid) next time. Wisdom accumulates not only by providing findings that improve management's marketing strategies, but also by improving the researcher's abilities to be an even more effective low-budget experimenter in the future.

8

Low-Cost Survey Designs

Many low-budget researchers automatically think of surveys and questionnaires as their only research alternatives. It is important to become aware of and appreciate the potential of other techniques before moving on to survey design.

Chapter Seven focused on one such possibility: experimentation. Experiments are relatively easy to do and, because they can determine cause and effect, usually give managers direct insight into what works and what doesn't. Thus, experiments are both cheap and usually highly practical. A researcher with a limited budget has little freedom to conduct research that is not practical.

Chapters Five and Six discussed two other alternatives to surveys: archives and observation. These techniques are sometimes less immediately practical since they do not easily lend themselves to assessing cause and effect. They still have the prime virtue of being very inexpensive. Despite inadequacies, they can often help give managers the small edge in decision making that can help them consistently outperform their competitors.

A major reason for considering these alternatives is that surveys are both costly and difficult to do well. It is not easy to design sensible samples and well-worded questionnaires. Unfortunately, this does not keep amateurs from barging ahead to get something into the field without proper attention to making the research valid. This book is devoted to *good* low-cost research, not just low-cost research.

Surveys are difficult for two major reasons. First, you must typically draw a representative sample, and this is not always an easy goal to accomplish. Second, you must ask people questions. There are a number of reasons that this can be a major source of problems. Asking questions is always intrusive. This means your subjects know they are being studied, and because they know they are being studied, they will usually speculate about why you are asking. This can have one of two effects. One is that it makes people suspicious of your motives, and they may decide either not to participate at all (thus fouling up a carefully designed sampling plan) or to withhold or distort important information. A friend always tells researchers studying fast food preferences that he is a heavy, heavy consumer (which he isn't) and that he really would like to be offered healthier ingredients in his burgers, chicken nuggets, and tacos. He always answers this way because he wants to encourage fast-food marketers to offer healthier fare to their *real* heavy consumers.

The second effect of the awareness of being studied is that some respondents try to please the researcher. Well-meaning respondents may try to be helpful and claim they have a very favorable opinion of whatever it is you are asking about. Or they may try to guess which behaviors you are interested in and try to slant their preferences that way.

Asking questions always involves respondents and their egos. Whether we are aware of it or not, we all attempt to influence the way in which others perceive us. We do this with our dress, our choice of our furniture, the way we speak, whom we associate with, and so on. It is therefore inevitable that when we tell researchers things about ourselves, we may answer subtly or directly in ways that will enhance our self-image. *Reader's Digest* fans will say instead that they only read the *New York Review of Books* or the *Atlantic Monthly*. The soap opera lover will swear to a preference for public television. The heavy beer drinker will develop a sudden taste for wine.

Asking questions always involves language, and words are slippery things. A favorite word in studies of retail and service outlets is *convenience* as in the question, "Do you find YMCA #2 more or less convenient than YMCA #1?" What the researcher means by *convenient* may be a lot different from what the typical respondent means. For example, the researcher may assume that respondents are being asked how close the location is to their home or normal commuting routes, whereas some respondents may think the question is asking how easy it is to park and get in and out of the building. Others may think it is referring to the particular YMCA's hours of operation. In such cases, differences across respondents may simply reflect differences in how they interpret the question. For example, executives may find YMCA #1 more convenient than YMCA #2, while homebodies may indicate the reverse. Executives interpret your question to mean ease of parking, and homebodies may interpret it to mean closeness to home. The difference in the results is merely an artifact of the language.

All of these types of problems are unavoidable in survey research. Questions will always crop up as to the validity of the study. You can try hard to minimize their effects, but the nasty problem is that you usually never completely know that you have eliminated potential biases or even whether you understand them. This is particularly the case if you try to save money in the design by not pretesting the questionnaire thoroughly or training interviewers carefully. Management needs valid research results on which to act. In the YMCA example, it would be a mistake to promote the nearness of your outlet to executives as well as to homebodies. The two are very different in their goals and interests.

Conducting surveys and asking questions is often essential to a specific management problem. Researchers must use these techniques in hundreds of situations. If, for example, you want data on attitudes, you have no other recourse. But when surveys are not essential, researchers should exhaust other nonintrusive methods before going forward with a full-blown survey study.

Survey Design

If asking questions is the best approach to helping management make a decision, three basic strategic design decisions must be made:

(1) how to ask questions, (2) what questions to ask, and (3) who should answer.

Methods of Asking Questions

Modern technology offers researchers a wide array of approaches to asking questions. They vary mainly in the extent to which the respondent and the question asker interact. To decide on an approach, the researcher should ask a number of basic questions:

- Should the respondent be given a significant amount of time and the opportunity to talk with others before answering?
- Can the answers to the questions be reduced to a few simple choices?
- Do the questions need to be explained to the respondent?
- Is it likely that the respondent's answers will often have to be probed or clarified?
- Does anything have to be shown to the respondent, such as an advertisement or a package or a set of attitude scales to be filled in?
- Is it likely that many potential respondents will be unmotivated or turned off by the questions or the issue without personal encouragement by an interviewer?

The answers to these questions and several others, including those relating to the availability of personnel and financial resources to carry out fieldwork, will determine the basic approach. In the majority of cases, the alternatives likely to be considered will be mail, Internet, telephone, and face-to-face interviews. However, there are other possibilities. For example, respondents can be interviewed in small groups, as in focus group studies. Or individuals can be queried in a shopping mall by a computer video screen or over the telephone by a prerecorded voice with pauses for answers. In some circumstances, a combination of methods may be the best approach. One could ask questions in person that require face-to-face contact and then leave behind a mail-back questionnaire on which respondents can record further details, such as purchase histories, personal preferences, and socioeconomic characteristics.

Mail Studies. To my continuing dismay, when researchers with low budgets think of surveys and asking questions, they inevitably think first of doing a mail study. Many think this is the only alternative possible given their meager resources.

You can see why they might think so. It is often not difficult to get a mailing list. There are many such lists for sale and many list suppliers that will provide labels for a mail sample and even do the mailing at a modest cost. Even without such a commercial list, many researchers feel they can always develop a list themselves using their own database, the Yellow Pages, or the regular white pages telephone directory. A photocopier is usually close at hand, or a print shop can run off hundreds of questionnaire forms at low cost. Staff at the office can stuff envelopes at little or no out-of-pocket cost. The office postage meter and bulk mail rates can be used to keep the outbound cost of mailed questionnaires low. Business reply envelopes can be used for the returned responses, which means paying postage only for questionnaires that are in fact returned.

Given these low costs, the neophyte researcher says, "Why not?" and sits down and designs a questionnaire and a compelling cover letter and sends out five thousand forms in the mail. If it is an average study sent to a randomly drawn but moderately interested audience, the researcher will be lucky to get 10 to 15 percent of the questionnaires back. (If the audience is not interested, 4 to 5 percent would be good.) Nevertheless, this can mean 500 to 750 responses returned. The researcher thinks, "Certainly this is a substantial basis on which to make statements about a market. Don't most CNN polls reporting the president's popularity ratings base these on only nine hundred to eleven hundred respondents?"

The major problem with mail questionnaire studies, however, is not the respondents: it is the *nonrespondents*. Professional pollsters who need results that can be projected to the entire population with a known level of error are very careful to develop probability samples and then attempt to interview everyone in their samples. Because they spend a great deal of money and use face-to-face or telephone interviewing techniques, they usually have high rates of cooperation. When they do not contact a respondent or are refused participation, they make very careful analyses of just who did not respond and either adjust their analyses accordingly or alert users of the results to potential problems through a "limitations" section in their report. With the typical cheap but dirty mail study with a low response rate, the nature of the nonresponse bias is usually unknown.

Nonresponse is not necessarily bad. If the nonrespondents would have answered the questions in the study in the same way as the respondents, then there would be no bias. Nonresponse can occur in telephone or face-to-face interview studies when a respondent refuses to cooperate or is out of town or busy for the moment or because the telephone number or address was wrong. Assuming that personal interviews were scheduled at random times on weekdays and weekends and there are several follow-up attempts, nonresponse is more likely to be a chance occurrence where one should not expect nonresponders to be greatly different from responders.

In mail studies, this is virtually never the case. Those who get something in the mail asking them to fill in a modest (or great) number of answers will inevitably feel imposed on. The same is often true with telephone interviews. In a face-to-face interview or telephone study, the personality and skills of a highly trained interviewer can often overcome these negative initial reactions. But at home at one's desk or at the kitchen table, it is very easy for a potential respondent to throw out a mailed questionnaire. Those who do not react this way are likely to be different in one of two important ways. One group of responders will have an inherent interest in the topic of the study. The second group will want to help the researcher out either because they are a helping kind of person or because they are for the moment swayed by the convincing argument in the study's cover letter. Those who are interested in the topic are likely to be further divisible into two additional types: those who are positively excited about the topic (for example, those who buy the product or use the service) and those negatively disposed toward the topic who see the study as a grand opportunity to get a few gripes off their chest. As an additional biasing factor, it has generally been found that the higher the education level, the higher the response rate.

What, then, does this imply about the 10 to 15 percent who do respond to the typical mail study? It means they are almost always not at all like the nonrespondents. Unfortunately, too many researchers do not attempt to assess these potential differences because they do not recognize the problem, do not know how to handle it, or feel they do not have the time or budget to do so.

Not too long ago, I was asked by the publisher of a series of magazines aimed at different types of retail outlets to give a speech discussing the value of their annual statistical profiles of each retail category. On reviewing the publisher's methodology, I discovered that the statistics were based on responses to a single mailing from their magazine publishers (with no follow-up) and that no checking had ever been made of those who didn't respond. Yet each magazine was publishing its study as a profile of its industry, reporting such data as average store sales, widths of product lines, numbers of employees, various expenses, and profits broken down by various outlet categories.

But what, I asked, did their profiles really describe? Their response rate was usually 50 percent, which is quite good and not uncommon when mailing to a highly interested group. However, they did not know who really did respond. Although I was not concerned with the response rate, I was concerned with possible biases at both ends of the distribution of outlet size. Did the largest outlets participate? They may not have, feeling either that they would be exposing too much internal information that could be identified with them or that they were already part of a large organization that had a great deal of its own internal archival data and so they didn't need to contribute to a magazine's profile. At the other extreme, smaller or marginal outlets may not have participated because they were new to the industry, lacked appreciation of the value of such co-operation, or perhaps were embarrassed by their small size or poor performance. If either of these groups was underrepresented, the profiles have very limited value. The magazines apparently shut their eyes to these problems, never investigating who did and did not respond.

As a consequence of this and a great many similar experiences, I am very reluctant to encourage the use of mail questionnaires for low-cost research.

Some steps can increase response rates, and we will note some of these. There are also ways to investigate nonresponse bias, although usually at considerable cost. For example, you can conduct telephone interviews of a small sample of nonrespondents to a mail survey if they can be identified. Alternatively, characteristics of respondents can be compared to census data or, in a business study, to government business censuses. If there is a close match between the sample characteristics and the universe from which it was supposedly drawn, researchers can be encouraged that their sample may be representative. However, such close matching does not *prove* that the results are valid.

Even when nonresponse rates are satisfactory or understood, mail studies have a great many other, and often fatal, flaws. For example, it is possible that someone other than the intended respondent may fill out the questionnaire. A wife may ask her husband to respond, or vice versa. An executive may delegate the task to a subordinate. A doctor may ask a nurse to give the necessary particulars. Each of these situations may seriously distort the findings.

Also, there are unlimited chances to improve answers before they are returned. For example, suppose a respondent is asked for "top-of-the-mind" awareness of various cancer organizations early in the mail questionnaire and then later recalls additional organizations. He or she may go back and add the newly remembered items. On the other hand, by the end of the questionnaire, he or she may have discovered the study's sponsor and go back to change certain answers to conform more to what is presumed to be the sponsor's objectives.

Despite these problems, there are still three situations in which mail questionnaires should be the preferred choice:

First, in some situations, the respondent will need time to gather information to report in the questionnaire. This might involve consulting with someone else. For example, if the researcher wished to know whether anyone in the household had bought a product, used a service, or adopted a new behavior, then time would have to be allowed for consultation with others. This usually would not be practical (or sometimes even possible, given people's schedules) in a telephone or face-to-face interview situation. A more common example is where records must be looked up, such as when organization executives are asked for performance details or when households are asked to report on last year's taxes or asked what safety equipment they currently have in their household inventories.

Second, in some situations, it is desirable to give the respondent time to come up with a well-considered answer. Many years ago, I participated in what is called a *Delphi study*. This is a technique where respondents (usually a small select group) are asked to make judgments about the future or about some existing phenomena. The answers of the group are then summarized by the researcher and fed back to the original respondents, who are then asked to revise their answers if they wish.

The study in which I participated was an attempt to forecast time usage (for example, how much leisure or work time we would have and how we would use it) twenty-five years in the future. The study went on over three rounds of feedback, and at each stage, respondents needed several hours, if not a day or two, to give the researcher our carefully considered opinions. This could be achieved only by a mail study.

Third, a mail questionnaire is probably the only form that many busy respondents would answer. If the survey has a great many questions, those surveyed may be willing only to respond to a written questionnaire claiming they do not have the time to participate in a telephone or face-to-face interview (and if they are a physician or busy executive, they usually expect to be paid).

Even when one or more of these conditions exists, a potential mail study should also meet the following requirements:

- The fact that respondents will have long time in which to fill in the answers is not a problem.

- It is not a serious problem if someone other than the addressee fills in the questionnaire.

- A mailing list (or a procedure for sampling) that is truly representative of the population of interest can be obtained.

- A careful attempt is made to estimate the nature of the nonresponse bias.

- The respondent population is literate and reachable by mail (requirements that may make mail surveys difficult in some developing countries).

- There is a high probability that a large proportion of the respondents will be interested in the topic and respond. Interest is likely to be high where the target population has a tie to the research sponsor—for example, for members of a trade association or a club, patients recently in a hospital, employees in the researcher's organization, holders of an organization's credit cards, or subscribers to certain magazines. Even in such situations, it is essential that an estimate of the nonresponse bias be made.

There are two conditions when a biased mail survey can be used. One is when the researcher really does not care about nonresponse. This would be the case whenever projectability is not important. In a great many situations, this is the case—for example, when one wants to learn whether there are any problems with a certain product or service or with the wording of a particular advertising message or product usage instruction. A second reason for using a biased study is when the study is exploratory, seeking a few ideas for an advertisement, testing a questionnaire, or developing a set of hypotheses that will be verified in a later nonbiased study.

If the decision is to go ahead with a mail study, there are a number of very important and basic techniques that should be employed:

- The cover letter asking for assistance should be made as motivating as possible (especially the first couple of sentences). The letter should (1) be enthusiastic (if you are not excited about the study, why should the potential respondent?); (2) indicate the purposes of the study, if possible showing how it will benefit the respondent (for example, by helping provide better products and services); (3) ensure anonymity (for all respondents or for those who request it); and (4) ask for help, pointing out that only selected individuals are being contacted and each answer is important.

- The cover letter and the questionnaire should be attractive and professional with dramatic graphics and color where possible.

- The letter should be addressed to a specific individual.

- If possible, a motivating or prestigious letterhead should be used.

- If the sponsor of the study can be revealed and awareness of it would motivate respondents (for example, UNICEF or a key trade association), the letter should do so.

- The questionnaire should be kept as brief as possible and easy to follow and understand. It should be accompanied by a self-addressed stamped return envelope or a fax number. If the budget permits, one or more follow-up contacts (even by telephone) should be used to increase response rates.

- Giving advance notification to the respondent by telephone (better) or by postcard (worse) that the questionnaire is coming has been useful to increase the total number of responses, the speed of response, and the quality of the responses.

- In some cases, offering gifts, cash, or a chance at a major prize to those who mail back the questionnaire (or including a coin or a dollar bill "for charity"), and using stamped rather than metered return envelopes increases the number, speed, and quality of responses.

Lovelock and his colleagues strongly urge the use of personal drop-off and pick-up of what otherwise would be a mailed questionnaire. They believe this technique is particularly appropriate for lengthy questionnaires where considerable motivational effort and perhaps some explanation needs to be carried out. The results of their study indicate that response rates can be as high as 74 percent. While this rate is achieved by incurring the costs of personnel to handle questionnaire delivery and pickup, they can be lightly trained and low cost (students fit this bill). Cost-per-returned-questionnaire was found to be no different from the traditional mail questionnaire. In addition, those delivering the questionnaire can eliminate individuals obviously ineligible for the study (if anyone is), and data about the respondent's sex, age, living conditions, and neighborhood can be recorded by observation to enrich the database. Reasons for refusals can be elicited, and because the fieldworker can observe and screen the respondents, fieldworkers can provide the researcher with a very good sense of the nature of the nonresponse bias.[1]

This approach requires that the study be done in a concentrated geographical area rather than nationally. The technique is particularly useful in organizational or office studies where respondents are easy to locate but so busy they would not ordinarily agree to a personal interview.

Internet Research. The Internet is another medium for contacting potential informants. Estimates by Nua Internet Surveys indicate that over 400 million people worldwide were on-line in early 2001, with over 40 percent of these in the United States and Canada. Internet surveys allow you to ask complicated series of questions tailored to each individual respondent. The Internet has additional advantages in that respondents can be shown visual and audio stimuli such as television commercials or print ads and asked their responses. Such research is difficult to design, but there are many organizations that can help design and implement Internet research projects. Among these are Nua Internet Surveys, ActivMedia Research, and Opti-Market Consulting.

The major caution when conducting such research is deciding whom to contact and then understanding who has responded. Clearly, those now on the Web are not representative of the entire population of a specific country, especially countries in early stages of Internet development. Furthermore, those active on the Internet are demographically skewed toward those who are young, better educated, and upscale economically. Finally, it is not possible to control who responds to an inquiry; the person claiming to be a forty-three-year-old woman with three children could well be her preteen son.

The Net can be an excellent medium to study a precise population known to be active on the Web, especially one with whom the manager has some sort of contact. For example, a nonprofit can study clients or partners with whom it has regular contact and achieve a reasonably representative profile of this group. In the same way, nonprofits could study donors who make their gifts over the Web.

Perhaps the best use of the Web is in formative research designed to get impressions, insights, and other guidance for managerial decisions. Where the manager is interested in getting help with directions to go in or for ideas to pursue with more formal research later, respondents on the Web can be very helpful.

Telephone Interviewing. Telephone interviewing with or without computer assistance is now the method of choice in most developed countries when a researcher needs to interact with respondents and achieve a projectable sample. A major reason is the lower cost. A large number of interviews all over the country or even internationally can be conducted from a telephone bank at one site in a very short period of time. Telephone interviewing also has some advantages that alternative techniques do not:

• The person-to-person contact yields all the advantages of motivating responses, explaining questions, and clarifying answers in face-to-face interviews. However, the number of cues that the interviewer as a person presents to the respondent are very few (sex, voice, vocabulary), yielding fewer chances for biasing effects than if the respondent also could react to the interviewer's clothes, facial expressions, body language, and the like.

• The facelessness of the telephone interviewing situation can loosen the inhibitions of respondents who might withhold a personally embarrassing piece of information if a flesh-and-blood person was standing or sitting opposite them taking down information.

• Appointments and multiple callbacks permit interviewers to find precisely defined individuals (for example, high-income potential donors).

• Because telephone interviews are conducted from one location, a supervisor can easily monitor the work of interviewees through systematic eavesdropping, thus greatly increasing quality control and uniformity of techniques.

Despite these advantages, telephone interviewing has three major drawbacks. First, it is harder to motivate and establish rapport with potential respondents over the telephone than in person; it is easier for them to hang up the telephone than to close the door on an interviewer. This problem is worsening in the age of telemarketing as more unscrupulous sales organizations use the pseudo–telephone interview as a technique for generating sales leads.

Second, some things cannot be done in a telephone interview that could be done in person. No visual props can be used (one can still test radio commercials, though), and certain sophisticated measurements, such as scales with cue cards, cannot be used.

The third drawback is that increasing numbers of telephones are not publicly listed, especially in major cities, and many households have multiple numbers for their kids and their home-based businesses. For these reasons, the telephone directory is not a good sampling frame for interviewing in most major centers. Telephone books, which typically are published yearly, tend to exclude three kinds of households: phoneless households, unlisted households, and not-yet-listed households.

Over 20 percent of all owners of residential lines choose not to be listed. In larger cities like Chicago, Los Angeles, and New York, this figure can be as high as 40 percent or more. These households are more likely to represent younger heads, single females, those with middle rather than high or low incomes, nonwhites, and those in blue-collar or sales and service occupations. Not-yet-listed households include those moving into an area or out of their parents' house since the last directory was published. These may be crucial targets for many marketing efforts, such as those aimed at immigrants, recently unemployed, or college graduates.

For these reasons, those planning to do telephone sampling are encouraged to use some variation on random digit or plus-one dialing. These approaches involve first randomly selecting listings from the existing directory to ensure that the researcher is using blocks of numbers the telephone company has released. At this point, the last one or two digits in the listing number are replaced with other randomly selected numbers. Alternatively, the researcher could simply add one to the last digit in the selected number. These approaches still omit blocks of numbers released since the previous directory was published, but this should be a nominal bias (mostly affecting new movers) when compared with that of using only numbers in the directory itself.

The random digit dialing approach has its drawbacks. Most important, the technique increases costs because often the randomly selected numbers turn out to be ineligible institutions or fax lines. (Indeed, in one unusual case, an interviewer randomly called a radio call-in show and, to the amusement of both the audience and the interviewer's colleagues and supervisor, proceeded to interview the host on the air.) However, this cost is one that most researchers are usually willing to bear.

Face-to-Face Interviewing.   After mail surveys, researchers planning original fieldwork consider face-to-face or telephone interviews. For a great many purposes, face-to-face interviews are the ideal medium for a study for several reasons. For example, respondents (once contacted) can be strongly motivated to cooperate. By choosing inter-viewers carefully, matching them as closely as possible to predicted re-spondent characteristics, and giving them a motivating sales pitch, the refusal rate can be kept very low. This can be critical, for exam-ple, when studying small samples of high-status individuals who must be included in the study and will participate only if a high-status in-terviewer personally comes to them and asks questions. Also, stimuli can be shown to or handled by respondents in particular sequences. This is very important where one wishes to assess responses to pro-motion materials such as advertisements or brochures or where a product or package needs to be tasted, sniffed, or otherwise inspected.

As in telephone interviews, there are opportunities for feedback from the respondent that are impossible in self-report, mail, or com-puter methods. This permits elaboration of misunderstood ques-tions and probing to clarify or extend answers.

The interviewer can add observation measures to traditional questioning. For example, if a set of advertisements is shown, the interviewer can informally estimate the amount of time the re-spondent spends on each stimulus. Facial expressions can be ob-served to indicate which parts of the messages are confusing to respondents and need to be refined. Respondents' appearance and the characteristics of their home or office can be observed and re-corded. Sex, race, estimated age, and social status can be recorded without directly asking respondents (although some measures, like social class, should be verified by alternative means).

Against these considerable advantages are some important, of-ten fatal, disadvantages. For example, because the interviewer is physically present during the answering process, two sorts of biases are very likely. First, the interviewer's traits—dress, manner, physi-cal appearance—may influence the respondent. The interviewer may be perceived as upper class or snooty, or slovenly or unintelli-gent, which may cause the interviewee to adjust, sometimes un-consciously, his or her answers. Second, simply because there is another person present, the respondent may distort answers by try-ing to impress the interviewer or hide something in embarrassment.

In addition, the fact that interviews are conducted away from central offices means that the performance of interviewers is very difficult to monitor for biases and errors (as compared to central office telephone interviewing). Also, physically approaching respondents can be very costly when there are refusals or not-at-homes. Callbacks that are easy by telephone can be very costly in face-to-face interviews.

Finally, delays between interviews are great. Telephone lines or the mail can reach anywhere in the country (and most parts of the world) very quickly and with relatively little wasted time. Travel between personal interviews can be costly.

The last two factors tend to make the field staffing costs for face-to-face interviews in most developed countries very high. They are so high that one-on-one personal interviews are probably prohibitively expensive for the low-budget researcher except where the technique's advantages are critical to the study (for example, graphic materials must be shown or handled or high-status subjects, such as doctors or lawyers, must be interviewed), the sample size is very small, or the study is local. Situations in which these criteria would be met include studies in local neighborhoods, malls, offices, or trade shows.

In the developing world, personal interviews are still relatively low cost and often the only way to reach target audiences. Furthermore, potential respondents often have limited education and reading and writing skills and thus may need help in answering even relatively simple questions (such as rating scales).

If the decision is to go ahead with personal interviewing, there are a number of low-cost sampling techniques to consider.

Low-Cost Sampling

If a researcher wishes to carry out a study that is projectable to some universe of interest, such as all adults in an area or all hospitals, each potential sample member must have a known probability of being selected. Two approaches are typically used. In a *simple random sam-*

pling study, a list (or sampling frame) is prepared and enough individuals selected on a probability basis so that, given expected rates of not-at-homes, refusals, and the like, the desired sample size can be achieved. A variation on this approach is called *stratified sampling*. This approach requires that the sample first be divided into groups or strata (such as census tracts or store size categories) and then either proportional or disproportional random samples drawn within each group. This approach has advantages over simple random sampling if there is special interest in some strata, the variation within strata is low compared to the variation across strata, or the costs of interviewing vary significantly across strata.

While simple random and stratified sampling are appropriate for projectable studies, they can raise costs dramatically beyond a limited-budget researcher's capabilities. When this is the case, the researcher should consider several techniques to cut down on personnel time and increase efficiency in studies that still must use face-to-face interviewing:

- Focus groups
- Mall intercepts
- Quota sampling
- Convenience sampling
- Judgment sampling
- Snowball and network sampling
- Sequential sampling

Some of these approaches will still yield statistically projectable results.

Focus Groups

One extremely popular low-cost technique for conducting face-to-face interviews is to do so in focus groups. These studies bring together eight to twelve individuals in a room (or more recently, by telephone conference call) to talk for sixty to ninety minutes about a specific research topic. The discussions are typically led by a trained moderator. Focus groups are qualitative and nonprojectable. They are typically used for the following purposes:

- Generating hypotheses
- Generating information helpful in designing consumer questionnaires
- Providing background information on an exchange category
- Securing reactions to new offerings, a proposed organization repositioning, communications messages, or other promotional materials
- Stimulating new ideas about offerings or communications
- Interpreting previously obtained quantitative results

Desirable Features of Focus Groups. While cost efficiencies are important reasons for using focus groups, they have other desirable features specifically attributable to the group interaction, which accounts for much of the technique's popularity among researchers. Even if focus groups were not cheaper per respondent, many researchers would still use them because of the following advantages.

- *Synergism.* Because each group member can respond to, elaborate on, criticize, modify, or otherwise react to the comments of other group members, focus groups can significantly increase the total volume of information gleaned over what would be the sum of eight to twelve individual interviews.
- *Minimal interviewer effects.* Although the moderator will act to stimulate the group at times or to move the discussion in a particular direction, participants will be responding to the remarks of others like themselves for the most part. For this reason and because focus group members are usually actively caught up in the discus-

sion, respondents are less likely to try to guess the purpose of the study or try to please or impress the moderator. The process will be less intrusive.

• *Increased spontaneity.* In an individual interview situation, the respondent has to pay attention and answer all questions. In a group situation, participants usually feel that they needn't speak if they don't want to. The lack of pressure tends to make respondents feel more spontaneous and enthusiastic in their participation.

• *Serendipity.* Because there are eight to twelve interviewees in the group, many more questions, perspectives, and comments may be introduced than the researcher and moderator would ever have thought of on their own.

• *Higher-quality interviewing.* Because several people are interviewed at once, the research organization can afford a more expensive moderator-interviewer than if hour-long interviews had to be conducted one by one. This is a very important point because the moderator's role is crucial in what is really a group depth interview. (A focus group session can sometimes appear not unlike a group psychotherapy session.)

• *Natural setting.* A one-on-one interview situation is usually highly artificial. In a focus group, one can create an atmosphere of a "bunch of people sitting around chatting" about a product, a health problem, or a set of advertisements. This will seem to the participants to be much more like the real world. The comments and reactions therefore will have much more projectability to the actual real world.

Guidelines for Focus Groups. High-quality focus group interviews are achieved by following a number of basic guidelines.

• Keep the group size from eight to twelve. Smaller groups tend not to have enough input to be valuable and run the risk of being dominated by one or two individuals. Larger groups are likely to find many members who are frustrated at not having enough time to talk or are just plain bored.

• Select participants carefully. Usually focus groups should be kept relatively homogeneous so that members share the same values, experiences, and verbal skills and so that some members do not intimidate others. Those with previous group experience should be avoided, and members should not be previously acquainted. In most major cities, there are commercial organizations that recruit focus group participants designed to meet precise specifications. One focus group I observed was composed of twelve women twenty-one to thirty-five years old who had two or more children and did not work outside the home. This group was asked to evaluate new cake mix products. A local focus group recruiter generated the group.

• Make the atmosphere for the group session as nonthreatening and natural as possible. Ideal focus group locations include a respondent's home or a hotel or motel room. Many research agencies maintain their own focus group rooms at their offices with comfortable chairs, cookies, soft drinks, coffee, and minimum distractions. Many agencies try to make the focus group interview area resemble a kitchen or living room as much as possible.

• Keep the session to two hours or less. Fatigue and repetitiveness set in quickly after two hours. The modal length of focus groups is around one and one-half hours.

• Hire the very best moderator the budget can afford. The moderator will be responsible for guiding (focusing) the discussion without seeming to and for catching hidden or subtle points and bringing them out for elaboration (for example, by saying, "I don't completely understand that point"). A good moderator also will draw out shy or inhibited participants and be able to quiet or distract those who wish to dominate the group. To establish and maintain a conflict-free, permissive environment, the effective leader will encourage participants not to criticize the thoughts of others but instead to elaborate on them or provide another perspective. Also, the moderator must stimulate participants to talk to each other (not always look to the moderator for guidance) and be able to close off the discussion at the appropriate moment. Last, a review and summary of the major findings after the session ends is the moderator's responsibility. Not just anyone can conduct a good focus group.

• Tape-record or videotape each focus group session if possible. This puts less pressure on the moderator to take notes or remember everything that goes on and allows concentration on group dynamics and the focus of the session. The existence of such a permanent archive also permits going back over tapes for additional insights or clarification of unclear points and having two or more experts review and summarize the same material. The archives can also be used for comparisons over time, for example, as the cake mix or advertising message is improved.

• Have two-way mirrors available for others to observe and hear the group without influencing the participants. This is usually possible only in specially constructed focus group rooms at research or advertising agencies. Many research clients like to observe focus groups, although one must be careful not to let an attending executive's "instant analysis" influence more carefully considered findings. Two-way mirrors also permit other focus group experts to watch the proceedings and share in the eventual interpretation. It also allows them to send in new questions that particularly interest them.

• Have clear objectives for each session, and, if possible, use a clear agenda of topic sequences. It is typical in focus groups to begin the discussion generally (such as discussing child care) and then gradually narrow the topic to the researcher's specific interest (perhaps awareness and use of specific sanitation practices). It is this aspect that led to the term *focus* group.

If the budget merits, conduct several focus group sessions. Some of the additional focus groups should replicate the original group's composition, and others should be quite different. This will allow the researcher some insight into the extent to which the original insights tend to generalize or have to be modified for specific populations.

Good focus groups are not particularly low cost, ranging from $1,000 to $3,000 each. Thus, research managers need to be frugal in their use and precise in their objectives.

Mall Intercepts

Mall intercepts are probably the second most popular technique for commercial survey research in the United States after telephone interviewing.[2] One researcher has referred to them as the modern equivalent of the old street-corner interview.[3] They are relatively inexpensive since interviewees in effect come to the interviewer rather than vice versa, significantly reducing travel costs and keeping the interviewer perpetually occupied with questioning.

Although the efficiencies are considerable, the major worry with mall intercepts is the quality of the sample. Two concerns are typically raised. First, it is suggested that those coming to a mall do not represent the population about which the study wishes to say something (such as all households in the community). It is argued that mall shoppers constitute a biased sampling frame of the universe; for example, they are more likely to have automobiles and are not bedridden. The second problem with mall interviews is that there is a danger that interviewers will choose to interview atypical people, such as those who are alone (without distracting children or friends); of the same characteristics as the interviewer in terms of age, race, sex, and social status; not in a hurry; or appearing to be the kind of person who would be unlikely to reject the interviewer's request.

Controlling for Sampling Frame Bias. Virtually all households shop in a shopping mall at least once a year and two-thirds have been there in the previous two weeks. So unless the population of interest is the very ill, the elderly, or the very poor, the mall sampling frame is in principle a reasonable one. Indeed, those who never go there may be of little interest to most marketers. The problem, then, is that if the researcher wants a projectable result, how can the fact that some people go to malls more often than others be accounted for?

In a mall study, two steps are taken to deal with this problem. First, malls in the study area can be selected on a probability basis, with their probability of selection proportional to the number of customers they serve. Second, a procedure can be developed to sample individuals on a random basis within each selected mall. (The terms *random* and *probability* sampling are used interchangeably here. In the strict sense, random sampling is a special case of probability sampling, where all member of the sampling frame have an equal probability of selection.) If done correctly, such a procedure would assume that everyone in the mall over a given time period has a nonzero chance of being in the sample. However, the more a given individual goes to shopping malls, the greater is his or her chance of selection. This possibility can be explicitly taken into consideration if, in the course of an interview, the researcher obtains an estimate of the respondent's frequency of mall shopping in a given period, say, the past year. All that is then necessary to get a projectable representative sample is to reweight the final sample proportional to the inverse of each respondent's frequency of visits. In this way, those who come rarely will receive greater weight than those who come often.

Controlling for Interviewer Selection Bias. Interviewers can sabotage a carefully designed mall sampling procedure if they tend to pick easy subjects. Basically, all that is needed to control for such potential interviewer selection bias is to develop and enforce a tightly specified procedure that allows the interviewer virtually no freedom in the choice of interviewee. People within a mall must be selected on a probability, not judgment, basis either when they arrive or while they are moving around the mall. If the latter is the approach used, several locations must be chosen to account for traffic patterns and the differential popularity of stores in the mall.

One needn't worry about how long the interviewee was in the mall if the researcher decides to sample people when they arrive. With such a procedure, it is necessary to select several entrances at random and then interview every *n*th arrival at each chosen entry. (Two persons will be needed: one to count and select arrivals and one to carry out the interviews.) This would effectively weight the entrances for the number coming through: there would be more respondents at busy entrances than at less busy ones. (If the goal were to have equal interviews per hour at an inlet, then a preliminary estimate of arrivals at each entrance would be necessary, with entrances then selected with a probability proportional to their volume and the fraction n established as inversely proportional to the entrance volume.)

Several entrances must be used because different types of customers may park at different sides of a mall (or arrive on public transportation) and because major retailers at different ends of the mall attract different clienteles. Finally, the researcher should be careful to conduct mall interviews on different days and at different times of the day. Again, it would be desirable to set the probability of selecting a day or time period proportional to the number of customers expected to be in the mall at that time. Malls that will cooperate often have already collected some of the preliminary data the researcher needs on number of customers per day and hour and perhaps even the proportion using each entrance.

If the sampling procedures outlined are followed and proper reweighting is introduced, mall surveys can often yield good population estimates plus the advantages of face-to-face interviewing at costs the low-budget researcher can afford.

Not all malls permit interviewing on their premises. Some malls restrict interviewing to commercial agencies or firms leasing a permanent interviewing site in the mall. In the latter case, it still may be economically feasible for the low-budget researcher to contract for these agencies' services.

Finally, malls have one advantage over in-home face-to-face interviews: large displays of products can be set up at mall sites, movies or television commercials run, and measurements taken with sophisticated equipment. It would be rather expensive for car manufacturers to bring two or three new test models to everyone's house to preview. But they can be brought to a central mall location (and also kept relatively well hidden from competitors, a nontrivial advantage) where interviewees can study and evaluate them.

Quota Sampling

A popular technique for keeping down field costs in commercial market research is quota sampling. Quota sampling, in fact, is frequently used in combination with convenience or mall interviewing. It is also very common in telephone studies. The approach is extremely simple, highly cost-effective, and, its advocates claim, virtually identical to results that would be obtained from a strict probability sample. However, quota sampling is *not* a probability sampling technique, and, strictly speaking, the researcher should not apply to quota studies statistical tests that require the assumption of random selection.

The procedure for developing a quota sample is to develop a profile of the population to be studied and then set quotas for interviewers so that the final sample is forced to fit the major characteristics of the population profile. For example, a researcher who wished a projectable sample of opinions of hospital senior executives in a town could use a chamber of commerce directory and note that 20 percent of local hospitals are religiously affiliated, 30 percent are for-profit, 10 percent are government, and 40 percent are nonprofit. A sample size of two hundred is set, and interviewers are sent out to interview forty managers in religious hospitals, sixty in for-profit hospitals, twenty in government facilities, and the remainder in nonprofits. The quotas may be more complex than this, however. The interviewers could be asked to meet the distribution while at the same time making sure that 30 percent of the respondents were female and 10 percent were ethnic minorities.

The advocates of quota sampling argue that if the quotas are complex enough and interviewers are directed not to interview just easy or convenient cases, the results will be as projectable as any probability sample, and the costs will be dramatically lower than probability sampling. The key to this cost saving is the fact that any forty managers from religious hospitals or any sixty female respondents will be as good as any others. Fieldworkers need not worry about sample members' refusals. They just keep trying to interview anyone who will cooperate until the various cells of the quota are filled.

There is a legitimate role for quotas in some telephone studies. Here, quotas can be used to help control for possible nonresponse biases. The initial sample may be drawn probabilistically, perhaps by random digit dialing methods. However, in some designs, to keep costs at a minimum, it will be desirable to conduct few or no callbacks. In other studies, callbacks may not be possible because of the topic under investigation, for example, instant reactions to a significant political or social event or a specific television show. In such cases, quotas are used to minimize the chances that the sample is grossly unusual.

The major risk of error in quota sampling is that the final sample members are still selected by the fieldworkers. If they are biased in their choices, the research will be biased. The answer to getting cheap but good quota research is, as usual, careful control and systemization of the process.

Convenience Sampling

Mall intercepts are efficient because they include a very high proportion of most populations of interest and because respondents come to the researcher rather than vice versa. There are a number of other situations in which the advantages of convenience may be important. Convenience samples include people in university classes, an office, or a social or religious organization or those coming daily to a clinic, the lobby of the organization's building, and so on.

Convenience samples may be useful for four kinds of occasions. First, there are a few rare occasions when the results of a convenience sample can be generalized to make some projectable statements. Second, convenience sampling can be used for some kinds of experiments where the researcher needs a reasonably representative group to assign randomly to various treatment and control conditions. Third, convenience samples can be useful when the researcher simply wants exploratory data. Finally, convenience samples may be used if the researcher wishes to conduct so-called depth interviewing.

Projectable Convenience Samples. If the researcher wishes to learn something about the convenience population itself, then there is every reason to study them. Obvious examples would be a study of those patronizing the client organization or one or more of its services, patrons at a single mall or neighborhood center, and those working in a given building or simply passing a particular location (for example, if a health program were planning to open a clinic there or to change an existing product or service mix there) or visiting a Web site.

It would be easiest to draw a projectable sample for such convenience samples with a list of possible respondents or an approximation to it. Suppose, for example, someone considering opening a health clinic or day care center in a specific office building wishes to sample the building's workers. It may be possible to obtain in advance a list of offices in a building and the number of employees in each office. Offices could then be selected with probability proportional to size, and for every nth worker on a list the office could supply then interviewed or given a questionnaire to fill out. If, in addition, the researcher wanted to study not just the workers in a building but also everyone entering it, the approach would be identical to that described for mall intercepts.

Finally, in some kinds of studies, any respondent will suffice. This would be the case in many exploratory studies where one can assume one brain processes information from the marketer in about the same way as any other brain, or where the relationships between, say, age, sex, and experience and some purchase characteristic can be assumed to be the same for the convenience sample as for any other. These arguments explain why many academic researchers are not at all apologetic about using student samples when seeking to understand the principles of basic consumer behavior.

Convenience Experimentation. Taste, feel, or sniff experiments or tests of advertisements or packages or even new-product concepts are naturals for convenience sampling if one can assume that the population conveniently nearby is not unusual in some obvious way. One simply needs to develop a procedure for randomly assigning subjects to treatments and ensuring that the presentation of stimuli is carefully controlled, that there is no cross-talk among participants during or after the study, and otherwise adhering to the tenets of quality laboratory experimental design outlined in Chapter Six.

Qualitative Research with Convenience Samples. Convenience samples are ideal for a great many qualitative research purposes. These purposes could involve developing a set of attitude or other scales or a set of questions to be included in a later questionnaire, learning what words people use to describe something, what features they evaluate, or what motives they bring to bear in a particular behavioral context.

It is also an effective method for pretesting the questionnaire for a later study or testing advertisements, brochures, or any other graphic or written materials. In this way, the researcher can determine whether there are glaring problems with the materials (for example, whether anybody notices the possible sexual connotation in a phrase or the portrayal of teenagers in an antidrug ad), whether a situation portrayed or the models used seem realistic, or whether a message seems to get across what the marketer intends it to. The convenience sample may also be used to develop hypotheses to be tested later.

In qualitative studies, it is merely necessary to use people without special traits, such as those especially knowledgeable about the subject matter.

Depth Interviewing with Convenience Samples. Many researchers advocate the use of lengthy in-depth interviews of a limited number of convenient individuals as a very valuable approach for drawing out deep-seated basic motivations, hidden meanings, or fundamental longings and fears that may be kept hidden from other researchers in group situations or inadequate responses to superficial questionnaires. In comparing these so-called depth interviews with focus groups, Sokolow suggests the following advantages:

- The respondent is not influenced by the need to conform to group norms or to avoid embarrassment for unusual thoughts or behaviors.

- The respondent is the sole focus of the interviewer's attention and therefore is more likely to open up.

- Because of the intense involvement of the interviewer, the respondent is highly focused and therefore yields richer data that are more clearly to the point of the study.

- Most interviews are brief, and the time a respondent may have to speak in a focus group is limited. In a depth interview, the respondent has ninety minutes or more to talk about the topic. This inevitably leads to richer data that are both broader and deeper than in the alternative format.

Solokow points out that depth interviewing is especially valuable for sensitive topics; for interviews with individuals, such as teenagers, who are especially likely to be influenced by group pressure; and for interviews with groups that may be especially worried about confidentiality. The last group would include staffers discussing their employers and media figures talking about those they rely on for information and leads.[4]

Judgment Sampling

Sometimes it is desirable to seek out particular informants because their answers are good predictors of what the general population would say. To develop a forecast of future general environmental trends, one might interview leaders in a particular industry or service category who are thoughtful, expert observers of the target population. Alternatively, one could simply concentrate interviews in an area of the country (or the world) that is seen as especially representative of the target market or is often a leading indicator of what will come about in future. To predict high-fashion trends, designers study

Paris, Milan, and New York. More adventurous designers study the market in Los Angeles. Political analysts look to key precincts to predict elections (quite accurately), and most marketers have their favorite test cities. In all cases, these researchers are judging that they will learn more from intensive study of a few nonrepresentative individuals than a broader, shallower study of a statistically representative group.

Another judgment sample that marketers often use is key informants. In many social and political sectors, key consultants, journal editors, staffers at think tanks, and knowledgeable academics or foundation leaders can often be the best source of trend information and descriptions of the current market environment. To tap this information, many organizations assign staffers routinely to conduct lengthy interviews with these individuals for insights about what might be happening in the next six to twelve months or longer. These interviews (often really structured conversations) can yield early warnings that the marketer can use to considerable advantage. What is critical is that they be conducted on a systematic, routine basis.

The major problems with judgment samples are two. First, there is the possibility of selection bias. Researchers may try to choose people who are easily approachable. Second, if experts are used, there is the danger that they may be too familiar with the subject to be objective about it.

Snowball and Network Sampling

Many techniques that involve probability sampling of the general population are very inefficient and costly for studying a small, very special population. For example, if one wished to study paraplegics, a high proportion of the telephone calls one would make in most markets would be wasted. Normally, one would use a procedure called *screening*: asking each randomly selected individual a set of qualifying questions that determines whether he or she falls within the population of interest (in this example, "Do you have a physical disability?"). In many studies, the researcher will reluctantly absorb high screening costs in order to get projectable results. But what if the research is about a topic such as prostheses or the use of hearing aids where screening would be prohibitively expensive because of the high proportion of ineligible respondents who would have to be contacted?

One technique to use in such cases is network sampling. The technique is based on the notion that individuals are involved in networks of other individuals who are like themselves in important ways. The researcher begins with a few respondents who possess the characteristic of interest and then asks them for the names of any others with the same characteristic within a precisely defined network (such as immediate family, uncles, aunts, grandparents, nieces, and nephews) who can be contacted later. This approach takes advantage of interpersonal networks. Not surprisingly, many people with unusual traits tend to know others with the same trait. The sampling approach is not only more efficient in finding potential sample members; it also makes it much more likely that those contacted on second or third waves will agree to cooperate since the researcher can say, "So and so suggested I contact you!" Sudman and Kalten have developed techniques whereby network sampling can yield projectable population estimates.[5]

A similar procedure can be used to obtain a sample to contrast with a convenience sample. For example, suppose a hospital does an attitude survey of its own past patients (sampled from accounting archives). But the hospital realizes that it is not studying potential new customers. To do so, it could ask its patient-respondents for the names of one or two friends who had not been patients. The advantage of this snowball approach is that the second sample will be closely matched socially and economically to the patient sample. Neither sample, of course, is projectable; the comparisons should be the key focus.

Sequential Sampling

This technique is a form of probability sampling that can yield projectable results while keeping costs low. Sequential sampling involves taking successive dips into the pool of randomly chosen respondents and checking the results after each dip. As soon as the results are acceptable in precision or some other dimension, the sampling stops. Often this occurs well below the sample size specified by conventional formulas, at significant savings in cost.

Sequential sampling is also appropriate in studies with largely qualitative objectives. If a researcher is seeking to learn about any problems with a hospital service or about the reasons people give for taking up exercise or going on a diet, sequential dips can be taken until the researcher stops getting any new insights.

Other Alternatives for Asking Questions

Mail or Internet surveys, face-to-face interviews, and telephone interviews are the major alternatives a researcher typically considers as a means of obtaining answers to questions from individuals. There are other low-cost approaches that may be valuable from time to time.

One of the most common is the so-called *self-administered questionnaire*, which is really a hybrid of a mail study and a face-to-face or telephone interview technique. The interviewer asks the respondent for cooperation personally (as in a store, office, shopping mall, or other public place) or by telephone. The questionnaire is then handed over or mailed out for prepaid return, often with a financial incentive. It is frequently used in hotels and restaurants. This hybrid technique has some obvious advantages:

- Respondents can be personally asked to cooperate.
- Any questions about the purpose of the study can be answered in advance.
- A large number of people can be contacted and recruited for relatively little cost in personnel time.
- Questionnaires (or stamps) are not wasted on those unlikely to respond.

One area in which the self-administered survey is used very effectively is in hospitals. Patients scheduled to be released are given satisfaction-complaint questionnaires by a nurse or customer relations specialist, who returns at a prearranged time to retrieve the completed instrument. Participation rates are extremely high in such studies, yielding extensive, valuable tracking data for hospital marketing managers.

Another approach to the self-administered questionnaire being used by some research organizations is the use of computer terminals. A few people are unfamiliar with computers, but where respondents will cooperate, the computer can be used to administer questionnaires to consumers in malls or offices. Laptops can be taken into the field and left for interviewees to use while the researcher sets up other interviews.

Computers also have important advantages in conducting interviews, and they are now also routinely used by telephone interviewing organizations. Perhaps the most prominent of computer-driven interviewing advantages are the following:

- Complex skip patterns can be handled without confusing respondents. One of the serious problems with self-administered and mailed questionnaires is that one can only use limited skips. Skips are necessary where respondents must be directed to different parts of the questionnaire depending on their answers to a specific question. For example, in an alcohol consumption study, the organization might wish to ask different questions of beer, wine, and scotch drinkers and those who don't drink at all. If a respondent is a wine drinker, the organization may wish to ask different questions of heavy and light consumers and different questions of those preferring foreign over domestic wines, those whose spouses or mates do or do not also drink wine, those who are recent wine converts, and those who are oenophiles. This complex set of subcategories requires a great many branching instructions—for example, "If you answered No to Question 6, go to question 23. If you answered Maybe, go to question 30. If you answered Yes and also answered Yes to question 5, go to question 15." It is difficult to get a respondent to follow all the implied arrows in such a written instrument. But with a computer, it is easy.

- The respondent does not know how long the instrument is and will not be intimidated by a long questionnaire that (because of elaborate branching) is really very short.

- Unlike traditional mail and self-administered questionnaires, respondents can't go back and correct an answer or can't skip ahead to see what is coming and anticipate it. Thus, in a computerized study, a sponsor could be revealed at the end of the instrument without worrying that this will cause bias in earlier answers.

- Inconsistent answers can be corrected on the spot. While the advantages noted also apply to telephone and personal interviews (skip patterning and disguising sponsors until later), catching inconsistencies may be very hard for interviewers to do. Furthermore, if the inconsistency is the interviewer's fault, the interviewer would not catch it. The computer would be infallible in this connection and could ask the respondent to indicate what the correct answer should be.

- The computer can instantly create the database for the analysis just as the respondent inputs the answers. This has two payoffs. First, it leaves out one or two steps in the typical research design that can cause errors. Where an interviewer transcribes the answer and someone else enters it into a computer, minor or major errors can creep in. In large studies, this will only create noise. In the small studies typical for low-budget researchers, errors made in the answers for only a few respondents may seriously distort the results.

The second advantage of creating an instant database is that management can get a daily (even hourly) summary of the results to date. This has three uses. First, analysis of early returns may suggest problems with the questionnaire. For example, if there are preset categories for, say, consumption of a product, the researcher may discover that 90 percent of the answers fall in one category. This may require changing the category boundaries for the study from that point on. The second possibility is that further questions may be suggested. For example, respondents may report large numbers of complaints about product or service features that management thought were noncontroversial. This could well prompt new questions probing the nature of the problem.

Third, the availability of daily analyses may permit the research manager to terminate the study with fewer respondents and less cost than originally planned. This is, in effect, an example of the sequential sampling method.

Computers are still only rarely used as a means of getting direct input from respondents. However, they are being used extensively to guide telephone interviewers through computer-assisted telephone interviewing (CATI) systems. The approach is increasingly being used to generate and manage questionnaire studies over the Internet. While not something a low-budget researcher could afford, computer-assisted research techniques can be a reason for choosing a specific supplier because of the complicated studies they will permit, the lower error rates, and sometimes the lower research charges.

PART THREE

Making Low-Cost Research
Good Research

9

Producing Valid Data

For any curious human being, asking questions is easy. But for professional researchers, it can be a daunting challenge fraught with innumerable chances to destroy a study's validity. The basic objective is simple: the researcher wishes to record the truth accurately. The closer the questioning process comes to this ideal, the more one is justified in claiming to have valid measurements of what one is trying to study. There are, however, a great many points where bias, major and minor, can creep into the process of transferring what is in a respondent's mind to numbers and symbols that are entered into a computer.

Consider the problems of measuring target audience preferences. Suppose a California householder has three favorite charities. She greatly prefers the American Red Cross to the American Heart Association and slightly prefers the latter to the American Cancer Society. All of the following things could go wrong in the measurement process:

- She may not reveal the truth because she doesn't understand the nature of her own preferences, wants to impress the interviewer, is trying to guess what the right answer is (that is, what the sponsor would prefer her to say), or simply misunderstands the question.

- The question used to measure the preference may be worded vaguely or not capture the true relationship of the charities.

- The interviewer may record the response incorrectly because he or she mishears the respondent, misconstrues what the respondent meant, or inadvertently records the wrong number or symbol (or someone else assigns the wrong number or code to what the interviewer wrote down).

- The data entry person may enter the wrong information into the computer.

If any or all of these events transpire (or many others pointed out below), the researcher will have a clear case of "garbage in." No amount of sophisticated statistical manipulation can wring the truth out of biased data; it is always "garbage out."

In keeping with the backward approach introduced in Chapter Four, we will first consider data entry and coding errors and then turn to the more complex problems of eliciting and recording human responses.

Nonquestion Sources of Error

Information from respondents does not always get transcribed accurately into databases that will be analyzed subsequently. There are several things that can go wrong.

Data Entry Errors

Data entry errors almost always occur in large studies. In expensive studies, entry error can be almost eliminated by verifying every entry (that is, entering it twice). This option is often not open to low-budget researchers.

Four alternative solutions exist. First, separate data entry can be eliminated by employing computers at the time of the interview, conducting surveys over the Internet, or having respondents sit at a computer terminal and record their own answers (the last two would also eliminate a lot of interviewer errors). Second, if more than one data entry person is used, a sample of the questionnaires entered by each operator can be verified to see if any one operator's work needs 100 percent verification. Third, a checking program can be written into the computer to detect entries that are above or below the valid range for a question or inconsistent with other answers (for example, the respondent who is recorded as having a certain health problem but records taking no medication). Finally, if it is assumed that the entry errors will be random, they may be accepted as simply random noise in the data.

Coding Errors

There are different kinds of values to assign to any phenomenon we can observe or ask about. They can be nonnumerical values, such as words like *positive* or symbols like plus or minus, or they can be numerical. Numerical values are the raw material for probably 99 percent of all market research analyses and all cases where statistical tests or population projections are to be made.

Assigning numbers (or words or symbols) is the act of *coding*. In a questionnaire study, coding can come about at various stages of the research process and can be carried out by different individuals. There are three major possibilities for coding. The first possibility is that precoded answers can be checked by the respondent (as in mail or Internet studies or any self-report instrument). Also, precoded answers can be checked by the interviewer (as in telephone or face-to-face interview studies). Finally, postcoded answers can have codes assigned by a third party to whatever the respondent or the interviewer wrote down.

Most researchers would, I think, prefer it if answers could be precoded and checked or circled by either the respondent or the interviewer on the spot. Precoding has several advantages, such as reducing recording errors and speed, so that a telephone interviewer, for example, can ask more questions in a given time period. Precoding makes mail or self-report questionnaires appear simpler for respondents, which increases their participation rate. Also, it permits data to be entered into the computer directly from the questionnaire (thus keeping costs down by eliminating a step in the research process).

Sometimes precoding helps clarify a question for the respondent. For example, it may indicate the degree of detail the researcher is looking for. Thus, if asked, "Where did you seek advice for that health problem?" a respondent may wonder whether the correct answer is the name of each doctor, neighbor, or coworker or just the type of source. Presenting precoded categories will help indicate exactly what is intended. It may also encourage someone to answer a question that he or she otherwise might not. Many respondents will refuse to answer the following question, "What was your total household income last calendar year?" But if they are asked, "Which of the following categories includes your total household income last year?" many more (but still not all) will reply. In addition, precoding ensures that all respondents answer the same question. Suppose respondents are asked how convenient several health clinics are for them. As suggested in the previous chapter, some respondents may think of convenience in terms of ease of parking or number of entrances. Others may think of it in terms of travel time from home. If you ask respondents to check whether the clinics are "10 minutes or less away," "11 to 20 minutes away," and so on, this will ensure that every respondent will be using the same connotation for the term *convenience*.

Suppose respondents are asked, "Where have you seen an advertisement for a cancer treatment program in the past three months, if anywhere?" Unaided by precoding, respondents will offer fewer answers than if offered a checklist. For example, the question can ask, "Have you seen an advertisement for a cancer treatment program in any of the following places: newspapers, magazines, billboards, or in the mail?"

There are two main drawbacks in using precoded questions. First, precoding assumes the researcher already knows all the possible answers or at least the major ones. While research can always leave space for an "other" category on a mail or Internet questionnaire, most respondents will ignore anything that is not listed.

Another drawback to precoding is that it may frustrate a respondent who does not quite agree with the categories or feels unduly restricted. For example, if someone is asked, "Do you think the President of the United States is doing a good job: Yes or no?" many respondents would like to answer "Yes, but . . ." or "No, but . . ." If they experience such frustration, many respondents will terminate an interview or not reply to a mail or Internet questionnaire.

Postcoding involves coding a set of answers after a questionnaire is filled in. It is typically necessary in one of the three major circumstances:

- The researcher does not know in advance what categories to use. For example, if the researcher is rushed or has a very limited budget, it may not be possible to conduct any preliminary focus groups or pretests to develop the appropriate precodes.
- The researcher is afraid that presenting precoded alternatives will bias the answers.
- The researcher wishes to accumulate verbatim answers that can be used to give depth and interest to a final report.

If a third party is brought in to do the postcoding, there is always the possibility that the wrong code will be assigned to a particular written answer (of course, the interviewer could make this mistake also). The main difficulties will crop up when the answers are ambiguous. Suppose a coder is asked to assign a "liking" rating for a series of physician descriptions. The coder has three categories: (1) likes a great deal, (2) likes somewhat, or (3) doesn't like. The description from the respondent is, "Doctor Arneson is very authoritative. He always has a solution and insists you follow it without a lot of backtalk." A coder would like to have the respondent nearby to ask a number of clarifying questions: "Do you prefer doctors who are authoritative? Is it important to you that the doctor have all the answers, or would you like to express your opinions? Are you frustrated by not being able to challenge a diagnosis?" Interviewers who do the coding on the spot can interrogate the respondent. Third-party postcoders may have to make intelligent guesses that can introduce bias into the study.

The example is truly ambiguous about whether the respondent likes the doctor and probably should be coded as a fourth category: "Not clear." In most studies, coding problems can be minimized by following some well-accepted procedures.

After a set of questionnaires is completed, it is helpful to review a sample of verbatim answers and, along with some or all of the prospective coders, develop a clear, exhaustive set of coding categories. If necessary, write these down in a codebook, with a number of examples for each category. It is important to make sure coders understand the categories and how to use the codebook.

Coders should practice on sample questionnaires to ensure they assign the correct codes. And if possible, use multiple coders and have them code a sample of each other's work to detect inconsistencies among coders or to discover questions where the coding scheme is producing a great deal of inconsistency among coders.

Asking Questions

Most of the threats to measurement validity discussed to this point are partially or wholly controllable. But even where control is minimal, their potential for bias pales in significance compared to the problems in eliciting the truth from respondents. Problems can arise from three sources: the interviewer, the respondent, and the instrument.

Interviewer-Induced Error

Respondents may report something other than the truth because they respond to the way the interviewer looks and how he or she asks the questions. Interviewers can induce respondents to exaggerate, hide, try to impress, or be distracted. As a general rule, one would like interviewers to be as unobtrusive as possible. This means that in face-to-face interviews, interviewers should possess socio-economic characteristics as much like those of their respondents as possible. A neat and unobtrusive appearance (while still being enthusiastic and motivating in behavior) is important. Personal interviewers with distracting characteristics (or unusual clothing or makeup) may be effective over the telephone but not in the field.

The interviewer should be physically and emotionally non-threatening to respondents and avoid body or vocal cues that may give away or distort answers. The more the interviewing involves difficult questions and interaction with the respondent over the course of the interview, the more the interviewer's characteristics, style, and specific actions can influence the results. If the interviewer must explain questions, probe for details, or encourage fuller responses, his or her manner of doing so can have profound consequences for both the quantity and quality of data elicited. For these reasons, the researcher should be very careful in selecting and training both telephone and personal interviewers. Someone with a limited budget may be tempted to hire low-cost (or free) amateurs such as their employees and think that minimizing training sessions is a good way to cut costs. This is usually *very* short-sighted behavior.

If the researcher is forced to use amateurs, then careful training, extensive use of precoded questions, and a detailed set of interviewer instructions ought to be built into the study design. Even then, the dangers of interviewer-induced error are great. In a classic study, Guest had fifteen college-educated interviewers apply the same instrument to the same respondent, who was instructed to give the same responses to all. The number of errors was astonishing. No questionnaire was without error, and the number of errors ranged from twelve to thirty-six. Failure to follow up questions for supplementary answers occurred sixty-six times.[1]

Another problem with amateurs is that there is always the small possibility that they will fabricate total interviews or responses to particular questions (for example, those they are fearful of asking, such as income, drinking, and sex habits). Fortunately, it is almost certain that such amateurs will not know how the results to particular questions should be distributed. Consequently, their answers will look markedly different from the rest of the study and can be detected in computer checks.

In a study I conducted many years ago on radio station preferences using student interviewers, one interviewer apparently chose to do his fieldwork in his dorm room. And, of course, when it came time to record station preferences, he used his own preferences, which, not surprisingly, were not at all like the general population in the area studied. Such cheating can also be controlled by recontacting respondents in a small percentage of each interviewer's work to verify that they were contacted. Postcards or brief telephone calls can serve this purpose. Such validation is routine in most commercial research organizations.

Respondent-Induced Bias

There are four major sources of respondent bias: forgetting, deliberately withholding information, simple mistakes or unintentional distortion of information, and deliberate distortion of information.

The largest source of respondent bias in surveys is forgetting. With time, subtle details of purchases can be lost, and even major facts, such as brand names or prices, disappear. Aided recall can help reduce this problem (although potentially introducing its own biases), as can carefully limiting the time period for recall to that for which the respondent's memory should be reasonably accurate. The low-budget researcher should guard against the tendency to be greedy for information, asking for recall of data further and further back in time where such recall may be highly suspect.

Mistakes or neglect of information can be minimized by proper questioning. First, one must make sure that definitions of each desired bit of information are very clear, possibly with the use of precoded answers. A frequent problem is household income. Respondents may not know what to include as household income or may forget critical components. Worse still, different respondents may have different definitions that could make them appear different when they are not. For example, there is the problem of whose income to include: spouses, teenage children, live-in parents? What if a household has a boarder? Is this person included? What about spending money earned by a child away at college? Are dividends included? What about the $1,000 lottery winning? Is social security included if one is over sixty-five or dividends from a retirement account? Although not all contingencies can be handled in a simple questionnaire format, questions can be worded so as to specify most of the information desired. In face-to-face or telephone studies, interviewers can be instructed about the real intent of the question and armed with prompts to make sure that respondents do not inadvertently give biased or incomplete information.

Another broad class of unintentional respondent problems is time distortion. Often a study will ask for a summary of past experiences. That is, a researcher may wish to know how many head colds respondents have had, or vacations they have taken, or doctors they have seen within some specified period. The typical problem is that people will telescope experiences beyond the specified time frame into the period in question. A questionnaire may ask about six months' worth of head colds and really get eight months' worth. If everyone used the same amount of telescoping (eight months into six), this would not be a problem. But if they differed, this will produce artificial differences across respondents.

The solution is again a matter of design. First, the study should have as few of these kinds of questions as possible. Second, questions requiring memory should ask only about relatively prominent events (for instance, do not bother asking how many cans or bottles of beer a respondent has consumed over the past six months). And third, whenever possible, each question should clearly bound the starting point of the period. This boundary would depend on the subject, the respondent, or the date of the study. For example, one could anchor the period to the start of the year, Thanksgiving, the beginning of the school year, or the respondent's previous birthday.

Telescoping is an unconscious distortion on the part of the respondent. Respondents can distort results in other ways. If given a scale of answers, some respondents will use the full range of the scale, and others may use only a small part in the middle. *Naysayers*, as they are called, will tend to use the negative end of the scale and *yeasayers* the positive end. These systematic biases can often be controlled by having the computer normalize an individual's responses after the data are collected, in effect rescoring each answer in terms of the respondent's answer tendencies (see Chapter Ten).

Harder to detect and control are deliberate efforts by respondents to portray themselves as they are not or to answer as they think the researcher would like them to answer. Deliberate response bias in general is much harder to analyze and adjust for because the researcher doesn't know what the truth would have been. About all that can be done is to make the stimulus (the question and the interviewer) as unlikely as possible to encourage such distortion and to stress to the respondent the importance to the study that they be as candid and objective as possible. Repeating the researcher's initial guarantee of anonymity when introducing particularly worrisome questions can sometimes help.

Questionnaire Design

This book is not intended to make an expert question writer out of its readers. To some extent, writing questions that both motivate and get at the truth is a skill acquired only by considerable practice. It is not something any intelligent person can automatically do. One way the low-budget researcher can appropriate experience quickly is to borrow questions from others, preferably questions used by several other researchers. Using questions from secondary sources not only ensures that the questions have been pretested; it also guarantees that a database will exist elsewhere to which the researcher can compare the present results.

The U.S. Census is a good source of such questions, in part because its categories (for example, for income or occupations) are the ones used by most researchers and in part because the Census Bureau provides vast quantities of data against which to validate the researcher's own work.

Once the borrowing possibilities have been exhausted, the neophyte researcher should seek the help of an expert question writer if the cost is affordable. Alternatively, once a questionnaire is prepared, the draft instrument should be reviewed by as many colleagues as possible, especially those who will be critical. Finally, the researcher should test the instrument with potential respondents even if it is only the office staff and in-laws.

I have never yet written a questionnaire that did not have major flaws, ambiguities, and even missing categories despite the fact I was sure that each time I had finally done it right. It takes a thorough pretest to bring these problems out. My own preference is to continue pretesting each redraft until I am confident the instrument is right. I keep reminding myself that if I do not measure whatever I am studying validly at the start, all the subsequent analysis and report writing I might do will be wasted.

Following are possible questionnaire biases that could crop up in research instruments.

Question Order Bias

Sometimes questions early in a questionnaire can influence later ones. For example, asking someone to rank a set of criteria for choosing among alternative service outlets makes it very likely that a later request for a ranking of these same outlets will be influenced by the very criteria already listed. Without the prior list, the respondent may have performed the evaluation using fewer or even different criteria. The solution here is to try different orderings during a pretest and see whether the order makes any difference. If it does, then the researcher should either place the more important question first or change the order in every other questionnaire (called *rotating* the questions) to balance the effects overall.

A more obvious questionnaire order effect is what might be called *giving away the show*. This problem seldom survives an outside review of the instrument or a pretest. However, I have seen first drafts of a questionnaire where, for example, wording that mimicked an advertising campaign was used as one of the dimensions for evaluating a political candidate. Later, a question asking for recall of advertising themes got a surprisingly high unaided recall of that particular theme.

A third kind of questionnaire order effect involves threatening questions that if asked early can cause a respondent to clam up or terminate the interview altogether. If a researcher must ask questions about sex, drugs, diseases, or income, it is better to leave these as late as possible in the instrument.

A final order effect applies to lengthy questionnaires. As respondents tire, they give shorter and less carefully thought out answers. Here again, put the more important questions early or rotate the questions among questionnaires.

Answer Order Bias

There is one major problem when respondents are given a choice of precoded categories to answer to a question: a tendency for respondents, other things equal, to give higher ratings to alternatives higher on a list than those lower on a list. In such instances, pretesting and (usually) rotation of answers are recommended. Practically, rotation is achieved during face-to-face or telephone interviews by having the supervisor highlight different precoded answer categories where the interviewer is to begin reading alternatives. (A CATI computer or Internet survey can do this automatically.) On mail questionnaires, the researcher must have the word processor reorder the alternatives and print out several versions of the questionnaire to be mailed out randomly.

Scaling Bias

Wording and formatting of individual questions that attempt to scale attitudes, preferences, and the like can be an important source of bias. If the researcher must construct his or her own scales, the best approach is to use one of a number of pretested general techniques that can be customized for a specific study.

Thurstone Scales. In this approach, a large number of statements about an object of interest (such as a company, a charity, or a brand) are sorted by expert judges into nine or eleven groups separated along some prespecified dimension such as favorableness. The groups or positions are judged by the experts to be equally far from each other. The researcher then selects one or two statements from each group to represent each scale position. The final questionnaire presents respondents with all statements and asks them to pick the *one* that best portrays their feelings about each object. Their choices are assigned the rating given by the judges to that statement. The ratings are assumed to be interval scaled (discussed in Chapter Ten).

Likert Scales. A problem with Thurstone scales is that they do not indicate how intensely a respondent holds a position. Likert scaling gives respondents a set of statements and asks them how much they agree with each statement, usually on a five-point continuum: (1) strongly agree, (2) somewhat agree, (3) neither agree nor disagree, (4) somewhat disagree, or (5) strongly disagree. Responses to a selected series of such statements are then analyzed individually or summed to yield a total score. Likert scales are very popular, in part because they are easy to explain and to lay out on a questionnaire. They are also very easy to administer in telephone interviews.

One problem with the technique is that the midpoint of a Likert scale is ambiguous. It can be chosen by those who truly don't know and by those who are indifferent. For this reason, some researchers allow respondents a sixth option, "don't know," so that the midpoint will really represent indifference.

Semantic Differential. Respondents are asked to evaluate an object such as a company, nonprofit organization, or brand on a number of dimensions divided into segments numbered from 1 to 9 or 1 to 11. In contrast to Likert scales, positions are not labeled. Rather, the scales are anchored on each end with opposing (semantically different) adjectives or phrases—for example:

Strong	1	2	3	4	5	6	7	8	9	Weak

Friendly										Unfriendly
Staff	1	2	3	4	5	6	7	8	9	Staff

Respondents indicate where on each scale they perceive the object in question to be. Two problems are common with semantic differentials. First, there is again the confusion of whether the midpoint of the scale represents indifference or ignorance. Second, there is the problem that the anchors may not be true opposites; for example, is the opposite of healthy "unhealthy" or "sick"?

Stapel Scale. Some dimensions on which the researcher may wish to rate something may not have obvious opposites, for example, "fiery," "cozy," or "classic." Stapel scales were designed for this contingency. The interviewer asks the respondents to indicate the degree to which a particular adjective applies to an object in question. Usually Stapel scales are easier to explain over the telephone than semantic differentials and require little pretesting.

Graphic Scales. If the respondent can be shown a scale graphically, for example, in a mail, Internet, self-report, or face-to-face interview study, then a scale where the positions look equal can be used. Researchers sometimes use a ladder to represent social class dimensions along which respondents are asked to place themselves. The ladder can also be used on the telephone, as can the image of a thermometer to give people unfamiliar with scales an idea of what they look like. Graphic scales are particularly useful for respondents with low literacy levels.

Threatening Questions

Studies may touch on issues that are threatening to some or all respondents, for example, topics like sex, alcohol consumption, mental illness, or family planning practices, all of which may be of interest to a marketer. These are touchy issues and hard to phrase in questions. Respondents usually do not wish to reveal to others something private or that they feel may be unusual. Some seemingly innocuous questions may be threatening to some respondents. For example, a man may not wish to reveal that the reason he gives blood regularly is that a nurse at the blood donation center is attractive. Or a housewife may not be anxious to admit she likes to visit the city art gallery so she can get a shopping bag in the gift shop to impress her middle-class neighbors.

There are several approaches to reducing threat levels. One is to assure respondents at the start of the study that they can be as candid and objective as possible since the answers will be held in complete confidence. This point can then be repeated in the introduction to a specific threatening question.

A second approach that tends to ease individuals' fears of being unusual is to preface the question with a reassuring phrase indicating that unique answers are not unusual for a specific question. Thus, one might begin a question about alcohol consumption as follows: "Now we would like to ask you questions about your alcohol consumption in the past week. Many have reported consuming alcohol at parties and at meals. Others have told us about unusual occasions on which they take a drink of whiskey, wine, or beer, like right after they get out of bed in the morning or just before an important meeting with a coworker they don't like. Could you tell us about each of the occasions on which you had an alcoholic beverage in the past week, that is, since last [day of the week]?"

Another approach is to use an indirect technique. Respondents may often reveal the truth about themselves when they are caught off-guard, for example, if they think they are not talking about themselves. A questionnaire may ask respondents to talk about "a good friend" or "people in general." In this case, the assumption is that in the absence of direct information about the behavior or attitudes of others, respondents will bring to bear their own perceptions and experiences.

Finally, the researcher could use so-called in-depth interviewing techniques (mentioned in Chapter Eight). Here, the interviewer tries not to ask intrusive questions. Rather the topic (perhaps alcohol consumption) is introduced, and the respondent is kept talking by such interjections as, "That's interesting" or "Tell me more." In the hands of a skilled, supportive interviewer, respondents should eventually dig deeply into their psyches and reveal truths that might be missed or hidden. However, such approaches are very time-consuming, can be used only with small (and probably unrepresentative) samples, and require expertise that is often unaffordable for low-budget researchers.

Constricting Questions

Respondents may withhold information or not yield enough detail if the questions do not permit it. They may also terminate out of frustration. The questionnaire should almost always include an "other" option, where there is the real possibility that all the possibilities have not been precoded. Multiple choices should be allowed where they are relevant, and people should be able to report that some combination of answers is truly the situation.

Generalization Biases

Bias can often creep into answers by respondents who are asked to generalize about something, particularly their own behavior. For example, neophyte questionnaire writers often ask respondents to indicate their favorite radio station, the weekly newsmagazine they read most often, or how often they exercise each month. The problem is that these questions require the respondents to summarize and make judgments about their own behavior, yet how they make these generalizations will be unknown to the researcher. For example, when asked for a favorite radio station, one person may report a station she listens to while in the car, another may report a favorite station at home, and a third may report one that pleases him most often rather than the one he listens to most frequently.

When asking questions about behavior, it is almost always better to ask about specific past behaviors than have a respondent generalize. Rather than asking about a favorite radio station, a respondent can be asked, "Think back to the last time you had the radio on at home, work, or in the car. What station were you listening to?" In this case, the respondent perceives the task as reporting a fact rather than coming up with a generalization. In such cases, the interviewer is likely to get much more objective, error-free reporting than if consumers are asked to generalize.

10

All the Statistics You Need to Know (Initially)

As we noted in Chapter Two, management's needs are for three types of information: descriptive, explanatory, and predictive. Management will want to know what something is, what caused it, or what it will be in future. Answering these kinds of questions correctly is a two-part process. First, managers must have the right raw material, that is, valid measurements. Second, the right meaning must be extracted from those measurements, so managers need valid descriptive summaries, valid measures of association and causation, and valid predictions. We considered some of the problems of developing valid measures in Chapter Nine. Now, we will explore the major analysis techniques, both simple techniques and a few of the more complex multivariate techniques for those who wish to extract even more from a given data set.

Fear of Statistics

Most people are frightened of statistics. They seem to think that statistical analysis is some kind of mystical rite not to be comprehended or used by ordinary people. They avoid statistics like the plague and take a curious pride in doing so. The view seems to be that those who avoid statistics are somehow more plain speaking and down-to-earth, while those who use statistics are either trying to make something simple appear unnecessarily complex and sophisticated or trying to hide something from others. One often hears, "Don't confuse me with all your statistics." In my view, this fear of statistics is irrational but understandable. Unfortunately, sometimes simple truths have been obscured by statistics and statisticians. But statistics can be very valuable tools for the budget-minded researcher. They make it significantly more likely that management will make decisions based on a valid interpretation of the information at hand.

Statistics, as we use the term here, can serve researchers and managers in two critical roles. First, there are *descriptive statistics:* simple frequency counts, measures of central tendency like the mean, median, and mode, and measures of variability like the range. These statistics do not frighten most people. However, some fancier descriptive measures, like *standard deviation* and *standard error,* do. Descriptive statistics perform a crucial function for harried managers: they provide ways of reducing large amounts of data to more concise, comprehensive values. A fundraising manager would rather not be faced with a report of funds raised for every volunteer in every city in every state through every medium (telephone, personal visit, and so on). Descriptive statistics such as means, modes, and ranges are much more manageable and therefore much more useful. By comparing these summary numbers, insights that would be lost in the mass of original data may become clear and courses of remedial or reinforcing action suggested.

The second, and more fearsome, connotation of statistics is more properly called *statistical testing.* Statistical tests are a bit intimidating if the researcher focuses on the method of applying the tests: the calculations, the theory, and the assumptions. We will try to avoid this as much as possible and instead will concentrate on the uses of statistical tests. These uses can be boiled down to one expression: statistical tests are designed to keep management honest. Statistical tests make sure that if management thinks that fundraising proceeds are up in Atlanta, or that Sally is really outperforming Irving, or that only middle-size cities respond positively to the new direct mail campaign, these conclusions are truly there and not artifacts of management's imagination. There is a great temptation to all of us to want to find something in a set of data, particularly if that something supports a prior assumption or will lend strong support to a course of action that management was planning to take anyway. But if that something has an unacceptably high probability of being a chance aberration, a manager would be ill advised to commit the organization to actions based on it. Statistical tests can keep management from unknowingly taking such chances: they keep one honest.

Managers should not fear statistics. Rather, they should be thankful they are there.

This chapter introduces the most important statistical tools likely to be used in an introductory program of low-cost research. I assume that research analysts will make extensive use of a computer to generate the statistics and conduct the statistical tests by using one of the myriad statistical packages currently available (such as SPSS, SAS, Minitab, or the statistical capabilities of spreadsheet software). All are available in versions for personal computers. The use of computers has two implications. First, it means that no researcher will actually have to calculate any of the statistics discussed here. Thus, we can focus on making sure you understand what the computer will produce.

The easy access of computers has a second implication, and one that presents a very serious danger for the naive researcher. Computers are dumb processors. They will take any set of values and crank out any statistics requested. Thus, if males are precoded as 1 in a study and females as 2, the computer can certainly tell you that the average sex of your respondents is 1.6239 with a standard deviation (presumably in sex-ness) of .087962. This, of course, is patently ridiculous. But there are many occasions on which a similar but not-so-obvious error can easily occur if the researcher asks for statistics that are inappropriate. It is the old problem of garbage in, garbage out. If statistics are to keep a researcher honest, the researcher must know when and where to use them legitimately. Thus, the goal of this chapter is to describe the use of different kinds of statistics so that they can be requested appropriately.

I purposely simplify many of the treatments in order to provide readers with a layperson's understanding that is not intimidating. I do not discuss any assumptions and variations in calculation methods and suggest that before using the statistics described here, the researcher either seek advice from a more experienced user or consult the Recommended Readings for this chapter found at the back of the book.

Input Data

If a researcher is going to use statistics properly, it is essential to consider the kind of data about which descriptive statistics are to be calculated or to which will be applied some kind of statistical test. Statistical analysis, even such simple analysis as counting, requires that each characteristic to be studied be assigned a unique value. Sometimes, especially in qualitative research with small samples, this value can be a word or a symbol. For example, the interviewer could assign the word *yes* or *positive* or the symbol + to indicate that a respondent liked a product, or a flavor, or a company. Analysis could then produce a statistic called a *frequency count* of these words or symbols to reveal overall perceptions of various stimuli or various groups of respondents. However, even in these cases, when the sample is large and we wish to do a lot of cross-tabulations or plan to use a computer, we will want to assign each measurement a number.

For the computer to prepare summary statistics or conduct a statistical analysis, each measurement of the sample population must be assigned a number. These numbers can differ significantly in their level of sophistication, and it is this level of sophistication that determines what should and should not be done to them. There are four categories in which numbers are generally grouped. In increasing order of sophistication, they are (1) nominal numbers, (2) ordinal numbers, (3) intervally scaled numbers, and (4) ratio-scaled numbers. We will examine each briefly, noting that numbers of a particular higher-order status can always be treated as if they had a lower-order status. For example, ordinal data can always be treated as if they were merely nominal.

Nominal Data

In a surprisingly large number of cases, the number we assign to some object, idea, or behavior is entirely arbitrary, although in some cases a tradition may establish the rules of assignment. If measurements are assigned arbitrary numbers, they are called *nominal* numbers, and their sole purpose in the analysis is to differentiate an item possessing one characteristic from an item possessing a different characteristic.

Consider, for example, the assignment of numbers to football players. Each player has a number that distinguishes one player from another. The numbers allow coaches and fans to tell them apart and allow referees to assign penalties to the correct person. The numbers here have no meaning other than differentiation. Despite what a boastful wide receiver may tell the press, players with numbers in the 80s are not necessarily smarter than those with numbers in the 70s, nor do they deserve bigger salaries. They are probably faster than those with numbers in the 70s, but not necessarily faster than those with numbers 16 to 20 or 30 to 50. The fact that someone has a higher number than someone else does not mean that he is more or less of anything.

Ordinal Data

Ordinal numbers are assigned to give order to measurements. In a questionnaire, we may ask two respondents to rank charities A, B, and C. Typically, we would assign a 1 to their most preferred charity, 2 to their second most preferred, and 3 to their third favorite. Note that if someone prefers A over B over C, we do not know how much A is preferred to B or how much B is preferred to C. For example, Gordon may prefer A a great deal over B, but Gary may be almost indifferent between the two, though giving a slight edge to A. Both would have the same rankings. It is perfectly permissible to assign any numbers to the respondents' first, second, and third choices as long as we retain the same ordering distinction.

Interval and Ratio Data

The next two classes of data represent a substantial jump in sophistication from the first two classes. Nominal and ordinal measurements are frequently described by researchers and statisticians as *nonmetric* numbers. Interval and ratio measurements are called *metric* (or parametric) numbers. Most of the sophisticated summary statistics and statistical tests strictly require metric measurements. For this reason, it is desirable, but not essential, for researchers to seek to develop interval or ratio data whenever possible. Experience has shown that assuming data are metric when they might be ranked only does not usually produce serious distortions in results. For example, if a magazine reader rates *Time* as 5 on an "informative" scale and *Newsweek* as 4, it may seem safer (more conservative) to interpret these results as saying only that the reader rated *Time* higher than *Newsweek* (that the data are really ordinal). However, making the stronger assumption that one has produced an interval scale will typically not materially affect any conclusions.

Interval data are similar to ordinal data in that the assigned numbers order the results. In this case, however, the differences between numbers have an additional meaning. In an interval scale, we assume that the distance or interval between the numbers has a meaning. The difference between interval data and ratio-scaled data is that the latter have a known zero point and the former do not. Thus, we may be able to say that on an "honesty" scale, charity A is as far from charity B as charity C is from charity D (the interval assumption). We cannot say that charity A seems to be four times as honest as charity D. The distinction may be made clear by using two common examples.

A Fahrenheit temperature scale is an example of an interval scale. Any four-degree difference in temperature is like any other four-degree difference. But since the zero point on a Fahrenheit scale is arbitrary, we can say that if the temperature rose from 76 degrees to 80 degrees in the morning and later dropped from 44 degrees to 40 degrees just after midnight, the changes were equal. However, we would be foolish to say that the morning was twice as warm as the night. Is 80 degrees twice as warm as 40 degrees? Is 10 degrees five times as warm as 2 degrees? We can speak confidently about temperature intervals and not temperature ratios.

In contrast, age is an example of a scale with a real, known zero. In this case, we can say that someone who is forty is twice as old as someone who is twenty. In many analyses in marketing, the distinction between interval and ratio-scaled data is not very important managerially.

Some examples of marketing measurements that fall under each of the four levels of numerical sophistication are given in Table 10.1.

Descriptive Statistics

The problem with much research is that it produces too many pieces of data. Some of the information we will wish to simply report just as it comes, and some of it we will wish to relate to other data to show differences, relationships, and so on.

For a great many decision problems, we may be satisfied with a description of the population under study. At the very least, merely

TABLE 10.1 Numerical Qualities of Some Typical Marketing Measurements.

Nonmetric	Metric
Nominal	Interval
Sex	Some rating scales (for example,
Marital status	semantic differentials, Likert
Store or brand last patronized	scales)
Ownership of various items	Knowledge and awareness levels
Employment status	Ratio
Ordinal	Age
Occupational status	Education
Service outlet preferences	Sales
Some rating scales	Time elapsed
Social classes	Income

looking over the data is a good starting point for more sophisticated analyses.

Descriptions of data can take many forms. Take the simple case of evaluations of a new home exercise video. We can report the scores that respondents give to the video as frequency distributions, or we can portray their scores graphically in a bar chart or histogram, as in Figure 10.1. The next step will be to summarize these data in more concise form.

This will be particularly desirable if we wish to compare a large number of different distributions, say, respondents' ratings of three alternative exercise videos on ten different dimensions each. In summaries, we are usually interested in three features: (1) the frequency counts of various measurements (how many people assigned a "3" on a value-to-cost ratio to video A), (2) some measure of central tendency (what the mean level was of the value-to-cost ratio assigned to video A), or (3) some measure of the spread of the measurements (whether the value-to-cost ratings of video A were more dispersed than the ratings of video B).

Central Tendency

The term *average* is loosely used by the general population to connote any one of the following:

- The modal value: the value most frequently reported

FIGURE 10.1 Ratings of an Exercise Video.

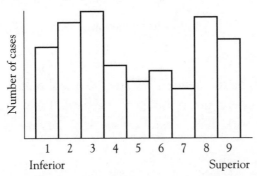

- The median: the value at the midpoint of a distribution of cases when they are ordered by their values
- The arithmetic mean: the result of weighting (multiplying) each value by the number of the cases reporting it and then dividing by the number of cases

Applying a measure of central tendency is not always straightforward. Suppose fifteen respondents rated the value-to-cost ratio of video A on a seven-point scale as follows (their ratings have been reordered for convenience):

1 2 3 3 3 3 4 4 5 5 6 6 7 7 7

Here, we can see that the mode is 3, the median is 4, and the mean is 4.4—all different. Which is the best measure of central tendency? To some extent, it depends on management's interests. If they want to know what was the most frequent rating of the video, they would use the mode. If they want to know at which point the sample was divided in half with respect to this measure, they would use the median. If they wanted to weight respondents by the scores they assigned, then they should use the mean.

Not all measures of central tendency can be applied to all kinds of data. The kinds you can use vary depending on the type of data you have, as follows:

Numbers	Permissible Measures
Nominal	Mode
Ordinal	Mode, median
Interval	Mode, median, mean
Ratio	Mode, median, mean

Although it is all too frequently done, no one should attempt to compute an arithmetic mean using ordinal data. It is not at all uncommon to hear untrained researchers speak of the *average* ranking of something. This is correct terminology only if the researcher is referring to the median or modal ranking.

Here are a few more important suggestions about measures of central tendency:

- Always compute and look at all the measures of central tendency you can. A median or mode may tell you something the mean does not.
- In computing a mode, do not neglect the possibility that a distribution is bimodal. The computer will typically report only one mode, but you should scan the frequency counts of all responses or have the computer produce a bar chart (histogram) in order to detect multiple modes where they exist. For example, it would be important to know whether scores of "liking" for your own nonprofit organization or for a major competitor were unimodal (one high point) or bimodal (two high points). If it were bimodal (see, for example, Figure 10.1), this would suggest that the nonprofit tends to polarize people into a group of likers and a group of dislikers (or "less likers"). This could suggest a possible vulnerability for the nonprofit and the need for a campaign to convert those who like it less.
- Do not be afraid to compute a median even where the data are grouped (for example, ages under ten, ten to nineteen, and so on). The computer will automatically do this.
- Be sure to compare the median to the mean when you have metric data. Since they are identical in a normal distribution, a comparison will tell you whether your distribution is skewed in any way. Some statistical tests have as an assumption that the underlying data approximate the well-known normal curve. The more the mean and median differ, the more the distribution leans one way or the other.

As shown in Figure 10.2, distributions can be skewed positively (curve A) or negatively (curve B). Several characteristics of interest to marketers, such as the quantity of a product bought per week or the size of a household's income, will be positively skewed.

FIGURE 10.2 Normal and Skewed Distribution.

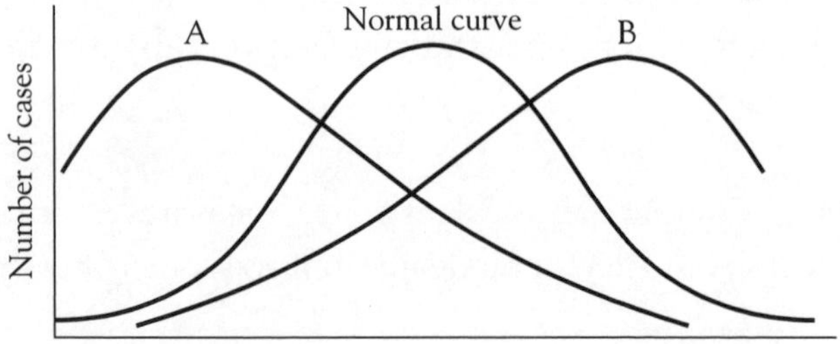

Measures of Dispersion

Measures of dispersion indicate the relative spread of the data we are studying. Heights of a line of chorus girls will be much less diverse (spread) than heights of children in a primary school. Measures of dispersion are relatively underused by neophyte marketing researchers. They form an important part of many statistical analysis procedures (such as testing whether an experiment's results were due to chance), and they can be useful in their own right.

There is, of course, no such thing as a measure of dispersion for nominal data. It makes no sense to talk about the spread of marital status data. Dispersion, however, can be computed for ordinal data. The most common dispersion measures here are the range from maximum to minimum, and the *interquartile range*, that is, the difference between the seventy-fifth and twenty-fifth cases. The interquartile range is often used because it produces a measure that eliminates the effects of extreme values at either end of the rankings, which would exaggerate the full range.

For metric data (interval or ratio scaled), the most common measure of dispersion is the *variance* or its square root, the *standard deviation*. Variance is computed by subtracting each value from the mean of all of the values, squaring the results, and then averaging these squared values (actually, dividing by one less than the number of cases). The variance has two virtues. First, it tends to weight values far from the mean more than those near the mean. This makes it a relatively stringent measure when incorporated in statistical tests of relationships or differences. The second virtue is that (assuming we have a normal distribution) it allows us to say something rather precisely about how many cases will fall within a certain distance from the mean (in standard deviation units).

The standard deviation or the variance can also be used to compare two distributions expressed in the same units. For example, we can compare perceptions of a Boys & Girls Club in one city with those of a Boys & Girls Club in another city on both mean and variance. It may be possible that the means are the same in the two cities but the variance is much higher in one than the other. This would suggest that the club's image is relatively clear in one city and pretty fuzzy in the other. (See Figure 10.3.) In the same way, we might compare variances within a city to see whether the club's image is fuzzier for some market segments than for others.

Another role for the standard deviation is to tell something about the typicality of a given case. Calculating how many standard deviations a case is from the mean will yield a quantitative measure of how typical or atypical it is. We could say, for example, that per capita tuxedo sales in Reno are a lot different from the average for the United States: only 2 percent of reporting cities have greater tuxedo sales. (Indeed, since the Greek symbol for the standard deviation is the letter *sigma*, it is not unusual to hear a member of the research community describe an offbeat colleague as being "at least five sigmas off center.")

A final role of the standard deviation for experienced researchers is in normalizing data. This process is described in Exhibit 10.1.

A final measure of dispersion that is of great interest to statisticians is the *standard error*. This measure has much the same meaning and use as the standard deviation, but it describes the spread of some summary measure like a mean or a proportion. Because we know the percentage of cases that fall within specific distances from the midpoint of a normal curve as expressed in standard errors, we can say something about the likelihood that the true mean we are

FIGURE 10.3 Ratings of Program Quality of Boys & Girls Clubs in Two Cities.

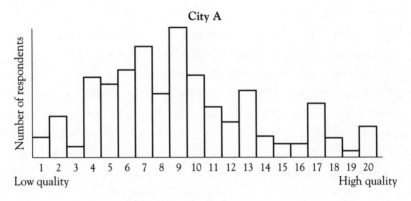

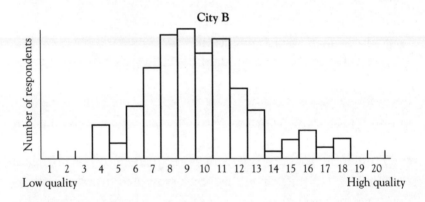

trying to estimate in a specific study is within a certain distance (in standard error units) from the mean we actually did find.

Assume that we studied a sample of heads of household in a community and found that the mean contribution to charity was $1,000 per year and the standard error was $10. We can say that we are 95 percent sure that the true annual household donation in this community is between approximately $1,019.60 and $980.40—the sample mean plus or minus 1.96 standard errors (the confidence level for two standard errors is 95.44 percent). This is because we know that 95 percent of all cases under a normal curve fall between the midpoint and points approximately 1.96 standard errors above

EXHIBIT 10.1 Normalization.

The fact that one can describe a particular case as being so many standard deviations away from the mean introduces one other important role that this dispersion measure can serve for researchers. A frequent problem when comparing responses to certain kinds of psychological questions across respondents is that people tend to differ in the proportion of a given rating scale they tend to use. For instance, when rating different stores on an 11-point interval scale, an extroverted respondent may use the full range from, say, 2 to 11, while more restrained respondents may venture ratings only between 4 and 7. If we were to compare only their raw scores, the computer would treat a score of 7 as being essentially the same for both. But as we have seen, a 7 for the extrovert is just barely above average; for the introvert, it represents outright enthusiasm, the highest score he or she gives.

To accommodate these basic differences across individuals (or sometimes across questions), it is customary to transform the original respondent scores into scores measured in terms of numbers of standard deviations. Thus, a computer would be instructed to divide each respondent's original score on a given scale by that respondent's personal standard deviation on all similar scales. This is called *normalization* of the data. By this procedure, the introvert's score of 7 will get transformed into a higher normalized score than the extrovert's score of 7.

Normalization is also a method for making many different kinds of variables comparable, that is, to express them all in standard deviation units. This approach is often used when employing multiple regression equations.

---

and 1.96 standard errors below that midpoint. The band expected to envelop the true mean is often called the 95 percent *confidence interval*.

Statistical Analysis

Statistical analysis helps researchers and managers answer one of two questions: Does a specific result differ significantly from another result or from an expected result, or is a specific result associated with or predicted by some other result or results, or is this just due to chance?

Such analyses are typically performed on one of three kinds of data: frequencies, means, or proportions. Do more people buy from a jumbled or a neat display? Is the proportion of target audience members noticing a newspaper ad different for men and women? Can mean donation levels be predicted from occupation, income, and family size?

The sections that follow introduce the major statistical analysis techniques that a beginning researcher may wish to use. The techniques are organized on the basis of the kinds of data for which they are most appropriate: nominal, ordinal, or metric. However, we need first to understand the concept of significance.

Levels of Significance

An important question in statistical analysis is what we mean when we say there is a very low probability of a particular result being due to chance. If a probability is very low, we may decide that our actual results are really different from the expected results and take some action on it. But suppose the analysis yielded a .15 chance that the results are really not different. Should we act on this, or do we act only if the probability they are not different is .05 or lower? That is, what is the appropriate *level of significance*? In classical statistics, statisticians tend to use either the .05 or the .01 level of significance as the cutoff for concluding that a result is significant. In my opinion, this classical notion is of little relevance to marketing decision makers, especially in this age of computer analysis.

Historically, statisticians have instructed us that good science involves the construction of hypotheses usually in *null form* (that there is no difference or association) before the results are in (so we are not tempted to test what we have in fact already found), and the setting, in advance, of a level of statistical significance level beyond which we would reject the null hypothesis. The cutoff is typically stated as the probability of rejecting this hypothesis. Classically, this probability was set at either .05 or .01 depending on how tough the researcher wanted to be before accepting a positive outcome.

But these levels are arbitrary. Why not .045 or .02, for example? Furthermore, they ignore the important managerial context. The real issue is not whether the data are sufficiently strong to permit us to make statements about the truth but whether the results are strong enough to permit the manager to take action.

Implicit in this action orientation is the view that (1) it is the manager's *perception* of the significance of the result that is relevant, not the researcher's use of some classical cutoff; (2) significance is really in terms of whether the result will lead to action; and (3) significance is ultimately a matter not just of statistical probability but also of the manager's prior information, prior conviction about which way to act, and the stakes involved. In this conceptualization, it becomes obvious that the researcher's responsibility is simply to report the absolute probability that a result is significant and then let the manager decide whether this is significant in terms of the decision at hand. Significance in some cases (for example, where the stakes are low and management is already leaning toward a particular course of action) may be acceptable with a .15 probability or better. In other cases where the stakes are larger and management is quite unsure what is best, only a .03 or better probability will decide the matter. In modern managerial decision making, the classical role of the .05 and the .01 levels of significance should be irrelevant.

Nominal Data: The Chi Square Test

Where we have nominal data, we are forced to analyze frequency counts since there are no means and variances. Two kinds of questions are typically asked of these frequency counts. When looking at only one variable, we usually ask whether the results in the study differ from some expected distribution (often referred to as the *model*). For example, we might wish to know whether the distribution of occupations in a target population is different from that found in the metropolitan area as a whole or in an earlier study. The second kind of analysis we may wish to conduct is to ask whether the distribution of one variable is associated with another, for example, whether occupation depends on the geographical area of the respondent. The appropriate statistical test to use for either type of analysis is called the chi square (χ^2) test. Because it is especially appropriate for nominal data and because it can also be used for higher-order numbers, chi square may well be the most frequently used statistical test in marketing research.

The chi square test is exceedingly simple to understand and almost as easy to compute. I have calculated the chi square on backs of envelopes on airplanes, on my pocket calculator during a client meeting, and countless times in the classroom. All that is needed is the raw frequency count (F_i) for each value of the variable you are analyzing and a corresponding expected frequency (E_i). The chi square technique then calculates the difference between these two, squares the result, and divides by the expected frequency. It sums these calculations across all the values (cells) for the variable to get the total chi square value. (Division by the expected frequencies is a way of making sure that a small absolute difference for a case with a lot of respondents expected in it is not given as much weight in the final result as the same absolute difference for a smaller cell.)

Comparison to a Given Distribution. Suppose that prior to an election a political candidate has her campaign staff interview a sample of shoppers outside a particular department store on a random sample of days and nights. The candidate wants to know whether the shoppers' party affiliations differ from what would be expected if her staff had obtained a random sample of all voters in her district. Of a sample of 130 shoppers, 80 said they were Democrats, 30 were Republicans, and 20 were listed as Independents. Suppose that voter registrations in the district show that 54 percent of all voters are Democrats, 27 percent are Republicans, and the rest are Inde-

TABLE 10.2 Actual and Expected Party Affiliation.

Party	Actual (F)	Expected (E)
Democrat	80	70
Republican	30	35
Independent	20	25
Total	130	130

pendents. The question is, Do the affiliations of the shoppers differ from the expected pattern? The chi square for this example is calculated from the data in Table 10.2.

If the analysis is done by hand, the analyst then refers to a chi square table that indicates the likelihood of obtaining the calculated total chi square value (or greater) if the actual frequencies and the expected frequencies were really the same. (If the calculation is done by computer, this probability will be printed on the output.) If the probability is very low, it means that results are clearly not what was expected. Conversely, subtracting the probability from 1 gives the probability that the results are really different. For example, a chi square probability of .06 means that there is a 6 percent chance the two distributions are really the same and a 94 percent chance they are not.

It is important to use the appropriate *degrees of freedom* when determining the probability. (The computer does this automatically.) *Degrees of freedom* is a measure that reflects the number of cells in a table that can take any value, given marginal totals. In the example, we estimated the expected number of cases for three cells. Since we started with 130 cases, once we had calculated the expected frequencies in any *two* cells, the remaining cell has no freedom to assume any value at all; it is perfectly determined. Thus, two of the cells were free to take on any amount and one cell was not. Therefore, degrees of freedom in this case is two: the number of cells minus one. In a cross-tabulation, degrees of freedom is $(r - 1)$

$(c-1)$, where r is the number of cells in a row and c is the number of cells in a column.

The chi square calculation for Table 10.2 is:

$$\chi^2 = \Sigma \frac{(E_i - F_i)}{E_i}$$

$$= \frac{(70-80)^2}{70} + \frac{(35-30)^2}{35} + \frac{(25-20)^2}{25} = 3.143.$$

Cross-Tabulations.   A second research issue involving nominal values is whether two or more nominal categories are independent of each other or are associated. In the example, we might ask whether the distribution of party affiliations differs between men and women. The chi square analysis procedure used in this case is very similar to that in the previous case, and the formula is unchanged. That is, we are again simply asking the chi square analysis technique to tell us whether the actual results do or do not fit a model.

Suppose we had surveyed eighty men and fifty women in the study, and their party affiliations were those reported on the left side of Table 10.3. Are these distributions affected by the sex of the shopper, or are they independent? To answer this question, we must first construct a set of expectations for each of the cells in Table 10.3 and then go through the cells and, one by one, compute chi square values comparing expected to actual outcomes. As in all other cross-tabulations, we are testing whether there is no relationship between the variables, that is, that they are independent. The first step is to figure out what the expected frequencies would be if the two variables were really independent. This is easy; if they were independent, the distribution within the sexes would be identical. Thus, in the example, we would hypothesize that the proportion of Democrats, Republicans, and Independents is the same for the two sexes.

In Table 10.3, we can see that only slightly over half the men (actually 54 percent) are Democrats, but three-quarters of the women

TABLE 10.3 Party Affiliation by Sex.

Party	Actual			Expected			
	Male	Female	Total	Male	Female	Total	Percentage
Democratic	43	37	80	49.2	30.8	80	61.5
Republican	22	8	30	18.5	11.5	30	23.1
Independent	15	5	20	12.3	7.7	20	15.4
Total	80	50	130	80	50	130	100.0

$$\chi^2 = \frac{(43-49.2)^2}{49.2} + \frac{(37-30.8)^2}{30.8} + \frac{(22-18.5)^2}{18.5} + \frac{(8-11.5)^2}{11.5} + \frac{(15-12.3)^2}{12.3} + \frac{(5-7.7)^2}{7.7} = 5.27$$

are (74 percent). Therefore, we must ask whether the proportion of Democrats depends on one's sex or whether any apparent association is due to chance. The expected frequencies based on a no-difference model are given on the right-hand side of Table 10.3. (Note that the marginal totals have to be the same for the actual and expected frequencies.)

The calculated chi square is 5.27. Is this significant? As noted, degrees of freedom refers to the number of cells in the rows minus one, multiplied by the number of columns minus one. In this case it is $(r - 1)(c - 1) = 2$. (The correctness of this can be seen by arbitrarily filling two cells of the expected frequency section of Table 10.3. Note that the other four cells can take on only one value given the marginal totals.) In this case, with two degrees of freedom, we would conclude that there is between a .9 and a .95 probability that the null hypothesis is not true—that there is a relationship between sex and party affiliation. It is now up to the manager to decide whether this is enough certainty on which to act (that is, to assume that female shoppers are much better targets for Democratic party candidates).

Some Caveats. There are two things to guard against in carrying out a chi square analysis since the computation of chi square is sensitive to very small expected cell frequencies and large absolute sample sizes. To guard against the danger of small expected cell sizes, a good rule of thumb is not to calculate (or trust) a chi square when the expected frequency for any cell is five or less. Cells may be added together (collapsed) to meet the minimum requirement.

With respect to total sample size, it turns out that chi square is directly proportional to the number of cases used in its calculation. Thus, if one multiplied the cell values in Table 10.3 by 10, the calculated chi square value would be ten times larger and very significant rather than barely significant, as it is now.

There are statistical corrections for large sample sizes that more experienced researchers use in such cases. Neophyte researchers should simply be aware that large sample sizes can result in bloated chi squares and for this reason should be especially careful when comparing chi squares across studies where differences in significance levels may be due to nothing more than differences in sample sizes.

Metric Data: *t* Tests

The next most frequently used statistical test in marketing is the *t* test. Because it is applicable only to interval or ratio data, it is called a *parametric* test. It is used to compare two population estimations such as means or proportions and assess the probability that they are drawn from the same population. It is computed in slightly different ways depending on whether one is analyzing independent or nonindependent measures.

t Test for Independent Measures. The *t* test can be used to compare means or proportions from two independent samples. For example, the *t* test can be used to indicate whether a sample of donors in New York gave larger average donations than a sample in San Antonio. The procedure to conduct this test is first to use a procedure to estimate the (combined) standard errors of these means. (Remember that the standard error is a measure of the spread of a hypothetical series of means produced from the same sampling procedure carried out over and over again, in this case, in New York and San Antonio.) One then divides the difference between the means by the combined standard error, which is actually a combined standard error of difference in means. (To combine the standard errors and conduct this test, the original data in the samples must be normally distributed and have equal variances. If these assumptions do not appear to be met, a more sophisticated analysis should be conducted.) This in effect indicates how many standard errors the two means are apart. The resulting figure is called a t statistic if the sample size is small (under thirty) and a z statistic if it is large. This statistic then allows us to say something about the probability that two means are really equal (drawn from a more general population of all customers). A low probability indicates they are different. The same analysis could be conducted comparing two proportions instead of two means.

Independent t tests can also be used for two other purposes that are often important in research. First, they can test whether a mean or proportion for a single sample is different from an expected value. For example, a researcher could determine whether the average household size in a sample differs from the Bureau of the Census figure for the area. Using this same logic, the t test can also assess whether the coefficients in a multiple regression equation are really zero as indicated in Exhibit 10.2.

Sometimes we wish to see whether the means or proportions for the answers to one question in a study are different from similar means or proportions elsewhere in the same study or in a later study of the same sample. For example, we may wish to know whether respondents' evaluations of one positioning statement for an organization are more or less favorable than another positioning. (Note that the means or proportions must be in the same units.) Since this procedure would compare respondents to themselves, the two measures are not independent. In this case, the computer takes each pair of respondent answers and computes a difference. It then produces a t statistic and an associated probability that indicates the

EXHIBIT 10.2 *t* Test for Dependent Measures.

Testing Regression Coefficients

Multiple regression equations are typically developed to produce a linear combination of significant predictors of some phenomenon. For example, one might develop an equation estimating the ability of age, family size, or education in combination to predict the average donation of a household.

The resulting equation will have coefficients for each factor (for example, age or family size) used to produce the predicted donation size for each respondent. For example, age might have an estimated coefficient of $23, saying that for every year a person ages, the individual will give $23 more in donations, with the other factors in the equation held constant. In the process of estimating this coefficient, the typical computer program will also produce a *t* statistic and probability that will help us conclude whether the coefficient of $23 is really zero. If the computer printout says that the probability is high that it is zero, then we should be inclined to conclude that age is not a valuable predictor and ought to be dropped from the prediction equation (which then should be reestimated).

---

likelihood that the mean of all of the differences between pairs of answers is really zero. If the probability is low, we would conclude that the respondents did perceive the concepts as different.

Metric Data: Analysis of Variance

Very often, managers are interested in learning about differences across many groups or cases. A useful tool for these purposes in *analysis of variance*. There are two main variations referred to as one-way and *N*-way analysis of variance.

One-Way Analysis of Variance. Suppose we want to compare three or more means. That is, suppose we want to ask whether mean donation levels are different across five cities. The parametric test to use here is the *one-way analysis of variance (ANOVA)*, which is, in a sense, an extension of the *t* test described above. For the *t* test, we compared the difference between two means to an estimate of the random variance of those means (expressed as the standard error of the difference). The more general ANOVA technique proceeds in essentially the same way. It calculates a measure of variance across all the means (for example, the five cities) and then compares this to a measure of random variance—in this case, the combined variances within the five cities. Specifically, ANOVA divides the variance across the cities by the variance within cities to produce a test statistic and a probability of significance. The test statistic here is called an *F ratio* (of which the *t* ratio or *t* statistic is a special case). Again, a low probability and a high *F* statistic is interpreted to mean that the variance across the cities is greater than chance.

Note that we did not conclude that any one city is different from any other specific city, only that there was significant variance among them all. We may have a hypothesis that a specific pair of cities are different. In this case, we would simply have the computer run a *t* test on the difference between the two means.

N-Way ANOVA. Analysis of variance is probably most often used as the primary statistical tool for analyzing the results of experiments. It is highly flexible and can be used for quite complicated designs.

Consider by way of illustration a simple study of the effects on museum gift shop sales of (1) offering or not offering free beverages and (2) using each of four different types of background music. Suppose the researcher conducted a fully factorial experiment (that is, every possible combination) in which each of the four kinds of music was tried out for a specified period of time at a sample of gift shops with and without a free beverage service. Hypothetical results for each of the eight combinations offered in five shops for each cell are shown in Table 10.4.

N-way analysis of variance proceeds to analyze these results in the same way as we did in one-way ANOVA. We first compute an

TABLE 10.4 Sales Results of Hypothetical Experiment (thousands of dollars).

Music Type	Beverages	No Beverages	Music Mean
Classical	122	98	
	136	106	
	153	111	
	109	103	
	120	94	
	$\bar{X}_{11} = 128.0$	$\bar{X}_{12} = 102.4$	$\bar{X}_{1.} = 115.2$
Semi-classical	136	111	
	127	119	
	104	104	
	131	121	
	136	110	
	$\bar{X}_{21} = 126.8$	$\bar{X}_{22} = 113.0$	$\bar{X}_{2.} = 119.9$
Middle of the road	97	110	
	110	120	
	95	113	
	107	131	
	122	106	
	$\bar{X}_{31} = 106.2$	$\bar{X}_{32} = 116.0$	$\bar{X}_{3.} = 111.1$
Contemporary pop	86	99	
	85	101	
	93	110	
	78	90	
	93	95	
	$\bar{X}_{41} = 87.0$	$\bar{X}_{42} = 99.0$	$\bar{X}_{4.} = 93.0$
Beverage mean	$\bar{X}_{.1} = 112.0$	$\bar{X}_{.2} = 107.6$	$\bar{\bar{X}}_{..} = 109.8$

estimate of random variance, in this case, the combination of the variances within each of the eight cells. We (actually a computer does this) then calculate three tests for significant effects. The computer program asks:

- Is there a main effect due to having the beverages present or not, that is, is the variance across the two beverage conditions significantly greater than the random variance when the music treatments are controlled?
- Is there a main effect due to the different music types (ignoring beverage treatment)?
- Is there an interaction effect due to the combination of music and beverage service; that is, are the results in each of the eight treatment cells higher or lower than would be predicted from simply adding the two main effects together?

In each case, the computer reports an *F ratio* statistic and a probability of *no* effects. A glance at the means for the various cells in Table 10.4 shows that (1) beverages yield more sales than no beverages, (2) semiclassical music yields the most sales and contemporary pop the least, and (3) beverages added to classical or semiclassical music increase sales, but when added to contemporary or pop music *decrease* sales. Are these results statistically significant? The ANOVA results for the data in Table 10.4 are as follows:

	Sum of Squares	Df	Mean Square	F Ratio	Probability
Music main effect	4151.0	3	1383.67	12.764	.000
Beverage main effect	193.6	1	193.6	1.786	.191
Interaction effect	2521.0	3	840.33	7.752	.000
Error	3468.8	32	108.40		

Here, we see that the type of music does have a significant effect: the differences in means with the beverage treatment controlled seem to be real. However, despite appearances, the presence or absence of beverages has no effect. Finally, there is an interaction effect indicating that the combination of beverages and classical or semiclassical music is the manager's best bet. It may be that the two create a much more desirable ambience. At least our statistics kept us from concluding that beverages by themselves would be a good addition.

Association: Nonmetric and Metric Data

In many cases, we wish to know whether variables are associated with each other, either singly or in sets. If variables are associated, we may be able to use one variable or set of variables to predict another. Furthermore, if we have some plausible prior theory, we may also say that one variable or set of variables explains or causes the other (although always remember that association is not causation). We have already discussed nominal measures of association using chi square. Other measures of association can be computed for both ranked data and metric data.

Ordinal Data: Spearman Rank-Order Correlation. Spearman's rank-order correlation procedure can compare the rankings of two variables, for example, a hospital's rankings on staff knowledge and friendliness. Spearman's rho coefficient indicates whether a higher ranking on one variable is associated with a higher (or lower) ranking on some other variable. If the two rankings move in the same direction, the sign of rho will be positive. If the rankings move in opposite directions, rho will have a negative sign. In either case, rho can range between zero and one; the closer to one it is, the more we can conclude that the rankings really are associated.

Metric Data: Pearson Product Moment Correlation. This approach seeks the same result as the Spearman analysis but is used for interval or ratio-scaled variables. The Pearson correlation coefficient, called r, can be positive or negative and range from 0 to 1. Most computer programs produce both the Pearson r and a probability that the actual value of r is zero. Its square, the Pearsonian r^2, is an indication of the proportion of the original variance explained by the relationship.

Metric Data: Simple Correlations. Another use of the Pearsonian correlation coefficient is as a measure of the extent to which a straight line plotted through the points representing pairs of measurements fits the data poorly (and has a low r) or rather well (and therefore has a high r). Figure 10.4 shows a line with a good fit (5a) and a line with a poor fit (5b).

Metric Data: Multiple Regression. If one variable is good at predicting another variable, the researcher may wish to look further to see whether a second or third variable will help improve this explanatory power. Multiple linear regression is the technique most often used for this. In a manner similar to simple two-variable correlation, multiple regression seeks to construct a linear combination of two or more independent variables (that may be metric or dichotomous) that predict the value of a dependent metric variable. (A dichotomous variable in a regression equation is a special case of a nominal variable where the values zero and one are used to indicate the presence or absence of some characteristic, for example, being a woman or being married.) An example would be using age, income, education, size of household, and sex to predict the number of hours a month a person would spend exercising.

FIGURE 10.4 Two Hypothetical Regression Lines.

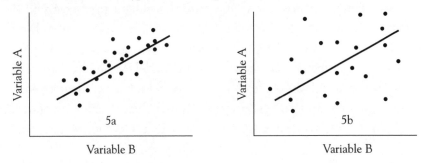

If a researcher has a great many variables that *might* be used in such a multiple regression but is not sure which to use, there are two basic approaches to finding the better set (using a computer). The first approach is theory driven. The researcher can specify the set of variables in advance, usually on the basis of some theory about which variables ought to predict well. Since the computer will print out a *t* statistic measure indicating the probability that the coefficient for any given variable is really zero, the researcher can then look at the initial output and eliminate predictors with high probabilities of being nonsignificant and rerun the analysis. This may have to be done two or three times before the final best set of predictor variables is determined.

Alternatively, the researcher can ask the computer to look for the best set of predictors among what is usually a very large set of candidate variables using a procedure called *stepwise regression analysis*. Under this procedure, the computer takes the original variance in the dependent variable and proceeds to enter into the equation the predictor with the highest explanatory power (for example, the highest simple *r*). It then subtracts out the variance explained by this variable, computes new correlations of each remaining potential predictor variable and the adjusted dependent variable, and then picks the variable with the highest correlation at this step. In this manner, variables from the candidate set are added to the prediction equation until they are all exhausted or some predetermined stopping point is reached (such as when the variance about to be explained at the next step is less than 1 percent).

Stepwise regression is a good technique at the exploratory stage of a study. However, care should be taken with it since it has properties that make it possible that a truly significant predictor will be missed because it happens to be highly correlated with a variable entered at an early step in the analysis. Furthermore, if the sample is large enough, researchers should test the model eventually discovered on a different subsample from the one on which it was developed.

Once the multiple regression analysis is done, the researcher will wish to look at three measures produced by the computer program:

- Multiple R measures how well the equation fits the data. The probability that this statistic is really zero is important as an indicator that the equation really does predict.

- Multiple R^2 is analogous to the Pearsonian r^2. It indicates the proportion of variance in the dependent variable accounted for by the linear combination of the predictor variables. It is as important as the probability of the multiple R being zero. If the data set is large, it is often possible to have a highly significant multiple R for an equation that explains very little of the variance in the dependent variable.

- Standardized variable coefficients. The researcher will also wish to know the relative contribution of each of the independent variables to the overall prediction equation. He or she could look at the relative size of the coefficients for each predictor variable to try to learn this, but this would be misleading because the variables are usually in different units; for example, the coefficient for income may be very small because income is expressed in thousands or tens of thousands of dollars, while sex may have a large coefficient because it can be only 0 or 1. The solution to this dilemma is to convert all of the variables into standard deviation units. The resulting *beta coefficients* (as they are called) are simply the original coefficients (often called *B coefficients*) divided by the respective standard deviations (see Exhibit 10.1). Variables with larger beta coefficients can be considered to make more of a contribution to the overall prediction than those with smaller coefficients.

Other Multivariate Techniques

Many researchers may already be familiar with the techniques just described and would like to move on to more sophisticated analyses. It is not appropriate to treat more advanced techniques in depth in this book. However, to acquaint the reader with some of the possibilities, several of the major alternatives will be described briefly. The Recommended Reading list at the back of the book cites other sources for detailed information on the various approaches. A general useful and nontechnical book for a good overview is *Multivariate Data Analysis*, by Joseph Hair et al.

Factor Analysis

Many measurements in a study are related. In studies with very large databases, it will often be very valuable to ask whether the measures obtained can be reduced to a smaller set of underlying factors to which each of a set of measurements is related. Factor analysis investigates the correlations among measurements and provides one or more factors that apparently underlie the data. Factor analysis looks at all the variables in a set simultaneously. None is specified as a dependent or independent measure.

An example of the use of factor analysis is that carried out by the United Way of America in the 1980s to help its 297 local chapters evaluate their performance against other comparable local chapters. In the past, chapters had been compared to others like themselves only in total market size. But United Way realized that comparing a city in an economically troubled part of Pennsylvania to a city of the same size in booming Arizona or Florida made little sense, so it sought to develop measures that would better describe differences in markets. To do this, its Research Division assembled ninety-two indicators on each of its 297 solicitation areas, in part using several of the secondary sources mentioned in Chapter Five. The Research Division then used a factor analysis computer program to reduce this unwieldy set of ninety-two indicators to a manageable set of five basic factors that seemed to capture much of the complexity of the local social and economic profiles:

- An income and affluence factor
- A type-of-employment and labor-force-structure factor
- A factor indicating the relative preponderance of impoverished and minority counties
- A growth rate factor
- A factor indicating the relative age of adults and presence of children in area households

These labels for the factors were added by the researcher and were not automatically produced by the computer program.

Cluster Analysis

Often marketers would like to know whether members of a large set of objects being studied (for example, respondents, government agencies, classical composers, and countries) clump together in groups exhibiting relatively homogeneous characteristics. Cluster analysis is designed for this type of problem. It takes whatever information the researcher has on each object and proceeds to develop groupings that maximize the homogeneity within the groups and heterogeneity across the groups. Again, no variable is dependent or independent.

In top-down clustering, the analysis begins with all objects in one large group and proceeds to split the group step by step until some homogeneity-heterogeneity ratio level is reached. In bottom-up clustering, the program begins with each object in its own group and proceeds to combine them into groups until the specified stopping point is reached.

The United Way used cluster analysis to partition its 297 local solicitation areas into 12 relatively homogeneous groups based on their scores on the five factors mentioned above. The clusters range in size from 7 to 51 communities. Organizations within clusters now could share performance data and experiences with greater confidence that they are dealing with others facing very much the same kind of market challenges they are.

Discriminant Analysis

Simple and multiple correlation analyses typically have metric measurements on their dependent variables, but sometimes marketers may have a nominal measure that is of interest. Discriminant analysis is a technique similar to regression in that it develops a set of variables that best help marketers predict whether a given case (that is, a respondent) falls into a particular nominal category.

For example, suppose the United Way wished to understand what variables differentiate three groups: nondonors, new donors, and repeat donors. Discriminant analysis can be used to determine the best combination of predictors of group membership. As with multiple regression, the analysis can also indicate the relative importance of each of the predictor variables in the final solution.

The equation that predicts group membership is called a *discriminant function*. One complication of discriminant analysis is that there can be more than one discriminant function if the researcher is trying to discriminate among more than two groups. A second important difference from regression is that discriminant analysis does not produce a statistic like R^2 that indicates how well the discriminant function predicts. Typically, researchers take as a measure of success how often the final function correctly predicts a subject's true group membership.

Multidimensional Scaling

Marketers are often interested in understanding how objects in a group are perceived in relationship to each other by target consumers. A strategic planner for the YMCA will be interested in understanding which other youth service organizations are most and least similar to it in parents' minds and what these consumers are using as the key dimensions in evaluating the entire set of organizations. Multidimensional scaling is a technique used to position objects in some physical or perceptual space. It does so by analyzing one of three kinds of measures: objective measures of an object's characteristics, such as the number of programs, number of employees, or square footage of buildings; subjective measures of an object's characteristics, such as perceptions of staff quality, equipment variety, or attractiveness of the premises; or subjective measures of similarity or dissimilarity among the objects, letting respondents use whatever dimensions they wish to use to determine those relationships. In all three cases, the computer analysis routine produces a map of the objects relating them in geometric space along one or more underlying dimensions (in a sense like factor analysis). It is then up to the researcher to label these underlying dimensions. When the raw data analyzed include subjective perceptions, the result is sometimes referred to as a *perceptual map*.

Multidimensional scaling studies that use subjective input in the form of either object ratings or similarities judgments can also ask respondents about their ideal object (such as their ideal youth center). A YMCA planner can then look at which respondents have ideal youth centers near to the researcher's own perceptual position (their natural constituency) or see whether there are sets of respondents with no youth centers near their ideal points. The latter would comprise a potential target for an entirely new type of youth center offering.

Conjoint Analysis

A great many consumer choices involve trade-offs between features possessed by different alternatives. For example, when considering which youth center to patronize, a young woman might have a real set of choices:

Option A: high fees, large variety of equipment, staff who are not very knowledgeable, poor parking, short driving time

Option B: medium fees, large variety of equipment, staff who are not very knowledgeable, great parking, short driving time

Option C: very low fees, average variety of equipment, staff who are very knowledgeable, average parking, long driving time

The consumer's preference ranking of these three alternatives will depend on the extent to which she is willing to trade off, for example, poorer staff knowledge and a longer drive for lower prices.

Conjoint analysis is a technique for exploring these trade-offs. In a conjoint study, objects such as products, services, or other choices are described in terms of attributes to be traded off. Consumers rank sets of these objects, and then the conjoint analysis routine proceeds to indicate the relative value respondents attach to each of the different dimensions. It will also indicate which combination of the specified attributes will be most attractive to the entire population (including combinations not offered in the study) and which consumers will find an existing or proposed combination of attributes most appealing.

Multivariate Analysis of Variance

Often a researcher in an experimental study may wish to see whether there are differences across groups in some set of metric characteristics rather than a single characteristic as in an ANOVA design. In the ANOVA example presented earlier (Table 10.4), the effects of beverage availability and music type were studied with respect to one outcome: total sales in a museum gift shop. But suppose the researcher wishes to look at the effect of the two types of treatment on:

- Average length of time spent in the store
- Total sales of high-priced merchandise
- Total sales of posters
- The ratio of items sold at full price to items sold at a marked-down price

The manager will be interested in this combination of outcomes. Multivariate analysis of variance (MANOVA) proceeds in much the same way as ANOVA with similar outputs to answer this question.

PART FOUR

Organizing Low-Cost Research

11

Organization and Implementation on a Shoestring

The preceding chapters have outlined both a procedure for planning and implementing a program of low-cost research and a wide-ranging set of techniques for carrying it out. It is now time to tackle the serious problem of how to get it all done, particularly within a very limited budget. The glib answer is to beg or borrow as much as possible and keep the costs of the research as low as possible, with the constraint that one always has an obligation to management to provide good as well as low-cost research. However, in reality, the task of system building is more complex. To see some of the ways in which it may be possible to keep costs down, we need to list the basic requirements for carrying out a beginner's research program. These requirements can be roughly divided into three categories: ideas, people, and things. A partial list of some of the requirements in each of these categories is outlined in Exhibit 11.1. We will consider some of the tactics available to low-cost researchers in each of the categories.

Financial Assistance

Assuming the research manager has been assigned a modest budget for a program of research, how can it be augmented? Several sources of additional funding can be explored.

EXHIBIT 11.1 Resources Needed for an Extended Program of Marketing Research.

1. Money to supplement the manager's limited budget.
2. Know-how to do the following:
   a. Learn from management what decisions they need to make and what information will help them make those decisions.
   b. Estimate the costs and benefits of research.
   c. Develop protocols for observation.
   d. Design experiments.
   e. Design sampling plans.
   f. Write questionnaires.
   g. Train a field force and their supervisors.
   h. Write coding manuals and schemes.
   i. Design and carry out statistical analyses (including any computer programming necessary).
   j. Run focus groups.
   k. Write reports (including preparation of graphics, possibly a separate skill).
   l. Present the results and see that they are implemented.
3. Personnel to do the following:
   a. Conduct and supervise interviews.
   b. Mail and follow up questionnaires.
   c. Carry out experiments.
   d. Conduct observations.
   e. Code results.
   f. Enter results.
   g. Run computer analyses.
   h. Produce final reports and presentation materials.
   i. Collect and analyze archives.
4. Equipment and facilities:
   a. Rooms for experiments or focus groups.
   b. Telephone equipment (including monitoring facilities for interviewing).
   c. Computers for:
      (1) Cover letters for mail studies.
      (2) Questionnaires.

(3) Statistical analyses.

(4) Report writing and graphic preparation.

d. Software for word processing, analyses, report publication and graph preparation.

e. Mailing lists or other materials for sampling.

f. Libraries and Web connections for secondary source material.

Immediate Superiors

Chapter Two outlined an approach in which the knowledgeable and persuasive research manager could demonstrate to management the benefits from additional expenditures on research that will more than justify those expenditures. The research manager needs to follow those steps to get the manager who approved the initial basic research budget to supplement it because of the value this will bring. The first step is to begin a long-term campaign to educate the manager in the benefit-cost approach to research funding developed in this book. The manager must learn to appreciate the extent to which the provision of some information in many situations will help make for better decisions even if the stakes are low. The manager must learn that inexpensive information can be very helpful in the face of uncertainty.

One problem is that the research manager's superiors may be inhibited by the myths outlined in Chapter One. The research manager should undertake a subtle but purposeful campaign to destroy them. In addition, management should become aware of many of the low-cost research possibilities outlined in this book. At the same time, following suggestions in Chapter Two, the researcher should constantly look for opportunities to point out over and over again how a particular problem can be helped by research. In a sense, the research manager should force serendipity.

One technique that may be helpful in this regard is the unauthorized low-cost research demonstration project. An occasion may arise when the research manager senses an opportunity to demonstrate (not just describe) how research can help improve a particular management decision. If at all feasible, the researcher should surreptitiously carry through a pilot study of modest proportions using existing funds focused on this decision. Although such a strategy is risky, the hope is that the results of the ad hoc study will be so compelling that management will grant ex-post authorization of the budget to the daring researcher. Peters and Waterman indicate that one of the hallmarks of a well-run organization is its tolerance of organizational mavericks.[1]

Other Organization Divisions

If the low-budget researcher is employed by a multidivision enterprise (say, a nonprofit with many regions or chapters), other low-budget researchers may well be hidden elsewhere in the organization. Jointly undertaken projects typically can achieve much greater payoff than would be possible from each budget separately. But it may be that other company divisions may not appreciate the possibilities of research at all. If this is the case, from time to time the researcher could add a few questions to planned studies to suggest the value of research to other divisions. Subsequently, financial contributions for projects could be solicited initially on a marginal cost basis. Once one joint venture is successful, other divisions could be enticed to join the enterprise.

Competitors

There may be certain kinds of projects where participation by competitors (who would obviously share in the findings) would be better than no research at all. For example, a cooperative effort by several charities or performing arts centers on the effectiveness of joint advertising might appeal to multiple participants. If such projects are to be mounted, any of the organizations could manage the research contemplated. Alternatively, a joint task force could be established. Although this can lead to conflict and, in my experience, will inevitably delay the project, it will at least ensure that each contributor has a voice in the final research design, thus increasing the likelihood each will participate. The disadvantage of this type of low-budget financing is that there is no confidentiality.

Other Partners

Other organizations with which the organization works may be persuaded to participate in a research project that would benefit mutual interests. Despite this mutuality, there is still the possibility that competitors would learn about the project. However, if projects can be designed that are of clear benefit to other partners, they may well be willing to maintain confidentiality.

Trade Associations or Universities

In the private sector, going to competitors for collaborative research may raise antitrust questions in addition to confidentiality problems. Furthermore, in any sector, joint projects may be aborted or compromised due to wrangling over who is in charge, what gets done, who does it, and how the results are to be used. If these are likely to be problems, it may be useful to induce a neutral entity like a trade association to take on the projects. If an association does not exist, an accounting firm or university may be persuaded to perform the same function. The obvious advantages are several, not the least of which is that there may be certain cost economies inherent in the tax-free status of the nonprofit association. Furthermore, to the extent that intraindustry data will be involved, having the project under the aegis of an association or university may increase respondent participation and candor. The association or university may be willing to commit its own resources if it sees a research study, especially a continuing study, as a benefit to its own mission. Universities often see research projects as opportunities to advance science—and academic careers.

Acquiring Knowledge

All of the activities of a year-long program of research activity can be carried out by the researcher and a separately dedicated staff. Alternatively, virtually all can be carried out by outside agencies. Full-service market research agencies can do virtually any activity a researcher wishes to carry out, as do organizations and individuals specializing in certain specific marketing research functions such as conducting focus groups (or focus group recruiting), telephone interviewing, laboratory experimentation, computer programming and statistical analysis, and preparation of graphics. Many of these outside suppliers have close competitors, and a few have their own proprietary approaches, such as unique methods of new product testing. The top fifty research organizations are listed in Table 11.1.

Unfortunately, there are no data indicating which functions are most often delegated to outsiders by major firms. In my experience, most organizations do not carry out their own field interviewing. Fieldwork requires specially trained people who would be put to work only from time to time as needed. Managing such a significant part-time labor force does not appeal to most firms. Outside field research agencies can achieve significant scale economies in such activities that individual firms cannot. Again, because of the specialized skills, focus group interviewing is also frequently contracted out, although here it is as often to individuals as to firms.

It is most likely, however, that a beginning researcher with a limited budget will have little financial capacity for hiring a great deal of outside know-how. However, there are a number of other lower-cost, and sometimes free, sources of assistance that can be used. Several of these are covered next, in an ascending order of difficulty of acquisition.

The Manager's Own Organization

If an organization has other divisions that work with or prepare analyses or reports, you may be able to secure their assistance. Some of the possibilities are:

TABLE 11.1 The Top Fifty U.S. Research Organizations, 1999.

Organization/Headquarters	Phone	Total Research Revenues (in millions of dollars)	Percentage of Revenues from Outside U.S.
1 ACNielsen Corp, Stamford, Conn.	203-961-3330	1,525.4	68.1
2 IMS Health Inc., Westport, Conn.	203-222-4200	1,275.7	60.7
3 Information Resources Inc., Chicago,	312-726-1221	546.3	23.7
4 NFO Worldwide Inc., Greenwich, Conn.	203-629-8888	457.2	61.3
5 Neilsen Media Research Inc., New York	212-708-7500	453.3	2.6
6 The Kantar Group Ltd., Fairfield, Conn.	203-255-7880	250.2	16.9
Diagnostic Research Int'l Inc., Los Angeles	323-254-4326	39.3	3.9
IntelliQuest Info. Group Inc., Austin, Texas	512-329-0808	26.9	14.8
Remaining Kantar Fairfield, Conn.	203-255-7880	184.0	20.0
7 Westat Inc., Rockville MD	301-251-1500	242.0	
8 The Arbitron Co., New York	212-887-1300	215.4	3.7
9 Maritz Marketing Research Inc., St. Louis	636-827-1610	174.3	31.0
10 Market Facts Inc., Arlington Heights, Ill.	847-590-7000	160.0	15.1
11 The NPD Group Inc., Port Washington, N.Y.	516-625-0700	143.4	18.4

TABLE 11.1 (*Continued*)

Organization/Headquarters	Phone	Total Research Revenues (in millions of dollars)	Percentage of Revenues from Outside U.S.
12 United Information Group USA, New York	212-627-9700	130.0	17.8
13 Opinion Research Corp., Princeton, NJ	908-281-5100	109.4	36.0
Opinion Research Corp., Princeton, NJ	908-281-5100	56.7	34.9
Macro International Inc., Calverton, MD	301-572-0200	52.7	37.2
14 Taylor Nelson Sofres Intersearch, Horsham, PA	215-442-9000	83.6	21.8
15 J. D. Power and Associates, Agoura Hill, Calif.	818-889-6330	75.4	12.5
16 Roper Starch Worldwide Inc., Harrison, N.Y.	914-698-0800	65.7	13.2
17 Ipsos-ASI Inc., Norwalk, Conn.	203-840-3400	64.1	47.6
18 Abt Associates Inc., Cambridge, Mass.	617-492-7100	50.8	15.1
19 Burke Inc., Cincinnati	513-241-5663	48.8	29.1
20 Total Research Corp., Princeton, NJ	609-520-9100	47.8	29.3
21 MORPACE International Farmington, Mich.	248-737-5300	44.4	19.5
22 M/A/R/C Research, Irving, TX	972-506-3400	38.8	4.4
23 C&R Research Services Inc., Chicago	312-828-9200	38.3	

24	Harris Interactive Inc., Rochester, N.Y.	716-272-9020	37.3	6.4
25	Market Strategies, Livonia, Mich.	734-542-7600	34.3	4.4
26	Wirthlin Worldwide, McLean, VA	703-556-0001	33.5	19.3
27	Lieberman Research Worldwide, Los Angeles	310-553-0550	31.2	23.7
28	Walker Information, Indianapolis	317-843-3939	29.1	23.8
29	Custom Research Inc., Minneapolis	612-542-0800	28.2	9.2
30	Yankelovich Partners, Inc., Norwalk, Conn.	203-846-0100	27.9	
31	Elrick & Lavidge Marketing Research, Tucker, GA	770-621-7600	27.2	
32	ICR/Int'l Communications Research, Media, PA	610-565-9280	25.3	1.5
33	RDA Group Inc., Bloomfield Hills, Mich.	248-332-5000	23.0	20.0
34	Media Metrix Inc., New York	212-515-8700	20.5	4.0
35	Data Development Corp., New York	212-633-1100	18.6	8.6
36	Lieberman Research Group, Great Neck, N.Y.	516-829-8880	18.3	2.8
37	Marketing and Planning Systems Inc., Waltham, Mass.	781-890-2228	18.2	30.2
38	National Research Corp. Lincoln, Neb.	402-475-2525	18.2	
39	Schulman, Ronca & Bucuvalas Inc., New York	212-779-7700	16.9	

TABLE 11.1 (*Continued*)

Organization/Headquarters	Phone	Total Research Revenues (in millions of dollars)	Percentage of Revenues from Outside U.S.
40 TVG Inc., Fort Washington, PA	800-368-7556	16.8	22.0
41 Ziment Associates Inc., New York	212-647-7200	15.9	1.9
42 Directions Research Inc., Cincinnati	513-651-2990	15.7	
43 Cheskin Research, Redwood Shores, Calif.	650-802-2100	15.0	30.0
44 Greenfield Consulting Group Inc., Westport Conn.	203-221-0411	14.7	4.8
45 Market Probe, Milwaukee	414-778-6000	14.4	42.2
46 The PreTesting Co. Inc., Tenafly, NJ	201-569-4800	14.3	7.0
47 Questar Data Systems Inc., Eagan, Minn.	651-688-0089	14.0	
48 The B/R/S Group Inc., Mill Valley, Calif.	415-332-4430	13.5	6.6
49 Marketing Analysis Inc., North Charleston, S.C.	843-797-8900	13.0	3.6
50 Savitz Research Cos., Dallas	972-386-4050	13.0	
Total		**$6,808.3**	**38.6%**

Source: Adapted with permission from Jack Homonichl, "2001 Study of U.S. Research Organizations," *Marketing News,* June 4, 2001 (Chicago: American Marketing Association, 2001), p. H4.

- *Long-range planning department.* There may be economists or others in a long-range planning group with advanced social science training who can be helpful with some kinds of statistical analysis. Economists in particular are likely to be familiar with regression, correlation, and such arcane topics as confidence intervals.
- *Quality control department.* Those who have been trained in this area may be familiar with concepts of experimental design and tests of significance (for example, whether twelve defects per hour constitute a serious quality control problem).
- *Advertising or marketing department.* Recently hired M.B.A.s with marketing majors may have been exposed to marketing research (possibly) or statistics (probably) courses in their graduate programs.
- *Information technology and accounting department.* These departments frequently have computer programming experts or individuals familiar with handling large data sets.
- *Public relations department.* These specialists are often skilled in producing newsletters and reports and may be able to help with graphics and report design. They may also be familiar with or can help the researcher evaluate desktop publishing computer software.
- *Secretarial and word processing department.* Here is a good place to get advice on word processing software. It may also be a place where one can find a secretary who is adept at producing attractive questionnaires, specialized research reports, and complex tables and figures.

Local Colleges and Universities

Institutions with programs in undergraduate or graduate business and economics can be very helpful in several ways.

Professors have been known to do consulting and may be hired at less-than-market rates (and sometimes for free) if the professor believes there will be some publishable outcome or something valuable for the classroom in the work. While clients are rightfully concerned about confidentiality of their own studies, most proprietary data can be well disguised for publication or classroom use (the professor will almost always agree to this in writing). The assistance may well be worth some very small potential that information will be leaked to competitors.

The researcher should not be limited for possible sources of help to business schools or economics departments. Psychology, social work, public health, and education departments may have people with skills in experimental design, computers, or statistical methods. They may also provide focus group leaders with good group dynamics skills and psychological insight. Anthropologists may be helpful in observation studies.

Beginning researchers should be cautious about some hidden costs of hiring professors. If the professors are not paid or are paid at below-market rates, they may not feel under pressure to meet deadlines the researcher sets.

At institutions with advanced degree programs, master's and doctoral candidates almost always need supplemental income. Graduate students can be particularly helpful in implementation (rather than design) roles, especially in areas where they may have technical training, such as computer programming or statistical analysis. However, be cautious about engaging students, even if they have an M.B.A. or are working on a Ph.D., to provide advice on problem formulation and research design where seasoned experience is a job requirement.

Special Assistance Available to Nonprofits

Researchers in nonprofit organizations can avail themselves of help unavailable to others except at considerable cost. An enterprising nonprofit researcher could tap the following sources.

Pro Bono Professionals. A selected number of professional fields have an ethic that encourages their members to donate their time to voluntary service in worthy causes. For example, the nonprofit research director could seek help from the major accounting firms since they have considerable experience at massive data handling. They typically have computer programmers and statisticians on staff and possibly specialists in report writing whom they may be willing to lend free of charge to nonprofit organizations. An area in which accountants can be of special help is in archival analysis. Auditors take great pride in being able to delve into records to learn the hidden secrets of an organization. They can have excellent suggestions on where to look for unsuspected marketing insights.

Volunteer Board Members. Key executives in the private sector have traditionally volunteered to serve on the boards of directors of nonprofit organizations. While some of these board memberships are intended more to add to the executive's resumé or to facilitate business contacts with other board members, in the main, board members can be very hard workers and very helpful. In my experience, nonprofit managers are much more likely to think of stocking their boards with politicians, lawyers, accountants, and heavyweight fundraisers rather than marketing experts. They rarely think of adding research experts. It may not be easy for research directors to convince nonprofit managers of the desirability of having the head of a local multiservice marketing research agency on the board, especially if he or she is seen as potentially taking the place of someone more valuable. However, such individuals can be immensely helpful to the research operation. They can provide direct advice themselves, encourage or assign their own junior staffers to provide technical advice, and provide volunteer staff for certain tasks, access to computer equipment and software, and opportunities for piggybacking research.

One of the most valuable roles they can serve for the research manager is in changing the attitudes of top management. The in-house research manager may have limited influence over the way the organization plans and sets policy. However, an independent, experienced outside director trained in marketing research can keep pointing out to top management how research can help this segmentation decision, that new service decision, that forecasting problem, and so on. This intervention will eventually do much to promote business for the research manager. At the very least, the researcher on the board will gradually change the climate so that the in-house research director's future proposals will be better understood and appreciated and, eventually, more often acted on.

Retired Executives. Many retired executives are eager to keep active and use their skills in work they feel is socially productive. In the United States, the Service Corps of Retired Executives has had a long tradition of providing government-sponsored help to small and nonprofit enterprises. They can be wise and experienced counselors for researchers thinking about different ways of formulating and researching management problems.

Acquiring Personnel

Research takes people, often a considerable number of them. It may be preferable for management to hire outside skills for certain research tasks because these tasks require unusual, precise skills or because these skills can be obtained at much less cost (including learning time) than would be involved if the researcher tried to do the task inside the organization. Several additional options are available for low-cost or even free help.

Volunteers

Most nonprofits and some for-profits (such as hospitals) have volunteers available to them who work anywhere from a few to many hours a week. These volunteers can be used for many of the low-skill research tasks described elsewhere in this book:

- Address and stuff envelopes for mail questionnaires, keep track of mail returns, and initiate follow-up-mailings
- Hand out or drop off self-report questionnaires

- Carry out simple observations such as counting customers stopping at a particular display, counting cars in a competitor's parking lot, or writing down (and later looking up the residence associated with) license plates in a mall parking lot
- Transcribe archival records, such as addresses in a visitor's guest book or information from expense account vouchers
- Clip competitive information, such as articles or advertisements from local newspapers or magazines
- Assist in experiments
- Do simple analyses if a computer is unavailable

With training, volunteers can be given more specialized and responsible tasks, such as conducting telephone or personal interviews, coding questionnaires, carrying out experiments, or processing data. The training component is crucial. At first appearance, volunteers would seem like the ideal low-cost resource. They are often over-educated for the tasks to which you wish to assign them. Some of them will be very dedicated.

Volunteers are not, however, without their costs. Those who volunteer often are very difficult to manage. One executive I know has said that he has a "rule of thirds" for volunteers: one-third work very hard without much supervision and encouragement, one-third work if given the right incentives and directions, and one-third hardly work at all. Part of the difficulty can be laid to the education, social status, and motivation of many volunteers. Many believe that the organization should be grateful for their help and so are patronizing in their attitudes. This often leads them to disdain certain kinds of work ("Stuff envelopes! Are you kidding; I have a graduate degree in art!"). Others, because they feel they earn more elsewhere or are better educated than the research manager, may argue about the way things are done or go off on their own and try to do things in a better way.

For many activities (stuffing envelopes, for example) relatively poor performance by volunteers may not matter greatly. However, it is more often the case in research that perseverance and attention to detail are critical in order to draw a representative sample, ask unbiased questions, prove causation, or perform a precise analysis. For this reason, be careful about using volunteers unless they are trained carefully, it is made perfectly clear to them what standards of performance are expected, and they are told that anyone not performing to the extent and at the quality level the research requires will be "fired." Volunteers usually respond favorably to being treated as responsible professionals who have an obligation to their organization to do excellent work.

Students

Advanced students can be hired by researchers who need specific knowledge skills. Students can also serve as temporary help in carrying out many (or all) of the day-to-day tasks on research studies. There are five academic vehicles for this:

- *Case studies*. Many professors in management or marketing classes require their students to undertake a real-world case study as a term project. These may be specialized in areas like consumer behavior or marketing research. Typically, these projects are required in advanced courses taken by senior undergraduates or second-year M.B.A. students. While many students will already know what organization or problem they wish to study, many are at a loss or are at least open to suggestions by a researcher who contacts them.
- *Work-study programs*. Some institutions have work-study programs in which students attend class part of the time and work part of the time. While the low-budget researcher would have to pay work-study participants to help out on a research project, such workers may command relatively low wages while having a sophistication and an intellectual interest not found in typical part-time employees.
- *Independent studies*. Many schools permit students alone or in teams to put together independent study projects equal to one or

two courses. These could be defined to incorporate a specific research project.

- *Community volunteering.* Many universities have vehicles for involving students in communities. Some require students to volunteer. Some M.B.A. programs have chapters of NetImpact, which will undertake volunteer consulting in the community.

- *Master's and doctoral theses.* Not all schools have master's thesis requirements anymore (they are more commonly found in Europe). Master's theses are typically less scientific and less often need to be intellectually earthshaking than do Ph.D. theses. A proper match with the low-budget researcher's needs may be possible. Such a match is usually much less likely for a doctoral dissertation. The objective of a doctoral dissertation is to advance some scientific theory or perfect some methodology. In some rare cases, a doctoral student may be interested in obtaining a real-world site at which to develop data or test a model or some methodology.

If these opportunities appeal to the low-cost researcher, the first step in securing student help is to write a general letter to the deans of local schools of business indicating an interest in matching organizational research needs and the academic needs of the school and its faculty. A brief description of the organization should be included, as well as a general overview of the kinds of projects in which the organization would be interested. An offer should be made to visit the school and discuss the possibilities with interested faculty. If the school is interested (the dean will likely pass your letter on to relevant staff), the researcher may be asked to come by or to write a more precise description of the company and its current concerns to be circulated to potentially interested students.

As in the case of volunteers, students do not come without costs. Although they are likely to be at advanced stages of a business program, do not expect great wisdom and experience or even a great deal of technical competence (except for doctoral students or individuals with special skills such as programming). Furthermore, there are some disadvantages to using students:

- Students will be interested in the project because of its potential for learning. Thus, the researcher should be prepared to waste some time with them to educate them about the organization and how research is carried out in the real world.
- They are not employees. Even with volunteers, the organization can exert a great deal of control over what is done. With students, there has to be mutual agreement as to objectives. Managers should be careful not to treat students as if they were employees and, especially, not leave them to do only routine jobs. Students will stuff envelopes if they see it as a reasonable cost of their real-world education or if they see that organization staff members are doing their share of the least interesting work.
- Students have other obligations. As a consequence, they may not work as fast as the organization wants and may miss meetings and deadlines that are important.
- Projects will have to fit into a semester or quarter timetable (except for theses and independent study projects). Students should not be expected to undertake major long-term projects.
- Students can sometimes be arrogant (especially those from elite institutions). They will have been exposed to what their professors have been telling them are the very latest management and marketing concepts and technology. If the researcher or organization is not using this technology or is not enthusiastic about it (or, worse still, doesn't *know* about it), students may become patronizing or attempt, none too subtly, to offer enlightenment. (This is sometimes also a problem working with the professors themselves.) For the new research manager, this may be a special problem if he or she is still a bit insecure in using new research techniques. On the other hand, a researcher may occasionally find the students to be adept teachers.

Government Services and Public Librarians

To the extent the organization is seeking secondary source data, public libraries and government organizations, such as the Departments of Agriculture and Commerce and the Bureau of Labor, may be willing to do some of the background legwork. Librarians with access to on-line database information retrieval systems may be able to provide the expertise needed to cope with these systems and may even carry out low-cost computerized information searches for a novice researcher.

Database Research Services

If a librarian cannot help, there are a number of services that the researcher can pay to do secondary source analyses or carry out archival research, for example, providing citations to articles by and about competitors or a new technology. Some services may also provide on-line reproduction of the articles themselves.

Customer-Contact Staff

It is tempting for a researcher with a low budget who wishes to get data from clients whom staff contact routinely to use the latter as field survey workers. There are obvious cost savings from such a move, and one would expect staff to have rather high response rates if they were asked to conduct formal interviews with selected clients. However, in this role, staff have a number of serious disadvantages:

- They are likely to resent the assignment or request. This means they may hurry the work and make major errors of commission and omission.

- If given latitude to select respondents, they may be expected to make choices that are easy to survey or who will either enhance or not detract from the staff person's own reputation. This will make it more likely they will pick their favorite customers or those they think will give the most upbeat answers. This selection will give an upward bias to many responses, including attitudes toward the firm and, especially, attitudes toward the staff.

- The staff person may well be tempted to turn the interview into a promotional opportunity. This will not only bias the immediate results, but also potentially lose the customer as a possible future research subject.

- Even if the staff person doesn't try to promote something, the customer may be suspicious that he or she is being set up for some purpose and hold back or distort answers.

This does not mean that staff cannot be trained to be effective field researchers. They may well see a research project as an opportunity to become involved in broader planning issues and thus enhance their skills and knowledge. However, on balance, because of their basic orientations, customer-contact staff should be used as interviewers only as a last resort. They may, however, be used to carry out observations of interest to the researcher, such as noticing which trade magazines are on a customer's desk.

Personnel Department

This department can assist in hiring and training part-time personnel and conducting evaluations of those in the research project.

Purchasing

This department can help when the researcher wishes to hire outside suppliers for research services. Purchasing professionals can seek out alternative suppliers, establish bidding procedures, and evaluate bidding submissions at least in terms of costs and fulfillment of bidding requirements. They can also (along with company lawyers) prepare a contract with the supplier that ensures that the researcher's needs are met as required, on time, and at the lowest possible cost.

Securing Low-Cost Samples from Outside Research Services

Several organizations maintain pools of respondents who have agreed in advance to participate in research studies, thus cutting nonresponse problems and achieving overhead efficiencies.

National Family Opinion. This organization has a large sample pool of over 400,000 families who have agreed to return self-administered questionnaires without compensation. Many are contacted over the Web and can be hired by the low-budget researcher. Since characteristics of the households are already known, the organization can also construct highly controlled panels of specific kinds of households for particular marketing research purposes, such as older women for a new health care program or families with young children for child care services. (Its URL is www.nfow.com.)

Market Facts Consumer Mail Panel. This pool of 70,000 will respond to mail questionnaires and test products. Respondents also keep records over time. Market Facts' system permits careful selection of a very specific sample or several matched groups that can each be exposed to different experimental treatments, such as different ads, products, or even questionnaire designs. (Its URL is www.marketfacts.com/products/cmp.)

Piggybacking. Many independent survey organizations, both locally and nationally, permit researchers to add (piggyback) a few questions onto a survey designed for other purposes. Sometimes this can also be done within the researcher's own organization, where marketing questions can be added to research done by other departments such as public relations or personnel. These other studies should be selected carefully to make sure the main topics don't influence marketing results.

Omnibus Surveys. A select number of research suppliers carry out studies in which a number of organizations pool their questions in a single omnibus instrument (or series of instruments). This permits the participants to share overhead costs. However, it also means that the researcher's questions will be mixed in with an unknown set of others, which could cause major or minor biases depending on the particular study. The Roper Organization administers Limobus, which interviews two thousand adult Americans in their homes face-to-face every month. In a 2001 ad, it claims, "Sample size, and composition are tailored to your needs. A simple question asked of 2,000 respondents costs 90 cents per interview, asked of 1,000 respondents, it's $1.10."

Outside Computerized Databases

Several organizations make available databases comprising various kinds of market data, Usually disaggregated at the city, census tract, or postal code level, these are often based on U.S. Census or other data. Specific secondary analyses can be carried out by suppliers of these data, or the raw data can be purchased for analysis on the researcher's own computer. The PRIZM system (mentioned in Chapter Five) works this way.

Cooperating Businesses

One final source of personnel for research available only to nonprofit organizations is the private business firm. Corporations have recognized the significant advantages of employee volunteering on morale and turnover. Many give employees paid time off and sometimes contribute in-kind or cash resources to the nonprofit with which the employee volunteers. Both employees and in-kind help can be applied to research.

Acquiring Equipment

Low-cost research usually does not require a great deal of physical hardware. Most equipment needs are for computers, telephones, software, and temporary facilities. The following possibilities may help keep these costs low.

Focus Group Rooms

One's own home or the company conference room or cafeteria can be used for focus group interviews. These locales obviously can bias respondents, and the spaces will not be equipped with the two-way mirrors or videotaping capabilities available in professional sites. Still, the ambience can be made very pleasant and audiotape recording is usually possible.

Telephones

Volunteers or staff may be willing to allow their home telephones to be used for limited interviewing provided their costs are reimbursed.

Computer Software

No one who wishes to undertake a continuing program of research should be without the following kinds of software. They are listed in decreasing order of importance.

Word Processing.   Word processing software is essential for drafting proposals, writing questionnaires, developing observation protocols, or coding manuals and preparing final reports. Word processing programs with mail-merge capabilities can prove especially valuable for mail studies to prepare labels and write cover letters customized to each respondent. Software capabilities to prepare tables or simple columns of figures are desirable features of chosen word processing software.

Spreadsheet Software.   Spreadsheet software such as Microsoft Excel can be used to record raw data from research and perform simple analyses. Most statistical software programs accept spreadsheet input. Spreadsheet software can also be used to generate attractive tables and graphs for reports and presentations.

Statistical Software.   For organizations planning a continuing research program, investment in a statistical package will be well worthwhile over the long run. The most extensive statistical software packages commonly found in the major research agencies are SPSS and SAS. All are available in PC versions. However, these systems are relatively complex and expensive, and they require some time to learn. The beginning researcher may want to start more simply. Less expensive statistical packages such as Minitab contain all of the major statistical procedures discussed in this book.

Investigate these programs to see which is most compatible with your organization's system and your own orientation to computers. Some of the less expensive programs have limits on the number of cases or the number of variables per case they can handle, so give some thought as to what the system's maximum capacity should be.

Graphics Software. Otherwise dull reports can be significantly improved in attractiveness and clarity through the use of effective graphics. A wide range of graphics software packages serves this purpose. Most do the standard bar and pie charts, and several produce dramatic three-dimensional presentations.

Review the alternatives, in particular paying attention to labeling capabilities and the complexity that can be obtained for related sets of data. Attention should also be paid to whether the graphics package is compatible with the organization's word processing and statistical software.

Desktop Publishing. Recent developments in desktop publishing offer a wide range of capabilities for composing final documents and questionnaires with elaborate and attractive headlines, borders, drawings, and flowcharts as well as the standard graphs, tables, and text. This software represents a significant advancement over early combinations of word processing and graphics programs. Desktop publishing can add considerable drama to each research report.

Other Software. Other kinds of software have also been developed that may save time and money. There are now programs and Web sites to help prepare questionnaires, develop and monitor samples, and guide and monitor telephone interviewers (as described in Chapter Eight).[2]

Choosing Software. Each software package has its own idiosyncrasies, so I advise researchers to take two steps. First, undertake considerable investigation among friends or through published independent evaluations, such as those in *PC World*, before making an investment. Second, pay attention to compatibility among software systems in both style of use and interchangeability of materials (such as data files, tables, text, and graphs). It is frustrating to prepare a table or graph in a statistical package and then find that it must be reentered to fit into a word processing program. The popularity of integrated systems like Microsoft Office reduces this annoying problem. Unfortunately, standard integrated programs do not yet contain very sophisticated statistical capabilities.

Notes

Chapter One

1. Amy Saltzman, "Vision vs. Reality," *Venture* (Oct. 1985): 40–44.
2. Ibid.

Chapter Two

1. For further discussion of influence decisions, see Alan R. Andreasen, *Marketing Social Change* (San Francisco: Jossey-Bass, 1995).
2. Philip Kotler and Alan R. Andreasen, *Strategic Marketing for Non-profit Organizations*, 5th ed. (Upper Saddle River, N.J.: Prentice Hall, 1995), pp. 74–78.
3. An inquisitive manager would do well in this regard to read some of the current popular predictions about the future environment, such as Faith Popcorn and Adam Hauft's *Dictionary of the Future* (New York: Hyperion Books, 2002) or Neil Howe and William Strauss's *Millennials Rising: The Next Great Generation*. (New York: Vintage Books, 2000).

Chapter Three

1. Benjamin Sackmary, "Deciding Sample Size Is a Difficult Task," *Marketing News*, Sept. 13, 1985, pp. 30, 33.
2. Ibid.

Chapter Five

1. Eugene J. Webb, Donald T. Campbell, Kenneth D. Schwartz, and Lee Sechrist, *Unobtrusive Methods: Nonreactive Research in the Social Sciences* (Skokie, Ill.: Rand McNally, 1971).

2. Lee G. Cooper and Masao Nakanishi, "Extracting Consumer Choice Information from Box Office Records," *Performing Arts Review* 8:2(1978): 193–203.

3. Bob Minzesheimer, "You Are What You ZIP," *Los Angeles Magazine* (Nov. 1984): 175–192.

4. *Online Access Guide* 2:2 (Mar.–Apr. 1987): 44.

Chapter Six

1. Amy Saltzman, "Vision vs. Reality," *Venture* (Oct. 1985): 40–44.

2. Russell W. Belk, John F. Sherry, Jr., and Melanie Wallendorf. "A Naturalistic Inquiry into Buyer and Seller Behavior at a Swap Meet," *Journal of Consumer Research* 14:4 (Mar. 1988): 449–470.

Chapter Seven

1. George D. Lundberg, "MRFIT and the Goals of the Journal," *Journal of the American Medical Association*, Sept. 24, 1982, p. 1501.

Chapter Eight

1. Christopher H. Lovelock, Ronald Stiff, David Cullwich, and Ira M. Kaufman, "An Evaluation of the Effectiveness of Drop-Off Questionnaire Delivery," *Journal of Marketing Research* 13 (Nov. 1976): 358–364.

2. Much of the material from this section is drawn from Seymour Sudman, "Improving the Quality of Shopping Center Sampling," *Journal of Marketing Research* (Nov. 1980): pp. 423–431.

3. Ibid.

4. Hal Sokolow, "In-Depth Interviews Increasing in Importance," *Marketing News*, Sept. 13, 1985, pp. 26–27.

5. Seymour Sudman and Graham Kalten, "New Developments in the Sampling of Special Populations," *Annual Review of Sociology* 12 (1986): 401–429.

Chapter Nine

1. L. L. Guest, "A Study of Interviewer Competence," *International Journal of Opinion and Attitude Research*, Mar. 1, 1977, pp. 17–30.

Chapter Eleven

1. Thomas J. Peters and Robert H. Waterman, Jr., *In Search of Excellence: Lessons from America's Best-Run Companies* (New York: HarperCollins, 1982).

2. Ellen Burg, "Computers Measures Interviewers' Job Performances," *Marketing News*, Mar. 14, 1986, p. 36.

Recommended Reading

Chapter One

Robert C. Blattberg, Rashi Glazer, and John D. C. Little. *The Marketing Information Revolution*. Boston: Harvard Business School Press, 1994.

Gilbert A. Churchill, Jr. *Basic Marketing Research* (4th ed.). Orlando, Fla.: Harcourt, 2001.

Rohit Deshpande and Gerald Zaltman. "A Comparison of Factors Affecting Researcher and Manager Perceptions of Market Research Use." *Journal of Marketing Research* 21 (Feb. 1984): 32–38.

Joshua Grossnickle and Oliver Raskin. *The Handbook of Online Marketing Research*. New York: McGraw-Hill, 2001.

Jack Honomichl "Growth Stunt: Research Revenues See Smaller Increase in '00." *Marketing News*, June 4, 2001, pp. H3-H37.

A Web directory of market research firms can be found at www.zarden.com.

Chapter Two

Vincent P. Barraba. "The Marketing Research Encyclopedia." *Harvard Business Review* (Jan.–Feb. 1990): 7–18.

Randall G. Chapman, "Problem-Definition in Marketing Research Studies." *Journal of Consumer Marketing* 6 (Spring 1989): 51–59.

Elizabeth C. Hirschman, "Humanistic Inquiry in Marketing Research: Philosophy, Method, and Criteria." *Journal of Marketing Research* 23 (Aug. 1986): 237–249.

V. Kumar, *International Marketing Research*. Upper Saddle River, N.J.: Prentice Hall, 2000.

Pnenna P. Sageev. *Helping Researchers Write, So Managers Can Understand*. Columbus, Ohio: Batelle Press 1995.

Chapter Three

Russell I. Ackoff. *The Art of Problem Solving*. New York: Wiley, 1978.

Howard Schlossberg. "Cost Allocation Can Show True Value of Research." *Marketing News*, Jan. 8, 1990, p. 2.

R. Kenneth Wade. "The When/What Research Decision Guide." *Marketing Research* 5:3 (Summer 1993): 24–27.

Chapter Four

Alan R. Andreasen. "'Backward' Marketing Research." *Harvard Business Review* 63 (May-June 1985): 176–182.

Lawrence D. Gibson. "Defining Marketing Problems—Don't Spin Your Wheels Solving the Wrong Puzzle." *Marketing Research* 10:1 (Spring 1998): 5–12.

Chapter Five

Diane Crispell. *The Insider's Guide to Demographic Know How*. Burr Ridge, Ill.: Irwin, 1992.

Lorna Daniels. *Business Information Sources*. Berkeley: University of California Press, 1985.

J. H. Ellsworth and M. V. Ellsworth. *The Internet Business Book*. New York: Wiley, 1996.

Gale Directory of Databases. Detroit, Mich.: Gale Research 1996.

Gordon L. Patzer. *Using Secondary Data in Marketing Research: United States and Worldwide*. Westport, Conn.: Quorum Books, 1995.

David W. Stewart and Michael A. Kamins. *Secondary Research: Information Sources and Methods* (2nd ed.). Thousand Oaks, Calif.: Sage, 1993.

Chapter Six

Paula Kephart. "The Spy in Aisle 3." *American Demographics Marketing Tools* Supplement. (May 1996): 16, 19–22. [http://www.marketingtools. com/publications/MT/96_mt/9605MD04.html].

Lee Sechrest. *New Directions for Methodology of Behavioral Science: Unobtrusive Measurement Today*. San Francisco: Jossey-Bass, 1979.

Chapter Seven

Bobby J. Calder, Lynn W. Phillips, and Alice M. Tybout. "The Concept of External Validity." *Journal of Consumer Research* 9 (Dec. 1992): 240–244.

Donald T. Campbell and Julian C. Stanley. *Experimental and Quasi-Experimental Design for Research*. Skokie, Ill.: Rand McNally 1963.

Geoffrey Keppel. *Design and Analysis: A Researcher's Handbook* (2nd ed.). New York: Freeman, 1995.

Douglas C. Montgomery. *Design and Analysis of Experiments*. New York: Wiley, 1991.

Chapter Eight

James H. Frey and Sabine Mertens Oishi. *How to Conduct Interviews by Telephone and in Person*. Thousand Oaks, Calif.: Sage, 1995.

Laurence N. Gold. "Do-It-Yourself Interviewing," *Marketing Research* 8:2 (Summer 1996): 40–41.

Thomas L. Greenbaum. *The Handbook of Focus Group Research* (2nd ed.). Thousand Oaks, Calif.: Sage, 1998.

Richard A. Kreuger. *Focus Groups: A Practical Guide for Applied Research*. Thousand Oaks, Calif.: Sage, 1994.

Richard L. Schaeffer and William Mendenhall. *Elementary Survey Sampling* (5th ed.). Belmont, Calif.: Wadsworth, 1996.

Chapter Nine

William Bearden, Richard Netemeyer, and May Ann Mobley. *Handbook of Marketing Scales*. Thousand Oaks, Calif.: Sage, 1993.

Gilbert A. Churchill, Jr. "A Paradigm for Developing Better Measures of Marketing Constructs." *Journal of Marketing Research* 16 (Feb. 1979): 64–73.

Arlene Fink. *How to Ask Survey Questions*. Thousand Oaks, Calif.: Sage, 1995.

Seymour Sudman and Norman M. Bradburn. *Asking Questions: A Practical Guide to Questionnaire Design*. San Francisco: Jossey-Bass, 1982.

Chapter Ten

L. Bruce Bowerman and Richard T. O'Connell. *Linear Statistical Models: An Applied Approach*. Boston: PWS-Kent, 1990.

Wayne W. Daniel. *Applied Nonparametric Statistics*. Boston: PWS-Kent, 1990.

Joseph F. Hair, Jr., Rolph E. Anderson, Ronald L. Tatham, and William C. Black. *Multivariate Data Analysis* (5th ed.). Upper Saddle River, N.J.: Prentice Hall, 1998.

John A. Ingram and Joseph G. Monks. *Statistics for Business and Economics*. San Diego, Calif.: Harcourt Brace Jovanovich, 1989.

Short articles on various measurement and analysis tools are available at www.marketfacts.com/publications.

Chapter Eleven

Lee Adler and Charles S. Mayer. *Managing the Marketing Research Function*. Chicago: American Marketing Association, 1977.

Paul Boughton. "Marketing Research Partnerships: A Strategy for the '90s." *Marketing Research* 4 (Dec. 1992): 8–13.

William D. Neal. "The Marketing Research Methodologist." *Marketing Research* 10:1 (Spring 1998): 21–25.

John Russell. *Strategic Database Management*. New York: Wiley, 1996.

Index

U

UCLA (University of California at Los Angeles), 40
United Way of America, 228, 229, 230
Universities: acquiring personnel via students of, 250–252; available consulting/knowledge acquisition using, 245–246; research collaboration with, 239
U.S. Bureau of the Census, 90, 190–191
U.S. Consumer Product Safety Commission (CPSC), 87
USA Data Web site, 93

V

Validity: answer order bias and, 192; coding errors and, 183–186; constricting questions and, 196; data entry errors and, 182–183; difficulties associated with, 181–182; generalization biases and, 196–197; internal and external, 124, 136; interviewer-induced error and, 186–188; question order bias and, 191–192; questionnaire design and, 190–191; respondent-induced bias and, 188–190; scaling bias and, 192–194; threatening questions and, 195–196. *See also* Data
Videotape recorders, 113
Volunteer board members, 247–248
Volunteer personnel, 248–250

W

Wall Street Transcript, 105
Web sites: government data sources using, 91–92; programmed to record items/information, 113; syndicated service, 92–98
Weighted average expected payoff, 53t–54
Word processing software, 257

Y

Yahoo!, 92
Yeasayers, 190
YMCA planners, 230–231